From Qom to Barcelona

Islamic History and Civilization

STUDIES AND TEXTS

VOLUME 178

The titles published in this series are listed at *brill.com/ihc*

From Qom to Barcelona

Aramaic, South Arabian, Coptic, Arabic and Judeo-Arabic Documents

Edited by

Andreas Kaplony
Daniel Potthast

BRILL

LEIDEN | BOSTON

Cover illustration: P.Vind.inv. A.P. 10126 recto + 10134 recto. © Austrian National Library, Vienna

Library of Congress Cataloging-in-Publication Data

Names: International Society for Arabic Papyrology. Conference (6th : 2014 : Munich, Germany), author. | Kaplony, Andreas, editor. | Potthast, Daniel, editor.
Title: From Qom to Barcelona : Aramaic, South Arabian, Coptic, Arabic and Judeo-Arabic documents / edited by Andreas Kaplony, Daniel Potthast.
Description: Leiden ; Boston : Brill, [2021] | Series: Islamic history and civilization. Studies and texts, 0929-2403 ; volume 178 | Includes bibliographical references and index.
Identifiers: LCCN 2020043003 (print) | LCCN 2020043004 (ebook) | ISBN 9789004443846 (hardback ; acid-free paper) | ISBN 9789004443877 (ebook)
Subjects: LCSH: Manuscripts, Arabic (Papyri and Papers)–Congresses.
Classification: LCC PJ7593 . I58 2014 (print) | LCC PJ7593 (ebook) | DDC 011/.31–dc23
LC record available at https://lccn.loc.gov/2020043003
LC ebook record available at https://lccn.loc.gov/2020043004

Typeface for the Latin, Greek, and Cyrillic scripts: "Brill". See and download: brill.com/brill-typeface.

ISSN 0929-2403
ISBN 978-90-04-44384-6 (hardback)
ISBN 978-90-04-44387-7 (e-book)

This book is printed on acid-free paper and produced in a sustainable manner.

Contents

Preface VII
Quoted Editions X
List of Figures XV
Notes on Contributors XVII

PART 1
Pre-Islamic Predecessors of Arabic Document Traditions

1 Aramaic Documents from Achaemenid Bactria: Connections to the West—and the East—and the Future 3
Peter T. Daniels

2 Semitic Documents on Wooden Sticks: Manuscript Writing in Pre-Islamic South Arabia 24
Peter Stein

PART 2
Papyri and Documents from the Early Islamic Period

3 Coptic Fragments in the National Library of Egypt (Dār al-Kutub) 57
Anne Boud'hors, Maher A. Eissa and Naïm Vanthieghem

4 The Second Source of Islam: Reconsidering Ḥadīth Papyri 73
Ursula Bsees

5 Using Papyri to Determine the Purchasing Power of a Dinar in Early Islamic Egypt 117
W. Matt Malczycki

PART 3
Fāṭimid Documents from the Cairo Geniza and Other Places

6 A 6th/12th Century Supplementary Deed of Sale for the Nubian Slave Woman Naʿīm (Gen. T-S 18 J 1.17v) 127
Craig Perry

7 Social Embeddedness in the Legal Arena according to Geniza Letters 152
Oded Zinger

PART 4
Mamlūk Documents

8 How Documents Were Quoted in *Inshā'* Literature: A Comparison of P.Aragon 145 and Its Quotation by al-Qalqashandī 185
Daniel Potthast

Index of Documents Quoted by Edition 217
Michail Hradek
General Index 220
Michail Hradek

Preface

This volume presents most of the academic outcome of the Sixth International Society for Arabic Papyrology (ISAP) Conference on "Writing Semitic: Scripts, Documents, Languages in Historical Context."[1] Organized jointly by ISAP and by the Committee on Semitic Philology (Bavarian Academy of Sciences, Humanities) and the Lehrstuhl für Arabistik und Islamwissenschaft (Institute of Near and Middle Eastern Studies, LMU München), the conference took place October 7–10, 2014 in Munich.

The long-term cooperation between the Academy and the Institute in the following three fields gave the Munich conference an inimitable flavor.

In *Qur'ān Studies*, Gotthelf Bergsträßer (1886–1933) and Otto Pretzl (1893–1941) here had built up a double collection of photographs of Qur'ān manuscripts and of wax drums of Qur'ān recordings, and using these, they had published the famous third volume of Nöldeke's *Geschichte des Qorāns* (1938). Here Angelika Neuwirth (now Berlin) wrote her Habilitationsschrift *Studien zur Komposition der mekkanischen Suren* (1981/2007). Much later, Bergsträßer's collection became the nucleus of the famous *Corpus Coranicum* project of the Berlin-Brandenburg Academy of Sciences and Humanities (2007–).

In the field of *Arabic poetry*, Anton Spitaler (1910–2003) here annotated his outstanding library, an extraordinary research tool still accessible in the basement of the Academy. Spitaler's work was and is continued by Werner Diem (Cologne), as well as by Reinhold Weipert and Kathrin Müller (both Munich). The Committee on Semitic Philology became home to the ambitious project of a *Wörterbuch der Klassisch-Arabischen Sprache*, of which, alas, only three volumes (Ullmann 1970–2009) were published.

Moreover, for those working in *Arabic papyrology*, i.e., on pre-16th century Arabic papyrus, parchment, and paper documents, Munich is the place where Werner Diem, in his pre-papyrology period, wrote his PhD thesis (1968) and his Habilitationsschrift (1974). It is also where the Lehrstuhl für Arabistik und Islamwissenschaft provides the community with much-needed infrastructure (www.naher-osten.lmu.de/papyrology). More than a thousand newcomers have fallen in love with Arabic documents while going through a web-based interactive introduction, and more than a hundred PhD candidates and postdocs have become devotees after attending one of the fifteen webinars offered

1 A contribution published elsewhere is Johannes Thomann. 2018. "Scientific and Archaic Arabic Numerals: Origins, Usages and Scribal Traditions of the Two *Abjad* Systems." In *SCIAMVS* 19: 167–200.

every second teaching term. Those working on editions of documents now use the full-text thesaurus of all former editions and the metadata register on (un)published documents, to which will soon be added the formal typology of documents. Finally, Munich cares for the annual bibliography of Arabic papyrology and diplomatics, and for the ISAP and the Munich papyrology websites.

Thus, for the participants in the 2014 conference, coming to Munich was, in a way, coming home. During the conference, we met one evening in the Institute library for tea, only to discover that those present in the form of their books were interrupting our conversions at least as much as those who were present physically! Another afternoon, our discussion took place in front of a number of well-chosen Sabaic wooden sticks and Arabic and Judeo-Arabic documents and manuscripts in the Manuscript Room of the Bavarian State Library.

As was the case at the five earlier ISAP conferences,[2] the program covered the first millennium of the Islamicate World from Spain to Central Asia, from the 7th to the 16th centuries CE, with a certain predominance of the first four centuries and a well-established presence of scholars working on Coptic, Greek, Judeo-Arabic, and Pehlevi documents, as well as on Arabic epigraphy. The distinctive goal of the sixth conference at Munich, however, was to place our work within the wider frame of more general Semitic Studies.

The conference was organized by Kathrin Müller (then of the Committee on Semitic Philology, Bavarian Academy of Sciences and Humanities) and by Daniel Potthast and Andreas Kaplony (Lehrstuhl für Arabistik und Islamwissenschaft, LMU Munich/ISAP). The Academy, the Carl Friedrich von Siemens Stiftung in Nymphenburg, and LMU Munich most kindly hosted us. Generous financial support came from the Academy and LMU Munich, as well as from the Deutscher Akademischer Austauschdienst (DAAD), the Gesellschaft der Freunde islamischer Kunst und Kultur, and the Münchner Universitätsverein. For this

2 For the proceedings of the 1st ISAP Conference (Cairo, 23–25 March 2002), see *Papyrology and the History of Early Islamic Egypt*, ed. Petra M. Sijpesteijn and Lennart Sundelin, Islamic History and Civilization, vol. 55 (Leiden: Brill, 2004); for the 2nd ISAP Conference (Granada, 24–27 March 2004), *From al-Andalus to Khurasan: Documents from the Medieval Muslim World*, ed. Petra M. Sijpesteijn, Lennart Sundelin, Sofia Torallas Tovar, and Amalia Zomeño, Islamic History and Civilization, vol. 66 (Leiden: Brill, 2007); for the 3rd ISAP Conference (Alexandria, 23–26 March 2006), *Documents and the History of the Early Islamic World*, ed. Alexander T. Schubert and Petra M. Sijpesteijn, Islamic History and Civilization, vol. 111 (Leiden: Brill, 2015); for the 4th ISAP Conference (Vienna, 26–29 March 2009), *From Bāwīṭ to Marw: Documents from the Medieval Muslim World*, ed. Andreas Kaplony, Daniel Potthast, and Cornelia Römer, Islamic History and Civilization, vol. 112 (Leiden: Brill, 2015); and for the 5th ISAP Conference (Carthago, 28–31 March 2012), see *New Frontiers of Arabic Papyrology: Arabic and Multilingual Texts from Early Islam*, ed. Sobhi Bouderbala, Sylvie Denoix, and Matt Malczycki, Islamic History and Civilization, vol. 144 (Leiden: Brill, 2017).

publication, our special thanks go to the editors of the series *Islamic History and Civilization* for accepting this volume into their series, to Victoria Scott for copy editing, to Teddi Dols from Brill for continuous support and patience, to Cas Van den Hof from TAT Zetwerk for his painstaking work, for Michail Hradek for compiling the Index, and first and foremost to all the authors!

Daniel Potthast and Andreas Kaplony
Munich, November 28, 2020

Quoted Editions

Chrest.Khoury I Grohmann, Adolf and Georges Raif Khoury. *Chrestomathie de papyrologie arabe: documents relatifs à la vie privée, sociale et administrative dans les premiers siècles islamiques*. Handbook of Oriental Studies, Ergänzungsband 2,2. Leiden: Brill, 1993.

CPR XXVI Thung, Michael H. *Arabische juristische Urkunden aus der Papyrussammlung der Österreichischen Nationalbibliothek*. München/Leipzig: Saur, 2006.

CPR XXXI Hasitzka, Monika R.M. *Koptische dokumentarische und literarische Texte "First International Summer School in Coptic Papyrology 2006"*. Berlin: de Gruyter, 2011.

O.Frange Boud'hors, Anne and Chantal Heurtel. *Les ostraca coptes de la TT 29: autour du moine Frangé*. Études d'archéologie thébaine, vol. 3. Brussels: CreA-Patrimoine, 2010.

P.AmariGenova Amari, Michele. "Novi ricordi arabici su la storia di Genova." In *Atti della Società Ligure di Storia Patria* 5 (1867): 1–39 and 549–635.

P.Aragon Alarcón y Santón, Maximiliano and Ramón García de Linares. *Los documentos árabes diplomáticos del Archivo de la Corona de Aragón*. Publicaciones de las Escuelas de Estudios Árabes de Madrid y Granada, Serie C, vol. 1. Madrid: Imprenta de Estanislao Maestre, 1940.

P.AragonGranada Giménez Soler, Andrés. *La Corona de Aragón y Granada: Historia de las relaciones entre ambos reinos*. Barcelona: Imprenta de la Casa Provincial de Caridad, 1908.

P.AbbottLiteraryPapyri I Abbott, Nabia. *Studies in Arabic Literary Papyri 1: Historical Texts*. Oriental Institute Publications, vol. 75. Chicago: University of Chicago Press, 1957.

P.AbbottLiteraryPapyri II Abbott, Nabia. 1967. *Studies in Arabic Literary Papyri 2: Qurʾānic Commentary and Tradition*. Oriental Institute Publications, vol. 76. Chicago: University of Chicago Press, 1967.

P.BaudenDueTrattati Bauden, Frédéric. "Due trattati di pace conclusi nel dodicesimo secolo tra i Banū Ġāniya, signori delle isole Baleari, e il comune di Genova." In *Documentos y manuscritos árabes del Occidente musulmán medieval*, ed. Nuria Martínez de Castilla, María Jesús Viguera Molins and Pascal Buresi. Colección Ductus, vol. 2. Madrid: Consejo Superior de Investigaciones Científicas, 2010, 33–86.

P.Berl.Arab. I Abel, Ludwig. *Ägyptische Urkunden aus den königlichen Museen zu Berlin: Arabische Urkunden*. Berlin: Weidmannsche Buchhandlung, 1896.

P.Berl.Arab. II Diem, Werner. *Arabische Briefe des 7. bis 13. Jahrhunderts aus den Staatlichen Museen Berlin*. Documenta Arabica Antiqua, vol. 4. Wiesbaden: Harrassowitz, 1997.

P.Brux.Bawit Delattre, Alain. *Papyrus coptes et grecs du monastère d'apa Apollô de Baouît conservés aux Musées royaux d'Art et d'Histoire de Bruxelles*. Académie royale de Belgique, Mémoires de la Classe des Lettres, 3e série, tome XLIII, no. 2045. Brussels: Académie royale de Belgique, 2004.

P.Cair Arab. Grohmann, Adolf. *Arabic Papyri in the Egyptian Library*. 6 vols. Cairo: Egyptian Library Press, 1934–1962.

P.ChampollionDocuments Champollion Figeac, Jean-Jacques. *Documents historiques inédits tirés des collections manuscrites de la Bibliothèque Royale et des archives ou des bibliothèques des départements: Tome second, 2e partie: Texte des documents*. Paris: Didot, 1843.

P.David-WeillLouvre David-Weill, Jean et al. "Papyrus arabes du Louvre." In *Journal of the Economic and Social History of the Orient* 8 (1965): 277–311; 14 (1971): 1–24; 21 (1978): 146–164.

P.DelattreEcrire Delattre, Alain, Boris Liebrenz, Tonio Sebastian Richter and Naïm Vanthieghem, "Ecrire en arabe et en copte: Le cas de deux lettres bilingues." In *Chronique d'Egypte* 87 (2012): 170–188.

P.DiemKhalili Diem, Werner. "Philologisches zu den Khalili-Papyri". In *Wiener Zeitschrift für die Kunde des Morgenlandes* 83 (1993): 39–81; 84 (1994): 57–93.

P.DiemVulgarismus Diem, Werner. 2012. "Zwischen hohem Stil und Vulgarismus: Ein Brief aus dem Ägypten des 10.–11. Jahrhunderts n. Chr." In *Autour de la langue arabe: Études présentées à Jacques Grand'Henry à l'occasion de son 70e anniversaire*, ed. Johannes den Heijer, Paolo La Spisa and Laurence Tuerlinckx. Publications de l'Institut Orientaliste de Louvain, vol. 61. Louvain-la-Neuve: Université Catholique de Louvain, Institut Orientaliste, 2012, 155–188.

P.Flor.Arab. Amari, Michele. *I diplomi arabi del r. archivio fiorentino*. Florence: Le Monnier, 1863.

P.GenizahCambr. Khan, Geoffrey. *Arabic Legal and Administrative Documents in the Cambridge Genizah Collections*. Genizah Series, vol. 10. Cambridge: Cambridge University Press, 1993.

P.GrohmannUrkunden Grohmann, Adolf. "Einige bemerkenswerte Urkunden aus der Sammlung der Papyrus Erzherzog Rainer an der Nationalbibliothek zu Wien." In *Archiv Orientální* 18 (1950): 80–119.

P.GrohmannWirtsch. Grohmann, Adolf. "Texte zur Wirtschaftsgeschichte Ägyptens in arabischer Zeit." In *Archiv Orientální* 7 (1935): 437–472.

P.Heid.Arab. II Diem, Werner. *Arabische Briefe auf Papyrus und Papier der Heidelberger Papyrus-Sammlung*. [Veröffentlichungen der] Heidelberger Akademie der Wissenschaften, Philosophisch-historische Klasse, Kommission für Papyrus-Editionen. Wiesbaden: Harrassowitz, 1991.

P.Heid.Arab. III Diem, Werner. *Arabische Briefe auf Papier aus der Heidelberger Papyrus-Sammlung*. Heidelberg: Winter, 2013.

P.HermitageCopt. Ernshtedt (Jernstedt), Petr V. *Koptskie teksty Gosudarstvennogo Ermitazha*. Leningrad: Izdelstvo Akademii Nauk, 1959.

P.Jahn Jahn, Karl. "Vom frühislamischen Briefwesen: Studien zur islamischen Epistolographie der ersten drei Jahrhunderte der Hiğra auf Grund der arabischen Papyri." In *Archiv Orientální* 9 (1937): 153–200.

P.Kellis V Gardner, Iain, Anthony Alcock and Wolf-Peter Funk. *Coptic Documentary Texts from Kellis I*. Dakhleh Oasis Project Monograph 9. Oxford: Oxbow, 1999.

P.Khurasan Khan, Geoffrey. *Arabic Documents From Early Islamic Khurasan*. Studies in the Khalili Collection, vol. 5. London: Nour Foundation, 2007.

P.LittlePurchaseDeeds Little, Donald P. "Six Fourteenth-Century Purchase Deeds for Slaves from al-Ḥaram aš-Šarīf." In *Zeitschrift der Deutschen Morgenländischen Gesellschaft* 131 (1981): 297–337.

P.Lond. IV Bell, Harold I. *The Aphrodito Papyri, with Appendix of Coptic Papyri*, ed. Walter E. Crum. London: British Museum, 1910.

P.Lond.Copt. I Crum, Walter E. *Catalogue of the Coptic Manuscripts in the British Museum*. London: British Museum, 1905.

P.Loth Loth, Otto. "Zwei arabische Papyrus." In *Zeitschrift der Deutschen Morgenländischen Gesellschaft* 34 (1880): 685–691.

P.Marchands I–III; V/1 Rāġib, Yūsuf. *Marchands d'étoffes du Fayyoum au IIIe/IXe siècle d'après leurs archives (actes et lettres), vol. I–III; V/1*. Suppléments aux Annales Islamologiques, cahiers 2; 5; 14; 16. Publications de l'Institut Français d'Archéologie Orientale, vol. 586; 631; 727; 768. Cairo: Institut Français d'Archéologie Orientale, 1982–1996.

P.MariageSeparation Mouton, Jean-Michel, Dominique Sourdel and Janine Sourdel-Thomine. *Mariage et séparation à Damas au moyen âge: un corpus de 62 documents juridiques inédits entre 337/948 et 698/1299*. Documents relatifs à l'histoire des croisades, vol. 21. Paris: Académie des Inscriptions et Belles-lettres, 2013.

P.RiberaTratado Ribera y Tarragó, Julián. 1910. "Tratado de paz ò tregua entre Fernando I el Bastardo, rey de Nápoles, Abuámer Otmán, rey de Túnez." In *Centenario della nascità di Michele Amari: Scritti di filologia e storia araba, di geografia, storia, diritto della Sicilia medievale, vol. I*, ed. G. Salvo Cozzo. Palermo: Virzi, 373–386.

P.RuizOrsattiTratadoDePaz Ruiz Orsatti, Reginaldo. "Tratado de paz entre Alfonso V de Aragón y el Sultán de Egipto, al-Malik al-Ašraf Barsbāy." In *Al-Andalus* 4 (1939): 333–389

P.Ryl.Arab. I Margoliouth, David S. *Catalogue of Arabic Papyri in the John Rylands Library Manchester*. Manchester: Manchester University Press, 1933.

P.Ryl.Copt. Crum, Walter E. *Catalogue of the Coptic Manuscripts in the Collection of the John Rylands Library*. Manchester: Manchester University Press, 1909.

P.SilvestredeSacyGenes Silvestre de Sacy, Antoine-Isaac. "Pièces diplomatiques tirées des archives de la République de Génes." In *Notices et extraits tirées manuscrits de la Bibliothèque du roi et autres bibliothèques* 11 (1827): 1–96.

P.SilvestredeSacyTraite Silvestre de Sacy, Antoine-Isaac. "Mémoire sur le traité fait entre le Roi de Tunis et Philippe-le-Hardi, en 1270, pour l'évacuation du territoire de Tunis par l'armée des Croisés." In *Histoire et mémoires de l'Institut royal de France* 9,1 (1831): 448–477.

P.Stras.Copt. Boud'hors, Anne. *Coptica Argentoratensia: Textes et documents de la troisième Université d'Eté de Papyrologie Copte (Strasbourg, 18–25 juillet 2010)*. Cahiers de la Bibliothèque Copte, vol. 19. Paris: De Boccard, 2014.

P.SultanMerinide Bresc, Henri and Yūsuf Rāġib. *Le sultan mérinide Abū l-Ḥasan ʿAlī et Jacques III de Majorque: du traité de paix au pacte secret*. Cahier des Annales islamologiques, vol. 32. Cairo: Institut Français d'Archéologie Orientale, 2011.

P.Rain.Unterricht.Kopt. Hasitzka, Monika R.M. *Neue Texte und Dokumentation zum Koptisch-Unterricht*. Mitteilungen aus der Papyrussammlung der österreichischen Nationalbibliothek in Wien, vol. 18. Vienna: Hollinek, 1990.

P.Vente Rāġib, Yūsuf. *Actes de vente d'esclaves et d'animaux d'Égypte médiévale*. Cahier des Annales islamologiques, vol. 28. Cairo: Institut Français d'Archéologie Orientale, 2002.

P.ViladrichSultan Viladrich i Grau, M. Mercè. 1999. "Jaque al sultán en el 'damero maldito': Edición y traducción de un tratado diplomático entre los mercaderes catalanes y el sultanato mameluco (1429)." In *L'expansió catalana a la mediterrània a la baixa edat mitjana: Actes del séminaire/seminari organitzat per la Casa de Velázquez (Madrid) ... celebrat a Barcelona, el 20 d'abril de 1998*, ed. María Teresa Ferrer i Mallol and Damien Coulon. Anuario de estudios medievales, Annex 36. Barcelona: Milà i Fontanals, 1999, 161–205.

SBKopt. Hasitzka, Monika R.M. *Koptisches Sammelbuch III*. Mitteilungen aus der Papyrussammlung der österreichischen Nationalbibliothek in Wien, vol. 23.3. Vienna: Holinek 2006.

Figures

1.1 Older and newer letter forms in roughly contemporary documents 9
2.1 Palm-leaf stalks are a welcome writing support © University of Jena (above), © Peter Stein (below) 27
2.2 Development of the Ancient South Arabian monumental (left) and cursive (right) scripts from the Early Sabaic (ESab) to the Late Sabaic (LSab) period (i.e., from the early 1st millennium BCE to the 6th century CE) © Peter Stein 29
2.3 Writing tablets with wax inlay from Ancient Yemen (ca. 1st century BCE, not scaled) © Mikael S. Gidada 32
2.4 Selection of inscribed wooden sticks of different size from the collection of the Oosters Instituut in Leiden, Netherlands © Oosters Instituut Foundation, Leiden, photo W. Vreeburg 33
2.5 Writing surfaces of cylinder-shaped manuscripts (left) and documents written on palm-leaf stalks (right). The red arrows indicate the direction of writing © Bavarian State Library, Munich (photo), © Peter Stein (drawing) 36
2.6 Manuscript with broad left margin that has been completely filled with text © Bavarian State Library, Munich (photo), © Peter Stein (drawing) 37
2.7 Two wooden documents with eyes for holding a string or perhaps even a seal © Bavarian State Library, Munich (photo), © Peter Stein (drawing) 38
2.8 Examples of individual signatures on wooden documents. In the picture bottom left, the signature repeats the prominent first letter of the author's name mentioned immediately before © Bavarian State Library, Munich (above); © Oosters Instituut Foundation, Leiden, photo W. Vreeburg (middle); © Peter Stein (drawing) 41
2.9 Annulment of wooden documents by carving and notching across the text © Bavarian State Library, Munich (photo), © Peter Stein (drawing) 44
2.10 Originally uninscribed raw material prepared for writing but never used (Mon.script.sab. 39 and 301 from the Munich collection). The "texts" on them are modern additions © Bavarian State Library, Munich 47
3.1 P.Cair.EgLib.inv. 29 verso / ID 3251 © Egyptian National Library, Cairo 62
3.2 P.Cair.EgLib.inv. 30 recto / ID 3252 © Egyptian National Library, Cairo 66
3.3 P.Cair.EgLib.inv. 30 verso / ID 3253 © Egyptian National Library, Cairo 67
3.4 P.Cair.EgLib.inv. 29 recto / ID 3250 © Egyptian National Library, Cairo 69
4.1 P.Vind.inv. A.P. 6666 verso © Austrian National Library, Vienna 77
4.2 P.Vind.inv. A.P. 10128 recto © Austrian National Library, Vienna 83
6.1 Gen. T-S 18 J 1.17 verso © Cambridge University Library 129
6.2 Gen. T-S 18 J 1.17 recto © Cambridge University Library 135

6.3 Gen. T-S 13 J 37.12 recto © Cambridge University Library 140
6.4 Gen. T-S 13 J 37.12 verso © Cambridge University Library 141
6.5 Gen. T-S. Ar. 53.61 verso © Cambridge University Library 144
6.6 Gen. T-S. Ar. 53.61 recto © Cambridge University Library 144
6.7 Gen. T-S. Ar. 53.70 recto © Cambridge University Library 145
6.8 Gen. T-S. Ar. 53.70 verso © Cambridge University Library 146
7.1 T-S 10J10.13 recto © Cambridge University Library 165
7.2 T-S 10J10.13 verso © Cambridge University Library 166
7.3 Gen. T-S NS J120 recto + Gen. T-S. Misc. 28.11 recto © Cambridge University Library 172
7.4 Gen. T-S NS J120 verso © Cambridge University Library 173
8.1 P.Corona de Aragón.inv. 145 © Archivo de la Corona de Aragón, Barcelona 193
8.2 P.Corona de Aragón.inv. 145 © Archivo de la Corona de Aragón, Barcelona 195
8.3 P.Corona de Aragón.inv. 145 © Archivo de la Corona de Aragón, Barcelona 197
8.4 P.Corona de Aragón.inv. 145 © Archivo de la Corona de Aragón, Barcelona 199
8.5 P.Corona de Aragón.inv. 145 © Archivo de la Corona de Aragón, Barcelona 201
8.6 P.Corona de Aragón.inv. 145 © Archivo de la Corona de Aragón, Barcelona 203
8.7 P.Corona de Aragón.inv. 145 © Archivo de la Corona de Aragón, Barcelona 205
8.8 P.Corona de Aragón.inv. 145 © Archivo de la Corona de Aragón, Barcelona 207

Notes on Contributors

Ursula Bsees
PhD (2015), is *Wissenschaftliche Mitarbeiterin* and Director of the Arabic Papyrology Research Group at the Institute for Near and Middle Eastern Studies, LMU Munich. Her main research interests include Arabic papyri (mainly literary and magical texts), Islamic manuscripts, the history of Medieval Egypt, and Islamic popular religion.

Anne Boud'hors
PhD (1984), Habilitation (2003), is Director of Research at the Institut de recherche et d'histoire des textes (IRHT) of the Centre national de recherche scientifique (CNRS) in Paris. Her main activities are editing Coptic texts, both literary and documentary, and doing research on Coptic language and manuscripts.

Peter T. Daniels
studied linguistics at Cornell University, and linguistics and Semitic languages at the University of Chicago (graduate studies). After nearly a decade as Manuscript Editor of the *Chicago Assyrian Dictionary*, he became a freelance editor and has concentrated on the study of writing systems, publishing in that field since the mid-1980s. He takes a comparative, typological, and theoretical approach to the nature and history of writing, observing parallels across writing systems that tend to go unobserved by specialists in one or another field. His books include *The World's Writing Systems* (coedited with William Bright; Oxford, 1996), *An Exploration of Writing* (Sheffield, 2018), and *Writing: An Introduction to Its Nature, Origins, and Development* (Cambridge, in preparation).

Maher A. Eissa
PhD (2009), is Professor of Coptology and Egyptology and head of the Egyptology Department at Fayoum University. His publications focus on Coptic papyrology and his main interest lies in the daily life of Copts.

Andreas Kaplony
PhD (1994), Habilitation (2001), is Chair of Arabic and Islamic Studies at Ludwig-Maximilians-Universität München and director of the *Arabic Papyrology Database*. He has published widely on Arabic-Islamic history, most recently on "Scribal Traditions in Documentary Arabic: From the One Imperial Standard Language to the One (Jewish) Language for Transnational Communication (7th–12th Centuries)" (2018).

W. Matt Malczycki
PhD (2006), is the Joseph A. Kicklighter Professor of History at Auburn University (USA). He also teaches Islamic history and serves as the director of the history BA program.

Craig Perry
PhD (2014), is Assistant Professor at Emory University in the Department of Middle Eastern and South Asian Studies and the Tam Institute for Jewish Studies. His research focuses on the social history of slavery and the slave trade in the medieval Middle East.

Daniel Potthast
PhD (2011), does research at the Institute of Near and Middle Eastern Studies at Ludwig-Maximilians-Universität München. His main interest lies in the history of Muslim-Christian contacts in the Middle Ages. Besides several papers on Arabic epistolography, practices of diplomatic exchange between Arabic and Latin empires in the fourteenth century, and translations from Arabic into Latin, he has published *Christen und Muslime im Andalus: Andalusische Christen und ihre Literatur nach religionspolemischen Texten des zehnten bis zwölften Jahrhunderts* (2013).

Peter Stein
PhD (2002), Habilitation (2009), is Associate Professor of Semitic Studies working in the Faculties of Theology at the Universities of Jena and Erfurt (Germany). His research focuses on the Arabian Peninsula in Antiquity, in particular on the epigraphic documentation in the Ancient South Arabian languages and in Aramaic.

Naïm Vanthieghem
PhD (2015), a papyrologist and historian of Egypt working with Arabic, Coptic, and Greek documents, is a Research Scholar at the Institut de recherche et d'histoire des textes (IRHT) of the Centre national de la recherche scientifique (CNRS) in Paris. He is the author of numerous articles on multilingualism, law, scribal practice, Early Islam, and governmental administration.

Oded Zinger
PhD (2014), is a post-doctoral fellow in the Martin Buber Society of Fellows at the Hebrew University in Jerusalem. In July 2020 he has started a tenure-track position in the Department of Jewish History at the Hebrew University. His research focuses on issues of gender and law in medieval Egypt based on

documents from the Cairo Geniza. He is working on a book tentatively entitled *Law, Gender, and Community: Jewish Women in the Legal Arena of Medieval Egypt*.

PART 1

Pre-Islamic Predecessors of Arabic Document Traditions

CHAPTER 1

Aramaic Documents from Achaemenid Bactria: Connections to the West—and the East—and the Future

Peter T. Daniels

1 Introduction: Aramaic and Iranian in the Ancient World

Archaeologists, philologists, and historians have long puzzled over the languages and literacies of what may loosely be called the Iranian world: in time and extent, from the rise of the Achaemenid Empire about 500 BCE until the Arab conquest nearly 1,200 years later; from Egypt to the frontiers of India. Some recent discoveries, emerging from turbulent Afghanistan in the 1990s, cast new light on some obscure corners of that bigger puzzle.

My topic here encompasses writing in most of Asia, during much of the first millennium BCE. In the beginning was cuneiform, and cuneiform begat hieroglyphs, and hieroglyphs begat letters; and letters spread through the Levant. Something over 3,000 years ago, a language family took shape near the northeast corner of the Mediterranean Sea: Aramaic (Gzella 2015). For a century and a half it has been known to have been a lingua franca of the Mesopotamian empires since at least the eighth century BCE, whether from rare notations on the edges of cuneiform tablets (Delaporte 1912) or the occasional ostracon, always alongside Akkadian, which was written with cuneiform on clay. Aramaic was written with ink usually on papyrus or leather, using a Northwest Semitic script very like the Phoenician. By the turn of the era, Aramaeans were using a great diversity of scripts (Klugkist 1982).

Early in the first millennium, Aramaeans were erecting monuments with substantial inscriptions. Perhaps because the Aramaic script on flexible materials was easier to learn and use than cuneiform on clay, the language soon appeared alongside Akkadian at least to keep administrative records, as is shown by the "epigraphs" or "dockets" on the edges of cuneiform tablets.

By the early first millennium, Aramaic was being used at least semi-officially in the capitals of the various empires that controlled Mesopotamia. During the first decade of the 20th century, the pieces of the so-called Assur Ostracon were found; it dates precisely in the middle of the 7th century BCE.[1] Such evidence

1 Gibson 1975: 100–101.

 | DOI:10.1163/9789004443877_002

for the use of Aramaic is sparse on the ground, but the coexistence of Akkadian and Aramaic scribes is well known in relief depictions. Papyrus and/or leather must have been more common than ostraca, or surely more ostraca would have survived.[2]

Aramaic papyri have been known from Egypt for 200 years, and a group of letters on then-supple leather turned up in the mid-20th century. It is not surprising to find Aramaic documents in the west, where the language was at home. But until now we had little to no evidence of its use in the east or the north. All three of these Aramaic uses—in the west, in the east, and in the north—are illuminated by the new discovery.

Along came the Achaemenid Empire. Between 559 and 539, Cyrus took Mesopotamia; Egypt fell to Cambyses in 525; Darius headed east a few years later; and Xerxes turned west, most notably in 480. One of the Achaemenid capitals, Persepolis, was renowned from the late 18th century for its trilingual inscriptions, in three different scripts. It was Georg Grotefend's conjecture that the most prominent of the three scripts in all the inscriptions would reflect the language of its rulers, whom Herodotus identified as Persians, and that their language would be a form of Persian. This turned out to be correct and the key into the decipherment of all three scripts. They turned out to record what are now known as Old Persian, Elamite, and Babylonian.

Old Persian may have been the language of the ruling family, the Achaemenids—Cyrus, Cambyses, Darius, Xerxes, Artaxerxes, and others of the same names—but it was of little account in the administration of the empire. This is demonstrated by the progress in creating the great trilingual inscription at Behistun. As summarized by Rüdiger Schmitt (1990), the first version, installed in 520 to accompany the relief of Darius receiving subjugated enemies, was the Elamite; then the Babylonian was added; and finally, the Old Persian script was devised for the purpose of including a version that could be read directly off in Persian; but then another vanquished enemy was added so the Elamite had to be rewritten, and then a sort of colophon. It has been suggested (Gershevitch 1979), and this is important for what follows, that the rulers did not speak Elamite at all, but dictated their letters, memoranda, and orders in Persian to scribes who took them down in Elamite (even after the Old Persian script was devised for use in monumental display).

In 1933, excavations at Persepolis by Ernst Herzfeld turned up more than 20,000 of what proved to be mostly low- and mid-level accounting documents

2 Far too many authors use "leather" and "parchment" interchangeably—the terms are not equivalent: they refer to very different ways of preparing animal skins for writing: tanning and liming, respectively.

of three types: individual "memoranda," summary "accounts," and "journals" that in turn collect information from "accounts." What language are they in? About one-quarter are impressed with seals but not inscribed. More than 70 percent—perhaps 18,000—are in Elamite, and up to 1,000 are in Aramaic, but they appear to serve the same function as the Elamite preponderance.[3] Recently, just *one* such tablet written in Old Persian script has been discovered—which could be either the tip of an iceberg of an entire other set of accounting documents or, more likely, just some scribe having fun or showing off (Stolper/Tavernier 2007). A number of these Persepolis Fortification Tablets refer to scribes writing on leather in Aramaic. A certain notation in Aramaic on some of these tablets has recently been taken as an indication that there is yet a fourth level of document that has not survived at all, precisely because it was written in Aramaic on perishable materials (Azzoni/Stolper 2015).

The climate of Egypt, of course, meant that papyri *could* survive there, and again around the turn of the 20th century, a considerable corpus of Aramaic papyri was recovered from Elephantine, or Syene, or Aswan, just north of the present-day border with Sudan. Two of them shed light on Jewish Diaspora communities, the "Passover Papyrus" of 419 BCE, and the "Temple Papyrus" of 407. But also from Elephantine, we know that not only *local* business was carried out in Aramaic. Most illuminative of imperial policy toward Aramaic is a translation of the Behistun inscription into Aramaic. This makes sense for the western part of the empire, where Aramaic was the lingua franca. But what of the east?

All we could say until very recently was that a few inscriptions had been erected in eastern areas. The Greek historians, who had little interest in distant lands, tell us almost nothing until Alexander's invasions. In 1996, Pierre Briant, whose voluminous account of the Achaemenid era is based largely on Greek and Roman sources, wrote:

> To return to the Bactrian example, it is important to realize that the problem it poses is unique: the history of this country, particularly during the reign of Cyrus and Cambyses, is known essentially from archaeological evidence. In fact, the Classical authors are hardly even interested in these regions before the conquest of Alexander. In the Greek imagination, these regions are located "at the extremities of the *oikumenē*," on which they had no real information anyway.[4]

---

3 Henkelman 2008: 90.

4 Briant 2002: 78, first published in French in 1996.

2 The Bactrian Aramaic Corpus

The situation has changed: an extensive (at least, as far as Northwest Semitic paleography is concerned) corpus of materials is now available, and doubtless will yield many new insights into the history and administration of the region. Such insights, though, are not my purpose here.

The 48 Aramaic documents from ancient Bactria were purchased by Nasser D. Khalili, of London, who had previously been known as a collector of Islamic and Japanese art; he himself says he took an interest in these pieces because of his Persian-Jewish heritage. He writes:

> Some years ago, when I saw the first few Aramaic documents surfacing on the market, I immediately realised their significance and started to make enquiries as to whether more were available, so that I could reunite them as a group, and be able to tell their story in full.
>
> I was told that they were to be found either in Central Asia, Mesopotamia or Afghanistan, but regardless of this, I pursued every single piece that I could. After years of hard detective work, I was able to bring together what you now see in this volume.[5]

However, we also have this note by Shaul Shaked: "New Aramaic documents from ancient Bactria bring further support …; the texts will be included in a forthcoming publication."[6] Does this mean that other documents have been acquired by a rival collector?

The Khalili documents were first brought to scholarly attention in a pair of lectures by Shaul Shaked at the Collège de France in 2003 (Shaked 2004). He had been shown photographs of four of them in London a few years earlier, and more and more were added. Shaked enlisted his Jerusalem colleague, the late Aramaist Joseph Naveh of the Hebrew University; and he had the benefit of earlier assessments (for the dealer) by the Iranist A.D.H. Bivar and the Aramaist J.B. Segal.[7] Their edition publishes 30 documents on leather[8] and 18 wood tally-

5 Khalili 2012.

6 Naveh/Shaked 2012: 261.

7 Shaked also gave rise to a decade of bibliographic confusion by claiming that the *editio princeps* by Naveh and Shaked, under the title *Ancient Aramaic Documents from Bactria*, was "in press" and would appear in the Corpus Inscriptionum Iranicarum. The copyright date of *Aramaic Documents from Ancient Bactria* is 2012, though it is not clear when it actually became available. It is in neither series, either the "Corpus" or the "Studies in the Khalili Collection."

8 None of the treatments of ancient documents on leather seems to identify the species of animal whose skins were used.

sticks. Ten of the documents relate to Bagavant of Khulmi, 10 are other letters, and 10 are lists of supplies and labels.

Already by 2003, Shaked, and presumably Naveh, had made considerable progress in interpreting the documents. There are in effect *three* layers of interpretation. In the first presentation, Shaked reveals that many of the letters are from a high official, Akhvamazda, the "Bactrian satrap" of his title, whose capital was at Bactra. He wrote to a subordinate, Bagavant, governor of the town of Khulmi and environs. The letters give strong evidence of being drafts rather than finished copies, so they must have come from Akhvamazda's archive, not from Bagavant's, meaning they came not from Khulmi but from Bactra.[9] Ancient Bactra is adjacent to modern Balkh, Afghanistan, and seems never to have been excavated.

The second layer of interpretation is the lengthy introduction to the book, which gives every appearance of having been written by Naveh—because there is a *third* layer, namely, the "Afterword" by Shaked, which takes issue with a number of points in the main text. Shaked is oriented more toward Iranian studies, and Naveh toward Aramaic, and this emerges in the three layers.

Shaked in his 2003 lectures makes some observations on the language and the scribes:

> Although the language of our documents is basically the same as is found in the other centers of the Achaemenid Empire, in these documents we can already detect some signs of the imminent collapse of proficiency in grammatically correct Aramaic.[10]

He gives only one example:

> We find some cases where 3rd person plural verbs of the type *ʿbdw*, "they made," lose their word-final waw and are written *ʿbd*, which strictly speaking means "he made." There is also one example of the converse, where a verb appears in the plural instead of the singular.[11]

9 Most of the toponyms in the documents, the editors say, are considerably to the north.

10 "Bien que la langue de nos documents soit en principe la même qu'on retrouve dans les autres centres de l'empire achéménide, ces documents nous permettent de détecter déjà quelques signes de l'effondrement imminent de la maîtrise d'un style araméen grammaticalement correct"; Shaked 2004: 23.

11 "Nous trouvons quelques cas où les verbes araméens au parfait à la troisième personne du pluriel du type *ʿbdw* 'ils firent' perdent leurs vav en fin de mot et sont écrits *ʿbd*, ce qui signifie à proprement parler 'il fit'. On trouve aussi un exemple inverse, où un verbe est utilisé au pluriel au lieu du singulier"; Shaked 2004: 26.

Naveh, on the other hand—before listing a considerable number of similar inconsistencies with Standard Imperial Aramaic—states simply,

> The Khalili documents are valuable as some of the earliest specimens of the writing of Aramaic for official purposes in a period when it was beginning to disintegrate and was on the way to becoming a mere writing system for conveying Iranian languages. This is *certainly not yet the case* with the documents published in this volume, but the occasional errors point to the direction which Aramaic writing would take some time after the period of these documents.[12]

But Shaked gives himself the last word:

> The various oddities noted in the use of Aramaic in these documents may suggest that the writers were not necessarily native speakers of Aramaic. This is also the conclusion reached by Henkelman for the Elamite scribes in Persepolis, cf. Henkelman 2008, 88, 348–350. The fact that the scribes normally carry Iranian rather than Semitic names, adds some weight to this hypothesis.[13]

More on this below.

In the 2003 lectures, Shaked wonders whether the scribes would have studied in Bactria itself, or perhaps in some administrative center elsewhere. He raises the possibility that the people given the title "scribe" were not those who actually wrote the documents, but rather the officials who dictated them to their amanuenses:

> There remains an alternative possibility, namely, that the individuals of the grade of "scribe" in the Achaemenid bureaucracy were high-ranking persons in the hierarchy, at too high a level, perhaps, to be bothered directly with writing letters. It is possible, in this case, that they did not know Aramaic but had at their side secretaries of lower rank, whose names are not given in the letters, who assisted in actual scribal duties.[14]

---

12 Naveh/Shaked 2012: 51–52, emphasis added.

13 Naveh/Shaked 2012: 261.

14 "Il reste cependant la possibilité alternative, à savoir que ceux qui sont appelés 'scribes' dans l'échelon de la bureaucratie achéménide étaient des personnes de haut rang dans la hiérarchie, à un échelon peut-être trop élevé pour s'occuper directement de la rédaction de lettres. Il est possible, dans ce cas, qu'ils ne connaissaient pas l'araméen, mais qu'ils

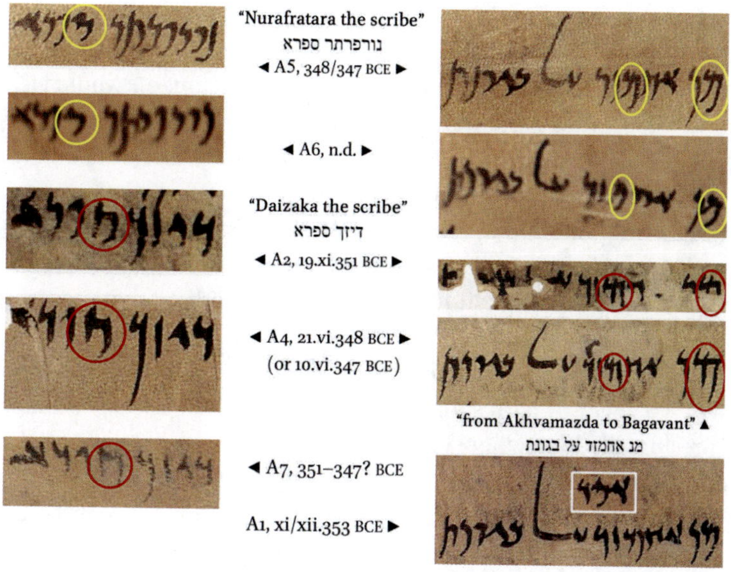

FIGURE 1.1 Older and newer letter forms in roughly contemporary documents

This is easily disposed of by looking at the documents themselves. The scribe is named on six letters. Hashavakhshu wrote just one of them (A1), so we set him aside for the moment. Nurafratara wrote two (A5 and A6), Daizaka wrote three (A2, A4, and A7). Figure 1.1 sets the signatures side by side (*left*), and also the names of the principals in the greeting (*right*). It is a bit less clear-cut here than it was when I studied the Brooklyn Museum Aramaic Papyri from this point of view thirty years ago (Daniels 1984), but a distinction can be seen in the two scribes' Samekhs: Nurafratara uses the more old-fashioned form with a squiggle at the top left (*circled in yellow*), but Daizaka makes it a separate vertical stroke (*circled in red*); and in their Mems: Nurafratara's are curved (*ovaled in yellow*), Daizaka's are straight and narrower (*ovaled in red*). As for Hashavakhshu's greeting, Samech is, as always, an infrequent letter, so his older form in the word *ʾsr*, "detained," is shown here as well (*boxed in yellow*). It thus seems clear that the named scribes are the men who actually did the writing. Adding another calligraphic note, the exuberant Lamed seen in all these greetings is a feature only of the *ʿal* of the greeting. Other Lameds, even in the first line with a wide top margin, do not extend that way.

avaient a leurs cotés des secrétaires d'un rang plus modeste, dont les noms ne sont pas cités dans les lettres, et qui les assistaient dans la tâche scribale proprement dite": Shaked 2004: 25.

3 The Connection to the West

It stands to reason that roughly contemporary Aramaic documents would yield mutual illumination. Shaked the Iranist mentions only the hallowed textbook by A.E. Cowley (Cowley 1923), from which generations of Aramaists studied the texts from Elephantine and elsewhere; additional corpora have come to light since, including the Brooklyn Museum Aramaic Papyri (Kraeling 1953), the Hermopolis Papyri (Bresciani 1960), and the Driver Letters (Driver 1957). Nor does Shaked cite the new standard edition (albeit without commentary) that includes all the named groups (Porten/Yardeni 1986–1999).

Naveh, however, goes immediately to the *most* comparable corpus, the Driver Letters,[15] a sheaf of correspondence, also on leather, also in Aramaic, discovered presumably somewhere in Egypt, from Arsames, the satrap of Babylonia, of the late 5th century BCE (just under a century earlier than the Bactrian material). Naveh's concern is the content of the two corpora. He reports that the grammar is almost identical. The script is so similar that the eminent epigrapher and paleographer Naveh has nothing to say about it. Nor does the paleographer Ada Yardeni discuss the scripts she was so long involved with; even her *Book of Hebrew Script* (Yardeni 1997), though it includes some of her Elephantine copies, does not display alphabets earlier than those of the Dead Sea Scrolls that were written several centuries later.

Despite the almost 2,100 km from Babylon to Bactra, and the great distance to Elephantine, the format of the two groups of letters is identical, including the way they are rolled and folded. The first similarity between the Bactra and Driver corpora, though, is purely external: the circumstances of their discovery. At some time after the First World War, the German archaeologist Ludwig Borchardt was shown a few photos by a nameless dealer, somewhere. He consulted specialists. He bought the documents, some time before he wrote about them in 1933. He sold them to the Bodleian Library, Oxford, and delivery was taken in 1944. Their publication was entrusted to G.R. Driver. His preliminary report (Driver 1950) noted that the documents were accompanied by a "tentative transcription and translation with notes" by Eugen Mittwoch, Hans Polotsky, and W.B. Henning. In the *editio princeps* of 1954, which included photographs of all the materials, and in the abridgment (Driver 1957), which includes none, the title page prominently acknowledges a "typescript" by these three—and Franz Rosenthal.

15 Porten/Yardeni 1986–1999, vol. 1: 102–129 nos. 6.3–16. A new text edition (Ma et al. 2013) is currently available on line.

Doubt, however, is cast on this account by Lindsay Allen (2013). She all but accuses Borchardt of inventing the entire story of purchase from a dealer and of instead having dug up the documents himself at Elephantine. Allen's view, however, is rather naive, especially given Emil Kraeling's account of the acquisition of the Brooklyn Museum Aramaic Papyri—that they were purchased from a dealer by the Egyptologist Charles Edwin Wilbour early in 1893 and lay neglected in a trunk until after the death of his daughter in 1947, who bequeathed them to the Brooklyn Museum.[16] Similarly, nothing is or can be known of the provenance of the Bactrian Aramaic materials; as Nicholas Sims-Williams observed with reference to the Bactrian Iranian documents mentioned below, it would be very much to the dealers' or middlemen's disadvantage to reveal their provenance (Sims-Williams 2015).

Naveh deals with the content of the Bactra letters, but not the diplomatics, i.e., the physical form of the documents. The Driver Letters were written in Babylon (and Susa). Babylon is almost 2,100 km from Bactra as the crow flies—and far more distant when deserts, mountains, and rivers need to be negotiated. Elephantine is more than 1,300 km from Babylon, again as the crow flies. But the format of the two groups of letters is identical.[17] Many of the letters in the two corpora are about 35 cm wide, and they all fall between about 30 and 37 cm in width, and so do most of the letters on papyrus. This strongly suggests that writing-leather was cut to conform to the existing papyrus standard, which was determined by the height of about 35 cm to which the usable stalk of the papyrus plant would grow.[18]

But documents other than letters can be even bigger. Document C4, a list of supplies disbursed, is 50 cm wide—and it is dated to the 15th of Sivan, year 7 of Alexander (June 8, 324 BCE). Documents in cuneiform dating to Alexander are rare enough, so the survival of a perishable one is a remarkable phenomenon. A bit of a cuneiform "astronomical diary" housed in the British Museum (BM 36390) mentioning Alexander is just a few centimeters in either direction, and the reverse bears 18 lines of tiny writing. Suggestions have been made as to how it was possible to read such small cuneiform writing, such as by using long thin hollow reeds (like drinking straws) somewhat like a *camera obscura* to magnify a tiny field of vision. But it does not seem to have been

16 Kraeling 1953: 9–11.

17 Neither the standard edition (Driver 1957) nor the new one (Ma et al. 2013) appears to include the dimensions of the Arsames corpus; the dimensions are registered in the *Textbook* (Porten/Yardeni 1986–1999), alongside the 1 : 1 facsimile drawings.

18 This is wider than the papyrus known to Classical authors; the stalk of the plant could grow up to 2 m tall (Lewis 1974: 22; 56).

shown that a cuneiform tablet could *not* be read by touch, just like Braille. Conversely, why are the leather and papyrus documents so *big*? In modern terms, Aramaic handwriting is equivalent to about 36 or 40 point type, well leaded. The reason for the large size would seem to be: they did not have eyeglasses.

4 The Connection to the East

The connection to the East is with the first script of India since Harappan times, which is known as Kharoṣṭhi. When it was deciphered,[19] in the late 1830s by James Prinsep (1799–1840), it was known as the "Bactrian alphabet," since it appeared almost exclusively on coins from the area of the "Greco-Bactrian" Empire (Prinsep 1838). Inscriptions were then found in Gandhara, in the far northwest of India, bearing the Edicts of Aśoka in the local Prakrit, or vernacular, from the mid 3rd century BCE, written with Kharoṣṭhi. Even farther to the west, at Kandahar, one such inscription was erected in Greek and Aramaic. Elsewhere in India, other local Prakrits were used for the Aśokan edicts, but they were written in the functionally more elaborated Brahmi script.[20] Brahmi gave rise to all the scripts of India, and beyond to Southeast Asia, but Kharoṣṭhi was confined to its limited area of origin—or so it was supposed until very recently: as recently, in fact, as the discovery of the Khalili Aramaic and Iranian documents. There are now several assemblages of manuscripts, on birchbark rather than papyrus or leather, retrieved from a number of locations along the Silk Road. Andrew Glass (2000) has studied the paleography of these manuscripts.

Ever since the 1890s, when Georg Bühler (1898) investigated the matter, it has been recognized that the inscriptional Kharoṣṭhi was closely related to the manuscript Aramaic—even though as yet very little manuscript Aramaic was available to him, and no manuscript Kharoṣṭhi. But now, not only has a century of discoveries brought Aramaic papyri from Egypt dating to the mid and late 5th century BCE, but we also have the Khalili documents from the third quarter of the 4th century, less than a hundred years before King Aśoka. When I called Andrew Glass's attention to the Khalili publication, he delightedly exclaimed

19 See Daniels 2019: 13–20.

20 Brahmi was also "deciphered" by Prinsep (Daniels 2019), but he observed that the historical development of the script could be followed back through the extant inscriptions, so that the characters were essentially readable by learned pandits. He had paved the way for the achievement by arranging the attested characters in a consonant × vowel matrix from which the similarities could be observed (Prinsep 1834).

that overall they looked just like the Kharoṣṭhi birchbark documents he had been studying. Not only the letterforms, as Bühler had recognized, but the ductus and the diplomatics display their kinship.

5 The Connection to the Future

"Connection to the future" refers to the use of so-called *Aramaeograms*, or *heterograms*, or simply *logograms* in writing Middle Iranian during the centuries after the Achaemenid Empire.[21] Now Iranian is probably the most neglected of the major branches of Indo-European, and Iranian writing, in all its multiplicities and complications, is even more neglected. The best known Iranian script (other than the Arabic-derived script of Modern Persian) is probably the Avestan, the alphabet of the Zoroastrian scriptures, the Avesta. Some of the Avesta may be as old as the Vedic Sanskrit texts of India, dating from the middle of the 2nd millennium, but they were not written down until the 5th century CE or so.[22]

Commentaries on the Avesta are composed in Pahlavi, the end point of several centuries of evolution of Middle Iranian languages and scripts.[23] The first Europeans to see this language were mystified: it appeared to be a "mixed language," comprising Aramaic and Iranian elements in seemingly equal measure. Its heterogeneous nature was never lost to its own scholars, who are represented in modern times by the Parsees of India and the diaspora. It is an ordinary Iranian language, but it is *written* with an Aramaic-derived script (in which a number of letters have merged in shape, so that it would be difficult to actually write Aramaic with it)—but not entirely according to the sounds of the Iranian language. The Aramaic connection had long been forgotten, however.

It is written with heterograms. The concept of heterogram is familiar to anyone who has learned a cuneiform-written language, or to anyone who has learned Japanese. Signs or characters that indicate a morpheme or word in one language (Sumerian, or Chinese) are used when writing another language (Akkadian or Hittite, or Japanese); in this second language, they indicate morphemes or words in the second language, without regard for the morpheme or word in the originating language.

---

21 Because the phenomenon in question here has parallels in other writing systems that involve different levels of representation of linguistic material, I prefer the term *heterogram* (Daniels 2018: 99–108).

22 Skjærvø 1996: 527.

23 Skjærvø 1996: 515–526; Skjærvø 2009.

The difference in Iranian is that the logograms are not seemingly indivisible units, but are complete words or morphemes *as spelled in Aramaic*. Thus the Europeans, who could read Aramaic, thought they were reading a text in weird Aramaic. Then, during the 18th century, inscriptions were found that seemed to represent similar mixed languages. Antoine Isaac Silvestre de Sacy (1758–1838) was the first to decipher some of them, on the basis of biscriptal coins with Iranian and Greek legends (Silvestre de Sacy 1793). The first to dimly illuminate the actual state of affairs was Martin Haug (1870). He provided a quotation from the 8th-century CE Arab historian Ibn al-Muqaffaʿ, who described the system,[24] and recounted his own experience studying in India, where he learned to interpret the Aramaic spellings as Iranian words, and seems to have convinced most of his readers; but he failed to convince himself, because at the end of his essay his Conclusions are still presented in terms of a "mixed language." This lengthy *Essay* of his is actually the introduction to an edition of the traditional glossary of Iranian readings for Aramaic spellings, which has about 1,000 entries.

The definitive explanation, however, is taken to be that of Herzfeld (1924), an archaeologist (not a philologist)—the same Herzfeld who, a few years later, was to be the excavator who found the Persepolis Fortification Tablets.

The most significant inscription, a trilingual in Parthian (early) Pahlavi, Middle Persian, and Greek, was erected by Shapur I (reigned 240/242–270/272) toward the end of his reign at Naqš-i Rustam (Sprengling 1953). Excerpts[25] show that (as in the other languages that use heterograms) there is nothing graphically distinctive about the stretches of text that are heterograms; the convention is to transliterate logograms with capital letters, and they are easily recognizable as Aramaic words. For the most part they are function words, but other frequent terms are also written with logograms.

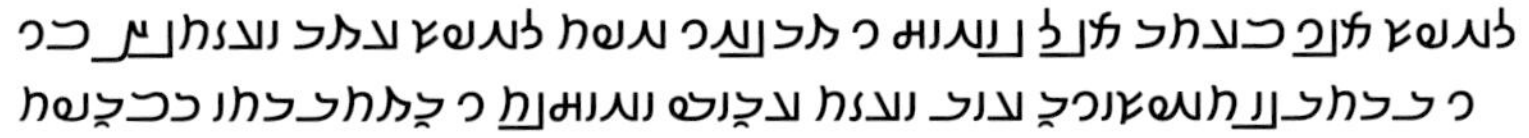

⟨LHWyš MNW BATR MN LN YHYE W prnhw HWYt LHWyš ʾpr yʾztn CBW
W krtkny twhšywd AYK yʾzt ʾdywr YHYEnt W dstkrty OBDWnt⟩

hawiž kē paš až amāh bawāδ ud parrox ahād haw-iž abar yazdān īr
ud kerdagān tuxšāδ kū yazd aδyāwar bawānd ud dastkerd karānd

24 Haug 1870: 38. The passage had been translated previously, but misinterpreted (Quatremère 1835: 256).

25 Skjærvø 1996: 522–523.

> He too who shall be after Us and shall be lucky, may he too toil in the matters and services of the gods so that the gods will be his helpers and make him their property.
>
> SHAPUR I, inscription at Naqš-i Rustam, Parthian, lines 29–30
>
> 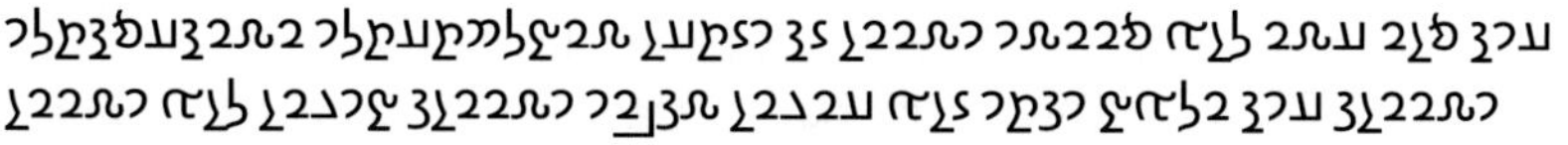
>
> ⟨AYK MNW AHR LNE MROHY YHWWN ZK yzt'n hwplst'tly Whwk'mktly YHWWNd AYK OLEc yzty ZNE 'wgwn hdbry YHWWNd cygwn LNE YHWWN
>
> *kū kē pas amāh xwadāy bawād ān yaz(a)dan huparistātar ud-hukāmagtar bawād kū ōy-iz yazd ēn-ōwōn hayār bawānd čiyōn amāh būd*
>
> So that whoever shall become lord after Us he will be more obedient and of better will toward the gods so that the gods will be his helpers too the way they have been Ours!
>
> SHAPUR I, inscription at Naqš-i Rustam, Middle Persian, line 35⟩

Additional Iranian languages using heterograms include the Sogdian of the "Ancient Letters," which date from the early 4th century, so not many decades later—and Sogdiana, north of the Oxus River, is a considerable distance from Shapur's realm; and Book Pahlavi, recording the language used for commentaries on the Avesta wherever Zoroastrianism was or is practiced. Skjærvø provides samples of these.[26]

Why, then, is this system used so similarly throughout the former Achaemenid area, even after it split into a number of jurisdictions? Precisely, I say, because of the uniformity revealed by the similarity of texts created in Egypt, in Babylon and Susa, and in Bactra. There must have been a rigid system of education for scribes throughout the immense realm.

A second question is, how far back does it go? The only synthetic treatment of all of Middle Iranian remains that of Henning:

> The coins of the minor kings of Persis … cover the entire time span of Arsacid [Parthian] rule (from the middle of the 3rd c. BCE to the beginning of the 3rd c. CE). They show most clearly when it was that Aramaic

26 Skjærvø 1996: 529; 526.

> was supplanted for general use. On the coins of both the first and second series ..., which were struck in the second century, the legends are written in correct Aramaic. In the third series, which begins somewhat toward the end of the second c. BCE [let us say 125 BCE], this is no longer the case; on its oldest coins ... the pure Aramaic *BR* is replaced by the form found in Middle Persian *BRH* "son" [i.e., not "his son"]. This is the oldest "Aramaic ideogram" on Persian soil; the legend proves that the changeover to ideographic writing was then complete.[27]

But this is from the Iranian point of view. Little attention seems to have been paid to this question from the Aramaic side, except for the occasional note in a commentary. As early as 1938, Franz Rosenthal[28] noted in the Driver Letters (Mittwoch had shown him Borchardt's photographs) the Iranism *bar beytā*, not a phrase otherwise used in Aramaic, clearly a calque, which later would be the logogram for *vispuhr*, "prince." Driver alludes to logograms in his introduction but is coy in his commentary—which for its Iranian aspects presumably relies on Henning (Driver 1957: vi). For example, Henning writes:

> The use of קדם in the sense of *apud* (cp. CA $_{10}$ B $_{54}$) is paralleled by its employment as an ideogram for *apar* 'at, on' in Pahl. texts (s. Andreas in *SbPAW, Ph.-h. Kl.* 1910, 871); so too קדמתה in the Parth. system of writing serves as an ideogram for the Parth. *parwān* 'before' (Rosenthal *AF.* 77–80), thus explaining how it comes to mean also 'in the eyes, opinion of' in the O.T. (Dan. iii 32 vi 2).[29]

27 "Die Münzen der Kleinkönige der Persis, deren Emission sich, wenn auch mit mehreren Unterbrechungen, über die ganze Zeitspanne der arsakidischen Herrschaft (von der Mitte des 3ten Jhdts. v. Chr. bis zum Anfang des 3ten nachchristlichen Jhdts.) erstreckt (am bequemsten bei G. F. Hill, *a.a.O.*, CLX–CLXXXII), zeigen am deutlichsten, zu welchem Zeitpunkt das Aramäische aus dem allgemeinen Gebrauch verdrängt wurde. Auf den Münzen sowohl der ersten Serie, die den sich פרתרכא זי אלהיא *prtrk' zy 'lhy'* nennenden Fürsten zugehören, wie auch der zweiten, deren Prägung ins zweite Jahrhundert fällt, sind die Legenden in korrektem Aramäisch geschrieben. Bei der dritten Serie, die etwa gegen das Ende des 2ten vorchristlichen Jhdts. beginnt, ist das nicht mehr der Fall; auf ihrer ältesten Münze liest man דאריו מלכא ברה ותפרדת מלכא *D'ryw MLK' BRH wtprdt MLK'* 'Darius der König, Sohn Autophradates' des Königs' (Hill, *a.a.O.*, 216 sqq.). Das hier reinaramäische *BR* ersetzende, mit dem späteren mittelpersischen übereinstimmende *BRH* 'Sohn' ist das älteste 'aramäische Ideogramme' auf persischem Boden: die Legende beweist, dass der Übergang zur ideographischen Schreibweise jetzt vollzogen ist": Henning 1958: 25.

28 Rosenthal 1939: 81.

29 *Apud* Driver 1957, 38. CA is Driver's siglum for Cowley's edition of the Words of Aḥiḳar (Cowley 1923: 204–248), CB is his siglum for Cowley's edition of the Behistun inscription

(As early as 1926, Driver in one of his first articles had shown, on purely linguistic grounds, that the Aramaic of Daniel dates no earlier than the Macedonian conquest of 333 BCE.) He has a lengthy discussion of בר ביתה, mostly not relevant to the passage it appears in, including:

> The Aram. sing. בר ביתה (cp. DL 5_1 10_1) with plur. בני ביתא (Cp 30_3) = N.-Bab. *mār bîti* 'the son of the house' is a literal translation of a Pers. expression designating a member of the royal family (Rosenthal *AF.* 81). The underlying Iran. word is the O.-Iran. **visō puϑra* ... The Aram. בר ביתה continued in use as an ideogram in Pahl. and Parth. texts meaning "prince of the royal house" ...[30]

Though I think he undervalues Rosenthal's remark:

> ... The Aramaic documents on leather provide another example in that they show that so remarkable a logogram as the title ברביתה = *vispuhr* = 'noble', 'prince' and the preposition בין in the meaning 'in' (as in Middle Persian), not previously attested in Aramaic, could already be used in Imperial Aramaic, and, one may say, only there within Aramaic.[31]

Driver's commentary lists some 15 Aramaic words and phrases that serve as heterograms in Iranian texts. Especially interesting is that fully one-third of them are Iranisms in the Aramaic text. Besides the two just cited, they are:

> The Aram. בין 'between' here means 'in' (cp. DL 2_2 5_5) like the Pahl. id. בין representing *andar* 'in, within, among, between' (Rosenthal *AF.* 81; s. Nyberg *HbP* II$_{10}$).[32]
>
> The substitution of על for אל, which is the norm in Eg. letters, is here due to Iran. influence, since על is still used as an ideogram for *ō* 'to' in Pahl.

Aramaic translation (Cowley 1923: 248–271). Driver refers to Cowley's edition of the non-literary papyri with Cp (Cowley 1923: 1–203).

30 Driver 1957: 40–41. DL is the siglum Driver uses for his numbering of the Letters.

31 "... haben die aram. Lederurkunden noch einen weiteren Beweis geliefert, indem sie zeigen, dass so merkwürdige Ideogramme wie der Titel ברביתה = vispuhr = 'Adliger', 'Prinz' und die Präposition בין in der sonst im Aram. nicht belegten Bedeutung 'in' (wie im Mittelpersischen) schon im Reichsaram., und, wie man wohl sagen darf, nur dort innerhalb des Aram., gebräuchlich waren": Rosenthal 1938: 81.

32 Driver 1957: 39. *HbP* is *Hilfsbuch des Pehlevi.*

texts (Nyberg *HbP.* II $_{164}$); and it sometimes serves simply to indicate the dat. case in late [i.e., post-Exilic, Iranian-influenced] parts of the O.T.[33]

The Aram. עבד לנפש as here used (cp. Cp 7 $_{6}$) is a verbal translation of the O.-Pers. *(h)uvāipašiyam akunauš* (cp. Pahl. *ō χ^{u}ēš kartan*) 'to make one's own' (Benveniste in *JAs.* CCXLII 305); and this *χ^{u}ēš*, for which נפשה serves as an ideogram, is the base on which *χ^{u}ēšīh* 'possession, property' is formed (Nyberg *HbP.* II $_{140}$).[34]

That is, Iranian forms were creeping into the Aramaic being written in Babylon and Susa—but not elsewhere—and in turn were fertilizing the stock of heterograms to be found later.[35] Moreover, 72 Iranian loanwords are identified in the (pre-Bactra) corpus of Egyptian Aramaic, and:

By far the largest number of [them] is to be found in the well-represented correspondence of the satrap Arsham (A6.1–16) and of the head of the Jewish community Jedaniah (A4.5, 7–8, 10). Almost every letter in the former collection contains one or more loan-words.[36]

As for syntactic influence:

The periphrastic construction of שמיע לי 'I have heard', of which this is the earliest known instance, is an East-Aramaic idiom reflecting Persian usage as seen in *עביד לי = *manā χšnūtam* 'it has been heard by me' = 'I have heard' (cp. Kutscher in 'JBL.' LXXVI 337); and it has passed thence into the Egyptian (Bresciani in *RSO.* XXXV 18–19 i R. 6) and other Aramaic and Syriac (Schlesinger *Satzl. d. aram. Spr.* 45–46 and Nöldeke & Crichton "Comp. Syr. Gr." $_{219}$) dialects. The same usage is reflected in the late Hebr. נשמע לסנבלט ... כי ... (Neh. vi $_{1}$); for the author may have learnt it at the Persian court.[37]

The construction had been registered, but not accounted for, in those earlier grammars.[38]

33 Driver 1957: 42.

34 Driver 1957: 83.

35 Nearly 400 Iranian words are discussed in the Bactra publication, along with nearly 150 forms from later Iranian languages: Naveh/Shaked 2012: 288–292 Index B.I.

36 Muraoka/Porten 1998: 370–373; 378. The sigla, from the *Textbook* (Porten/Yardeni 1986–1999), refer respectively to the Driver Letters and to Cowley 1923: nos. 27; 30; 31; 33.

37 Driver 1957: 100, among the Addenda of 1965.

38 The review by Kutscher cited by Driver (Kutscher 1957) contained the first adumbration of

These data, which have been available for more than half a century, should be at least considered to be evidence that already in the late 5th century BCE, officials in the Achaemenid capitals were dictating their correspondence in Persian to scribes who also may not have been native speakers of Aramaic. The new Bodleian edition (Ma et al. 2013) appears not to mention heterograms at all.

The expression *bar beytā* does not appear in the Bactra letters, but many of the features Naveh lists[39] as "bad Aramaic" are exactly what would turn up in the heterograms not many decades later. Notably, these are lack of number concord between subject and verb, some lack of gender or state concord, and uncertainty as to grammatical suffixes. So it is even more likely that they too were dictating in Persian to scribes writing in Aramaic, as in the earlier period they may have dictated in Persian to scribes writing in Elamite. These texts need to be examined from this point of view.

6 Conclusion

Finally, the conjunction of scripts in this part of the world confirms the old observation that "script follows religion." The Aramaic scripts remained in use in Zoroastrian and Manichaean areas;[40] Kharoṣṭhi spread along the Silk Road with Buddhism and lasted much longer there than in its homeland; and Brahmi was used in Hindu areas (Salomon 2007). But the other old observation, that "script follows politics," is also illustrated. When the "Greco-Bactrian" Empire arose from the dregs of the Successors of Alexander, eventually morphing into the kingdom of Bactria between the Hindu Kush to the south and the Oxus to the north, their (Iranian) Bactrian language came to be written with the Greek alphabet (Sims-Williams 2012).

---

the language-contact explanation for this "ergative"-looking Aramaic construction that is fully incorporated into the Modern Aramaic verbal paradigm, which is usually cited from an article a decade later (Kutscher 1969). Kutscher also observed other syntactic features of the Driver Letters in which they differ from the Cowley corpus and used their eastern provenance as evidence that the split between Western and Eastern Aramaic languages had begun earlier than was previously evident in the data and could be attributed at least in part to Iranian influence—and that these syntactic features could also be recognized in the "literary" texts from Elephantine (Cowley 1923: 204–271), namely, the Ahiqar story (but not the proverbs) and the translation of the Behistun inscription.

39 Naveh/Shaked 2012: 52–53.

40 It has been observed that the elaborate inherited script, with its merged letters and heterograms, prevailed in state affairs, and in the state religion, where intensive scribal training was available; but the simpler Syriac-based script used in Manichaean writings is the one that led to many national scripts of Asia (e.g. Durkin-Meisterernst 2005).

Once again it is the Khalili collection that has gathered at least 150 leathern documents in Bactrian (Sims-Williams 2000–2007)—a language that had hitherto been barely known from a handful of inscriptions—and they exhibit a complete break with the past. The Bactrian materials are formatted differently and sealed differently: they are tied shut with a sort of thong made by slitting a strip almost off the bottom of the leather piece. And their invocations and theophoric names are Zoroastrian. Only a handful of Bactrian documents reflect Buddhist concerns—and one is on birchbark like Kharoṣṭhi, and one is on cloth, a material that survives so sparsely that nothing can be said about its connotations at all.

This chapter has given some hint of the questions that are raised when we pay attention to the writing systems of the documents that are usually studied for their content alone. The Achaemenid Empire must have had an educational system, or a scribal training system, far more uniform than those of the preceding Mesopotamian empires, or of the contemporary Greek civilization, or of the succeeding Roman Empire, so that, even though its letter shapes diversified as the Iranian empires broke up, its orthographic practice remained constant. I hope that at least some of the pieces of the puzzle are beginning to fall into place.

Bibliography

Allen, Lindsay. 2013. "The Bodleian Achaemenid Aramaic Letters: A Fragmentary History." In *The Arshama Letters from the Bodleian Library*, ed. John Ma, Christopher Tuplin, Lindsay Allen, and David Taylor, vol. 1: 45–49. Oxford. http://arshama.bodleian.ox.ac.uk/publications/; last accessed 6 May 2019.

Azzoni, Annalisa, and Matthew W. Stolper. 2015. "The Aramaic Epigraph NSYḤ on Persepolis Fortification Elamite Tablets." In *Achaemenid Research on Texts and Archaeology* 2015.004. http://www.achemenet.com/document/ARTA_2015.004-Azzoni-Stolper.pdf; last accessed 6 May 2019.

Bresciani, Edda. 1960. "Papiri aramaici egiziani di epoca persiana presso il Museo Civico di Padua." In *Rivista degli Studi Oriientali* 35: 11–24.

Briant, Pierre. 2002. *From Cyrus to Alexander: A History of the Persian Empire*. Translated by Peter T. Daniels. Winona Lake: Eisenbrauns. (French original 1996.)

Bühler, Georg. 1898. *On the Origin of the Indian Brāhma Alphabet: Together with Two Appendices on the Origin of the Kharoṣṭhī Alphabet and the Origin of the So-Called Letter-Numerals of the Brāhmī*. 2nd ed. Strassburg: Trübner.

Cowley, A.E. 1923. *Aramaic Papyri of the Fifth Century B.C.* Oxford: Clarendon.

Daniels, Peter T. 1984. "A Calligraphic Approach to Aramaic Paleography." In *Journal of Near Eastern Studies* 43: 55–68.

Daniels, Peter T. 2018. *An Exploration of Writing*. Sheffied: Equinox.

Daniels, Peter T. 2019. "Indic Writing: History Typology Study." In *Handbook of Literacy in Akshara Orthographies*, ed. R.M. Joshi and C. McBride. Dordrecht: Springer, 11–42.

Delaporte, Louis. 1912. *Épigraphes araméens: étude des textes araméens gravés ou écrits sur des tablettes cunéiformes d'après les leçons professées au Collège de France pendant le semestre d'hiver 1910–11*. Paris: Geuthner.

Driver, G.R. 1926. "The Aramaic of the Book of Daniel." In *Journal of Biblical Literature* 45: 110–119.

Driver, G.R. 1950. "New Aramaic Documents." In *Zeitschrift für Alttestamentliche Wissenschaft* 62 = N.S. 21: 220–225.

Driver, G.R. 1954. *Aramaic Documents of the Fifth Century B.C.* Oxford: Clarendon.

Driver, G.R. 1957. *Aramaic Documents of the Fifth Century B.C.* Abridged and revised edition. Corrected 2nd impression, 1965. Oxford: Clarendon. ("With help from a typescript by E. Mittwoch, H.J. Polotsky, W.B. Henning, F. Rosenthal"; 1st ed., 1954.)

Durkin-Meisterernst, Desmond. 2005. "Manichean Script." In *Encyclopedia Iranica*. http://www.iranicaonline.org/articles/manichean-script.

Gershevitch, Ilya. 1979. "The Alloglottography of Old Persian." In *Transactions of the Philological Society* 77: 114–190.

Gibson, J.C.L. 1975. *Textbook of Syrian Semitic Inscriptions, Vol. 2: Aramaic Inscriptions including Inscriptions in the Dialect of Zenjirli*. Oxford: Clarendon.

Glass, Andrew. 2000. "A Preliminary Study of Kharoṣṭhi Manuscript Paleography." M.A. thesis, University of Washington, Department of Asian Languages and Literature. https://gandhari.org/bibliography?bib_id=Glass_2000.2; last accessed 26 September 2020.

Gzella, Holger. 2015. *A Cultural History of Aramaic: From the Beginnings to the Advent of Islam*. Handbuch der Orientalistik, section I, vol. 111. Leiden: Brill.

Haug, Martin. 1870. *Essay on the Pahlavi Language*. Stuttgart: Grüniger.

Henkelman, Wouter F.M. 2008. *The Other Gods Who Are: Studies in Elamite–Iranian Acculturation Based on the Persepolis Fortification Tablets*. Achaemenid History, vol. 14. Leiden: Netherlands Institute for the Near East.

Henning, W.B. 1958. "Mitteliranisch." In *Iranistik, part 1: Linguistik*, ed. Carl Hoffmann. Handbuch der Orientalistik, section I: Der Nahe und Mittlere Osten, vol. 4. Leiden: Brill, 20–130.

Herzfeld, Ernst. 1924. "Essay on Pahlavi." In *Paikuli: Monument and Inscription of the Early History of the Sasanian Empire*, by Ernst Herzfeld. Forschungen zur islamischen Kunst, vol. 3,1. Berlin: Reimer, 52–73.

Khalili, Nasser D. 2012. "Foreword." In *Aramaic Documents from Ancient Bactria from the Khalili Collections*, ed. Joseph Naveh and Shaul Shaked. London: The Khalili Family Trust, ix.

Klugkist, A.C. 1982. *Midden-Aramese schriften in Syrië, Mesopotamië, Perzië en aangrenzende gebieden*. Ph.D. dissertation, Rijksuniversiteit te Groningen.

Kraeling, Emil G. 1953. *The Brooklyn Museum Aramaic Papyri: New Documents of the Fifth Century B.C. from the Jewish Colony at Elephantine*. Publications of the Department of Egyptian Art. New Haven: Yale University Press.

Kutscher, E.Y. 1957. "Review of *Aramaic Documents of the Fifth Century B.C.* (1954) by G. R. Driver." In *Journal of Biblical Literature* 76: 336–338.

Kutscher, E.Y. 1969. "Two 'Passive' Constructions in Aramaic in the Light of Persian." In *Proceedings of the International Conference on Semitic Studies Held in Jerusalem, 19–23 July 1965*. Jerusalem: Israel Academy of Sciences and Humanities, 132–151.

Lewis, Naphtali. 1974. *Papyrus in Classical Antiquity*. Oxford: Clarendon.

Ma, John, Christopher Tuplin, Lindsay Allen, and David Taylor. 2013. *The Arshama Letters from the Bodleian Library*. 4 vols. Oxford. https://wayback.archive-it.org/org-467/20190828084238/; last accessed 6 May 2019.

Muraoka, Takamitsu, and Bezalel Porten. 1998. *A Grammar of Egyptian Aramaic*. Handbuch der Orientalistik, section 1, vol. 32. Leiden: Brill.

Naveh, Joseph, and Shaul Shaked. 2012. *Aramaic Documents from Ancient Bactria (Fourth Century BCE) from the Khalili Collections*. London: The Khalili Family Trust.

Porten, Bezalel, and Ada Yardeni. 1986–1999. *Textbook of Aramaic Documents from Ancient Egypt: Newly Copied, Edited and Translated into Hebrew and English*. 4 vols. in 7 parts. Texts and Studies for Students. Jerusalem: Hebrew University, Department of the History of the Jewish People.

Prinsep, James. 1834. "Notes on Inscription No. 1 of the Allahabad Column." In *Journal of the Asiatic Society of Bengal* 3: 114–123.

Prinsep, James. 1837. "Note on the Facsimiles of Inscriptions from Sanchá near Bhilsa." In *Journal of the Asiatic Society of Bengal* 6: 451–477.

Prinsep, James. 1838. "Additions to Bactrian Numismatics, and Discovery of the Bactrian Alphabet." In *Journal of the Asiatic Society of Bengal* 7: 636–655.

Quatremère, M. 1835. "Mémoire sur les nabatéens." In *Journal Asiatique* 15: 5–271.

Rosenthal, Franz 1939. *Die aramaistische Forschung seit Th. Nöldekes Veröffentlichungen*. Leiden: Brill.

Salomon, Richard G. 2007. "Writing Systems of the Indo-Aryan Languages." In *The Indo-Aryan Languages*, ed. George Cardona and Dhanesh Jain. Routledge Language Family Series. London: Routledge, 67–103.

Schmitt, Rüdiger. 1990. "Bisotun, iii: Darius's Inscriptions." In *Encyclopedia Iranica*, ed. Ehsan Yarshater. New York: Columbia University Center for Iranian Studies, vol. 4: 299–305. http://www.iranicaonline.org/articles/bisotun-iii; last accessed 6 May 2019.

Shaked, Shaul. 2004. *Le satrape de Bactriane: Documents araméens du IVe s. avant notre ère provenant de Bactriane: Conférences données au Collège de France 14 et 21 mai 2003*. Persika, vol. 4. Paris: De Boccard.

Silvestre de Sacy, Antoine Isaac. 1793. *Mémoires sur diverses antiquités de la Perse*. Paris: Imprimerie Nationale.

Sims-Williams, Nicholas. 2000–2007. *Bactrian Documents from Northern Afghanistan*. 3 vols. Studies in the Khalili Collection, vol. 3. Corpus Inscriptionum Iranicarum, vol. 2,6. London: Nour.

Sims-Williams, Nicholas. 2012. "New Light on Ancient Afghanistan: The Decipherment of Bactrian." In *The Silk Road: Key Papers, Part 1: The Pre-Islamic Period*, ed. Valerie Hansen. Leiden: Brill, vol. 1, 95–114.

Sims-Williams, Nicholas. 2015. "Peoples and Places in Pre-Islamic Afghanistan: The Evidence of the Bactrian Documents." Lecture, April 23, Institute for the Study of the Ancient World, New York University, New York.

Skjærvø, P. Oktor. 1996. "Aramaic Scripts for Iranian Languages." In *The World's Writing Systems*, ed. Peter T. Daniels and William Bright. New York: Oxford University Press, 515–535.

Skjærvø, P. Oktor. 2009. "Middle West Iranian." In *The Iranian Languages*, ed. Gernot Windfuhr. Oxford: Routledge, 196–278.

Sprengling, Martin. 1953. *Third Century Iran: Sapor and Kartir*. Chicago: Oriental Institute.

Stolper, Matthew W., and Jan Tavernier. 2007. "An Old Persian Administrative Tablet from the Persepolis Fortification." In *Achaemenid Research on Texts and Archaeology* 2007.001. http://www.achemenet.com/document/2007.001-Stolper-Tavernier.pdf; last accessed 6 May 2019.

Yardeni, Ada. 1997. *The Book of Hebrew Script: History, Palaeography, Script Styles, Calligraphy and Design*. Jerusalem: Carta.

CHAPTER 2

Semitic Documents on Wooden Sticks: Manuscript Writing in Pre-Islamic South Arabia

Peter Stein

لِمَن طَلَلٌ أَبصرتهُ فشجانى كخطِّ زَبورٍ فى عَسيب يمانِ

li-man ṭalalun ʾabṣartuhū fa-šaǧānī / ka-ḫaṭṭi zabūrin fī ʿasībi yamānī[1]

Die Wohnspur wessen seh' ich, die mich bekümmert hat, / Wie Schriftzüg' eines Buches auf Jemens Palmenblatt![2]

Cui (pertinent) rudera quae conspicio, et moerore afficior, / (quae fere deleta sunt) sicut scriptura libri in palmae folio Yamānensi?[3]

… … / Like the writing of the Psalter on a Yamanite palm-leaf.[4]

∴

This famous verse by the 6th-century poet Imruʾ al-Qays tells us almost everything about the mode of writing in pre-Islamic Yemen: the geographical setting, the common writing material, and the name of the particular script. However, when we look at the select translations of the verse as quoted above, a couple of

1 Imruʾ al-Qays 1990: 85. The edition renders the last but one word with *tanwīn* (thus *ʿasībin yamānī*, "a Yemenite *ʿasīb*"), however, refers in the notes to the alternative spelling as a construct state. The metric structure of the verse supports neither of these alternatives since the particular syllable may be spelled either long or short. I owe my gratitude to Tilman Seidensticker (Jena) for a fruitful discussion on this issue.

2 Rückert 1843: 116.

3 Conti Rossini 1931: IX.

4 Krenkow 1927: 930, rendering only the second half of the verse. At another place, the same author translates as follows: "To whom belong the traces of a dwelling-place which I saw and which filled me with sorrow, resembling the hand-writing of a book upon South Arabian palm-bast?" (Krenkow 1922: 265).

 | DOI:10.1163/9789004443877_003

questions arise about the actual meaning of the particular terms listed there: Was the writing really done on palm leaves, as we know them, for instance, from Southern Asia?[5] Was the material considered characteristic for the country of Yemen, or rather its script, or a combination of both?[6] And what, after all, is *zabūr*—a script, some scripture, or even a psalm book, as suggested by its specific usage in the Qur'ān?[7]

It is not necessary, of course, to discuss these issues here, since the answers to these questions have already been given by the material evidence we have available now. Unlike the interpreters of the 19th and early 20th centuries, we know for sure that the inhabitants of Ancient Yemen used wooden sticks and palm-leaf stalks—those *ʿusub* (sing. *ʿasīb*)—as writing material. The first evidence for this came to light in the 1970s.

It was Sergio Noja who identified these palm-leaf stalks with the *ʿusub* from Arabic literature as early as the late 1980s—only few years after the first publications on this new material had appeared.[8] Moreover, he not only gave the correct rendering of the term *ʿasīb* in the context of our verse but succeeded in finding a plausible explanation for the second term in question, *zabūr*—before a single word of this new genre of writing, let alone a translation from it, was published! Of the different meanings attested for the root *z-b-r* in Arabic, he singled out the basic meaning "to write (particularly by engraving in stone),"[9]

5 Thus unanimously in the earlier translations (cf. the quotations above), in spite of the clear statement of the Arabic dictionaries for *ʿasīb* denoting the palm-leaf stalk (e.g., Lane 1863–1893: 2041: "*ʿasīb* A palm-branch from which the leaves have been removed", cf. also the respective observation by Noja 1988: 2). Indeed, in another poem, Imru' al-Qays mentions traces of a camp that are "like the *zabūr* script in books of monks" (*ka-ḫaṭṭi zabūrin fī maṣāḥifi ruhbānī*, Imru' al-Qays 1990: 89). Other poets take writings on parchment as a means of comparison in the same context (cf. Grohmann 1967: 109 note 5). A *muṣḥaf* is basically a book; the word is borrowed from Ethiopic (cf. Stein 2010b: 261–262 with note 20). However, the Ethiopic script, derived from the South Arabian and topographically settled in the very same region (from 525 CE onward, South Arabia was occupied by the Christian Abyssinians!), had probably the same enigmatic appearance for the poet as the Yemenite script.

6 Cf. the analysis of the second part of the verse by Müller 1994: 38. According to him, the attribute *yamānī* is not to explain the foregoing *ʿasīb*, but rather the particular script, *ḫaṭṭ zabūr* (thus, "like the lines of Yemenite script on a palm-leaf stalk"). Yet the word *yamānī* need not be taken to be an attribute at all (cf. note 1 and our proposed translation in the Conclusion at the end of this chapter).

7 For the divergent meanings of *zabūr* in the Arabic literature, cf. Horovitz/Firestone 2002 and Müller 1994. Of course, the particular Qur'anic usage in a sense of "psalms" seems to be influenced by a mingling with Hebrew *mizmōr* and the like (cf. also Jeffery 1938/2007: 148–149).

8 Noja 1988, referring to the most recent publications by Lundin 1989 and Ryckmans 1986.

9 For the meaning "to write" of the root *z-b-r* and its use in Arabic literature for describing the particular writing culture of Yemen, see Müller 1994 and Maraqten 1998: 301–305. Cf. also below with note 33.

the *zabūr* then, being the stylos, the particular tool used to do so. Whether or not *ḫaṭṭ zabūr* really means "engraving by a stylus," as Noja proposed, is of secondary relevance. What is important is the clear identification of what Imruʾ al-Qays describes in his verse with the actual reality that lies behind it.

This reality is the writing culture of Ancient South Arabia, in particular, its manuscript writing, which forms the scope of our presentation. To avoid misunderstanding, it should be stated first that the term "manuscript" is used here in its literal sense, designating all that is, more or less fluently, "written by hand" (*manu scriptum*) on a portable support—in contrast to "inscriptions," which are of completely different purpose and style (cf. below, with note 10). Manuscripts thus comprise all kinds of documentary texts, correspondence, and ultimately even literary compositions—if these were documented at all (cf. below, with note 21). Before going into detail, we will give a brief introduction into Ancient South Arabian epigraphy as a whole.

1 Epigraphy in Pre-Islamic Yemen

The civilization of so-called Ancient South Arabia existed over 1,500 years—from the early 1st millennium BCE (or even earlier) up to the late 6th century CE. Consequently it witnessed the Ancient Mesopotamian culture, starting with the Neo-Assyrian Empire, then the Hellenistic–Roman period, and finally Late Antiquity with its fundamental religious change toward monotheism. Although not unaffected by cultural impacts from these neighboring civilizations in the north and northwest, the remote region at the southern end of the Incense Road remained basically secluded. As a result of this seclusion, the South Arabians preserved their ethnic and linguistic identity, as well as their particular mode of using script.

The South Arabian alphabet, derived from some Canaanite model in the late 2nd millennium BCE, developed into a unique script which would retain its basic characteristics up to the end of the civilization immediately before the rise of Islam. The abundant documentation in this script that has survived to the present, consisting of more than 12,000 inscriptions of quite different contents and style, reveals a vivid picture of South Arabian history and society before Islam. Spread over an area that is even smaller than the present-day Republic of Yemen, these texts are nevertheless found to be written in four different languages (and a number of dialects), named according to the ethnic entities behind them: Sabaic, Minaic, Qatabanic, and Ḥaḍramitic.

Most of the extant texts represent epigraphy in a strict sense: monumental inscriptions, carefully chiseled in geometrically shaped letters in rock sur-

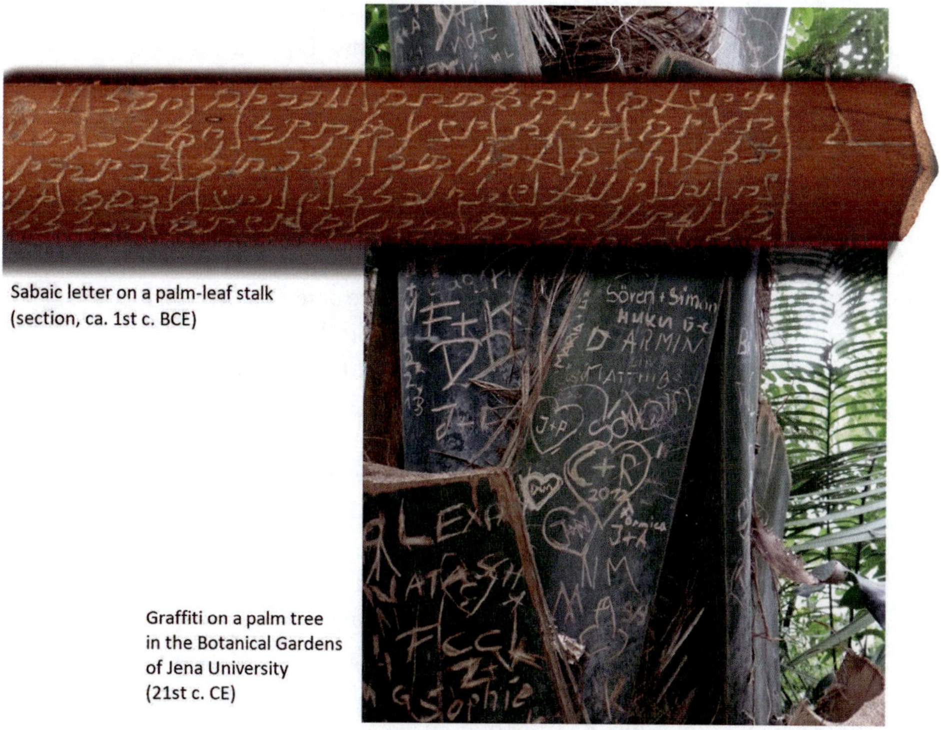
Sabaic letter on a palm-leaf stalk
(section, ca. 1st c. BCE)
Graffiti on a palm tree
in the Botanical Gardens
of Jena University
(21st c. CE)

FIGURE 2.1 Palm-leaf stalks are a welcome writing support
© UNIVERSITY OF JENA (ABOVE), © PETER STEIN (BELOW)

faces and stone blocks, or cast in metal objects. These are, of course, not made for recording business affairs or writing letters, two of the main scopes of using manuscript writing in other cultures. A manuscript for everyday purposes requires two basic things: a cheap and easily prepared support, and a script that allows a rather fluent writing.

And what, then, is cheaper than a piece of wood, quickly cut off the branch of a tree and ready to write upon, like the Yemeni *ʿusub* already described (Fig. 2.1)? One actually wonders why this material has won no recognition in other cultures of the Near East. Is it because sticks are not really appropriate to write on with ink? In South Arabia, at any rate, it seems to have been the only material for manuscript writing. Alternative supports such as leather, papyrus, and the like are not documented at all—which is perhaps no surprise since the established mode of writing by *incising* the script with a pointed stylos does not allow a too fine or soft material. Incising the script, not applying ink or paint, however, is the distinctive peculiarity of Ancient South Arabian writing. And in this respect, manuscript writing is indeed related to monumental epigraphy.

The basic relationship between the two fields even affects scholarly terminology, for the texts on wooden sticks have always been called "inscriptions" and not "manuscripts."[10] Leaving the specific feature of incising the script aside, however, it will easily become clear that writing on wooden sticks is *manu scriptum* in the best sense of the term: fluent writing by hand in a particular cursive script.

This cursive with inclined and sweeping signs clearly following a base-line is, of course, the product of a long-lasting development (Fig. 2.2). In the earliest stage, the letters in the manuscripts had more or less the same shape as those in the monumental inscriptions. Dependent on the needs of fluent writing, and influenced by the specific surface of the writing support, however, they developed consequently into a real cursive. In the later stages of this development, after a couple of centuries, this cursive appears to have nothing in common any more with the contemporary monumental script—just as is the case, for instance, with handwriting and print in modern European writing systems.

In consequence, a scribe had basically to learn two types of script: one for everyday correspondence, and one for epigraphy in the public sphere. It is interesting to note that both scripts would not have been mixed up in terms of their specific purpose. In fact there is no single instance of "monumental" letters on the wooden sticks, whereas cursive inscriptions on stone or rock occasionally occur, but rarely and in rather marginal contexts.[11] The generally crude ductus of cursive graffiti on stone easily reveals that the cursive script was simply not appropriate for being carved in hard surfaces. These short graffiti can thus be interpreted as but occasional attempts by professional scribes to execute their skill of handwriting on a material other than wood.

10 Although J. Ryckmans adapted the term "manuscript writing" to the texts on wood in one of the earliest publications on the matter (Ryckmans 1984: 79), no terminological distinction has hitherto been made between monumental inscriptions on stone and everyday correspondence on wood in Sabaean studies in general (cf. the term "Minuskelinschriften" still used in the title of the present author's 2010 publication). The same terminological weakness may be attributed to the term "minuscule script," which is used alternating not with "majuscule" but rather "monumental script" designating the contemporary script of the stone inscriptions. Since these terms are unmistakably used in Ancient South Arabian philology, however, there is no need to completely replace them. Alternatively, the Arabic terms *zabūr* and *musnad* could be used for the ("minuscule") manuscripts and the monumental inscriptions, respectively.

11 For the evidence of cursive inscriptions on stone known so far, see the references in Stein 2010a: 18 notes 15 and 47, and 47 note 204. Some additional examples are illustrated in Yule 2013: 178 and 181, Figs. 10.7,1 (upside-down) and 10.10,6. Maraqten 2014: 45f. with note 17 reports several short cursive inscriptions on stones found by the American excavations in the Awām temple in Mārib, among them one written with black ink(!), which has never been found on a wooden stick.

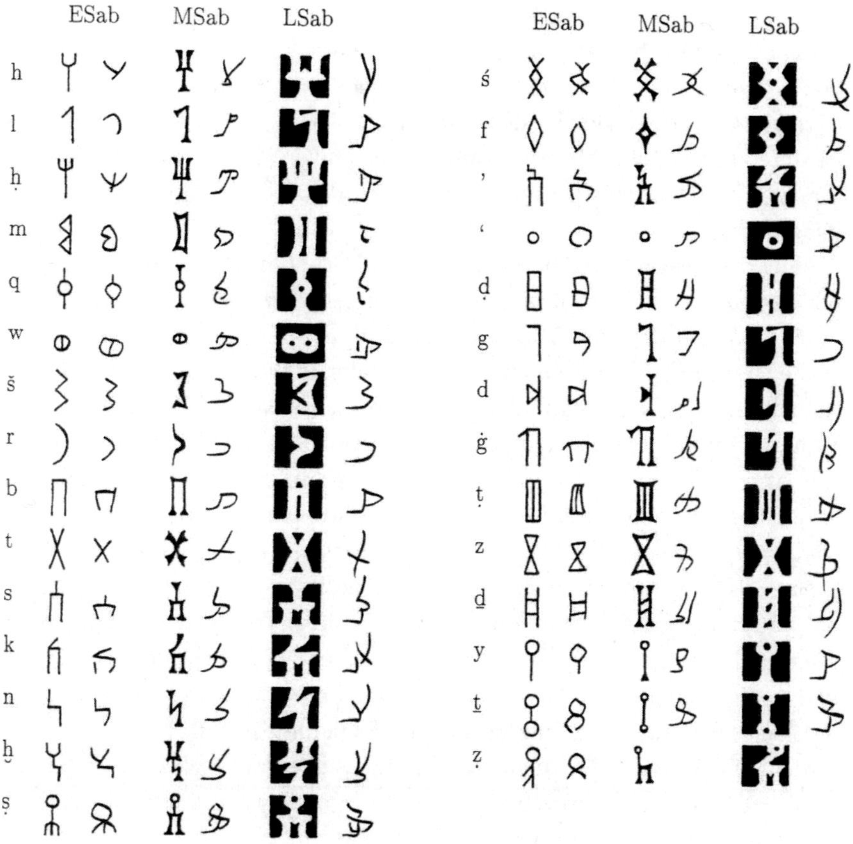

FIGURE 2.2 Development of the Ancient South Arabian monumental (left) and cursive (right) scripts from the Early Sabaic (ESab) to the Late Sabaic (LSab) period (i.e., from the early 1st millennium BCE to the 6th century CE)
© PETER STEIN

2 From *ʿUsub* to *ʿUšar*—the Wooden Material Used for Writing

Coming back to the material support of the manuscripts, what kinds of wood were used? We have spoken about the palm-leaf stalks, the Arabic *ʿusub*. And, as a matter of fact, the vast majority of the manuscripts from Ancient South Arabia were written on these stalks, particularly in the Early Sabaic period, i.e., from the 10th to the 4th century BCE. This is not surprising since the find-spot of our texts[12] lies in the ruins of the ancient city of Naššān (today as-Sawdāʾ), in

12 In fact almost all documents known so far appear to come from one and the same find-spot in that city of Naššān. For some implications of this, see the last section below.

the Wādī al-Ǧawf, a huge irrigation plain at the northern fringe of the Yemeni highlands. As in the oasis of Mārib with its famous dam, periodic monsoon floods coming down from the mountains twice a year enabled the inhabitants of this wadi to cultivate, besides other crops, date palms in huge plantations. As stated before, a freshly cut palm-leaf stalk, taken as a byproduct of agricultural activity, is the cheapest and most easily prepared writing support one can imagine.

However, bearing the topographical situation of the country in mind, we will notice that a number of South Arabian settlement centers are located not in the oases at the northeastern fringe but rather in the highlands themselves, such as the later capitals Ṣanʿāʾ and (Ḥimyarite) Ẓafār. In these mountain areas more than 2,000 meters in height, date palm produce is hardly not possible due to climatic conditions. Consequently one has to look for alternative writing material. And in fact we find documents incised in different sorts of wood, such as species of juniper (e.g., *Juniperus excelsa* M.Bieb.) and the butterfly bush (*Buddleja polystachya* Fresen.),[13] which are domestic in the highlands up to the present day, partly forming regular forests. Unlike the date palm, however, they are not cultivated and therefore had to be collected outside the agricultural domain. There was another slight restriction: in order to be inscribed, they first had to be stripped of their bark. After that, however, they provide a suitable writing surface in no way inferior to that of a palm-leaf stalk.[14]

Being neglected in the highlands for climatic reasons, palm-leaf stalks also eventually fell out of use even in the oases—probably conditioned by climatic changes as well. From the 4th century CE onward, in the Late Sabaic period, they appear to have been completely replaced there by another sort of wood—the so-called Sodom's apple, or *ʿušar* (*Calotropis procera* R.Br.), a wild scrub that grows and spreads widely around the oases in Arabia and beyond. That this mellow wood with a rather fibrous surface and covered with a thick bark was to replace the smooth palm-leaf stalks can only be explained by the fact that date palm cultivation had declined considerably by that time—a fact that is reflected in literary and epigraphic sources as well.[15]

13 For details, cf. Stein 2010a: 24–26 with references.

14 Wood of other trees has not yet been identified under the extant documents. Since Arab authors report that branches of *ʿilb* (*Zizyphus*) and *bān* (*Moringa*) were used as writing material in pre-Islamic Yemen, one may assume that the occasional rumors by locals about the existence of these species among the inscribed sticks could be justified (cf. Maraqten 1998: 294). However, a palaeobotanical analysis, as in the other cases mentioned above, would be required to confirm such an assumption.

15 See Sima 2000: 235 and 238–239, cf. Stein 2010a: 25 with note 64.

Summing up all the evidence, it will become clear that writing material in South Arabia was not restricted to a certain kind of wood, as the *ʿasīb* tradition in the Arabic literature suggests, but was taken from different species, with regional and chronological variation in preference for particular practical reasons.

3 Stylos or Kalamos? Writing Instruments

Incising script requires a special tool, a stylos (στύλος), on which we are going to say a few words now. Interestingly, the word used by Arab writers when referring to *zabūr* written on *ʿasīb* is *qalam*, the word for the kalamos (κάλαμος), or reed-pen.[16] It is difficult to judge whether this can be taken seriously because we do not know the indigenous terminology for a stylos in the Ancient South Arabian languages.[17] However, some material relics of what were apparently *styloi* have been found among the inscribed sticks: a number of pointed pins made of different materials, such as iron and bronze, but also wood and ivory.[18]

While pieces of metal are basically appropriate to incise in wood, wood and ivory certainly are not, since a stylos should, of course, be considerably harder than the material to which it is applied. What, then, could have been the purpose of these rather weak pins? Was there another, softer material to be inscribed—in addition to the wooden sticks we have been talking about? Indeed there was—though one that is still most sporadically attested and not yet published at all.

Some years ago, a number of small tablets came to light in the Wādī al-Ǧawf—in the same region as the wooden sticks and like these unearthed by

16 Thus Labīd, in one of his poems, speaks of a Yemeni child who is used to writing texts in *zabūr* by again and again applying with his hand a *qalam* on *ʿasīb* (*zuburun yuraǧǧiʿuhā walīdun yamānī / mutaʿawwidun laḥinun yuʿīdu bi-kaffihī qalaman ʿalā ʿusubin*, ʿAbbās 1984: 138, cf. Maraqten 1998: 294).

17 One might argue whether the term *mizbar*, which is used alternating with *qalam* for the reed-pen in Arabic, could be of South Arabian origin, evolving together with the particular concept of *zbr*, "to write" (cf. Müller 1994: 37). As mentioned above, S. Noja suggested an identification of the Arabic term *zabūr* with the particular writing tool. In the written sources from South Arabia, however, no allusions at such identification have so far been observed.

18 Five of them from the Ṣanʿāʾ collection have been illustrated by Ryckmans et al. 1994: 82. In fact the editors of this volume presumed already the existence of wax tablets on the basis of this evidence (Ryckmans et al. 1994: 28).

FIGURE 2.3 Writing tablets with wax inlay from Ancient Yemen (ca. 1st century BCE, not scaled)
© MIKAEL S. GIDADA

clandestine excavations (Fig. 2.3).[19] These diptych-like pieces, cut in wood or bone, are clearly writing tablets modeled on the pattern that is well-known from the Mediterranean and beyond. In one case even the wax inlay has been preserved, containing the text of a letter in the Amiritic dialect of Sabaic (Fig. 2.3, right part). According to its palaeography, the text may be dated to the last centuries of the 1st millennium BCE.[20] These unique pieces testify to an actually broader employment of the South Arabian manuscript tradition than the wooden sticks alone imply. However, the actual mode of writing—incising the script with a pen into the surface of a comparatively soft material—remains basically the same in both cases. Using wax tablets for writing is at any rate much less surprising here than in a culture that is accustomed to write with pen and ink. Since the evidence is still too meager to allow a representative evaluation of this find, however, we will now turn back to the main scope of this chapter.

19 The discovery has been reported by the present writer at the 5th Colloquium of the Arbeitsgemeinschaft Semitistik in the Deutsche Morgenländische Gesellschaft in Basel in February 2012 and at the Rencontres Sabéennes 16 in Pisa in June 2012; a publication has meanwhile been prepared (Stein forthcoming). The objects, of which only photographs have been made accessible, are in the possession of a Yemeni collector. Apart from this single find, no comparable objects have come to the author's attention so far.

20 The script is quite similar to that of two letters on palm-leaf stalks from the Munich collection, X.BSB 96 and 97 (cf. Stein 2010a: 340; Stein forthcoming).

FIGURE 2.4 Selection of inscribed wooden sticks of different size from the collection of the Oosters Instituut in Leiden, Netherlands
© OOSTERS INSTITUUT FOUNDATION, LEIDEN, PHOTO W. VREEBURG

4 Format, Size, and Margins—General Appearance of the Writing Support

Basically, the wooden sticks are suitable to provide a writing surface of (almost) any size. Several pieces are up to half a meter long! Figure 2.4 shows a random selection of inscribed sticks (most of them palm-leaf stalks) from the collection of the Oosters Instituut in Leiden, all to the same scale. Most of the documents, however, have an average size of 15 to 20 cm length and 2 cm diameter, providing space for about 10 lines of script. The actual size of a text differs depending on the size of its script, which can vary considerably.

Some school exercises inscribed on sticks are recorded in a regular microscript, offering, at least in theory, the possibility of writing down lengthy records and even works of literature. Combining several sticks into a convolute would in fact meet the requirements needed to compile a book comparable to a papyrus scroll or a codex. Nevertheless, literary compositions in a strict sense have not been found among the manuscripts. This complete lack of literature is characteristic for Ancient South Arabian writing and obviously due to the fact that cultural memory was orally transmitted there, just as it was in other parts of the Arabian Peninsula.[21] In order to give an impression of what kinds of text can be expected among the material, one may consult the following statistics:

Text genre	Collections	
	OI Leiden	BSB Munich
Legal and business documents	128	157
Letter correspondence	74	106
Writing exercises	31	67
Texts from religious practice	12	20
Unspecified fragments	95	44
Total	340	394

The table shows the composition of the two major collections in Leiden (Oosters Instituut) and Munich (Bayerische Staatsbibliothek).[22] In spite of different times and conditions of acquisition,[23] both collections reveal a remarkable correspondence in the distribution of genres. This could be taken as an indication that the original composition of the archive (or whatever it was) from which the documents stem was more or less the same.

About 40 percent of all the texts consist of legal and business documents, such as contracts, promissory notes, and settlements, but also simple accounts and mere lists of goods or names. The second important group is correspondence by letter, followed by records from school practice (alphabets and other exercises). The least important group is texts from the religious sphere—main-

21 On the lack of literary texts among Ancient South Arabian documentation, cf. Stein 2010b: 267–269. Only one genre of literature occurs occasionally in written form, mainly on rock or stone: hymns addressed to certain deities. The particular inscriptions have the character of a dedication.

22 These are the only collections with sufficient representative material available. On the state of research for the Leiden collection, cf. Stein 2015b and Drewes et al. 2016 (with a complete transliteration of all texts); the first half of the Munich collection has been published by Stein 2010a. The selective publication of 100 documents from the National Museum in Ṣanʿāʾ by Maraqten 2014 shall not be compared here since it gives no representative cross-section of this still important collection (cf. Stein 2015a).

23 Whereas the Leiden sticks were purchased on a single occasion in 1993, the Munich collection was gathered in several tranches between 1987 and 1994.

ly reports from the oracles. These contain as well requests addressed to the deity and the respective answers—the latter in a rather short and laconic form. It is important to note that the overall appearance of the manuscripts is basically the same, regardless of the particular genre of each single text. This appearance is characterized by a rectangular writing surface that is determined by the outer margins on both ends of the stick (Fig. 2.5). Additionally, the writing surface may be limited by vertical lines drawn by the scribe—leaving a blank margin that can be used to better handle the stick, but also to hold additional features such as the characteristic symbol that is applied to the right of the first line(s) of many documents. The purpose of this symbol, which is actually found as frequently on legal documents as on letters, still remains uncertain. Since it appears to have basically the same shape in most of the documents, it could stand for the particular location from which the texts come—perhaps being some kind of identification mark of the office that issued the documents.

On wooden sticks of circular diameter, one needs, of course, to indicate the starting point for reading (Fig. 2.5, left part). This is always given by a horizontal line which must first have been drawn along the whole stick (indicated by yellow markers in the picture). The text starts then in the upper right corner of the resulting surface and is written between the margins from right to left (as is usual also in monumental epigraphy)[24] continuously line by line around the stick—as far as necessary.

In contrast to this, the surface structure of palm-leaf stalks is somewhat different (Fig. 2.5, right part). Segments of a palm-leaf stalk consist of two separate surfaces—one larger and smooth, and one smaller and rougher. They are separated from each other by the small side faces that produce the leaves. Since these faces (equally highlighted in yellow in Fig. 2.5) are rather fibrous, they are never found to be inscribed.[25] The larger side of the palm (which is in fact

24 In monumental inscriptions, the text starts in the upper right corner and continues to run over the rectangular writing surface. Apart from right-to-left, the text is often written *boustrophedon* in inscriptions of the older period (up to the 4th/3rd century BCE). This feature, however, is not applied on the manuscripts. The only example for *boustrophedon* text on wooden sticks, recently published by Maraqten 2014: 298 f., is probably a copy of (or even a model for) a legal deed to be set up in monumental epigraphy (cf. Stein 2015a: 80).

25 Among the several hundreds of inscribed palm-leaf stalks published so far, only one could be found that proves to have some text written on one of the side faces. In the private letter published by Stein 2016, the last word of the closing formula was in fact written on the face since the scribe had no space left either on the regular surface or on the (not marked) margins (Stein 2016: 26 f. with Figs. 1–2).

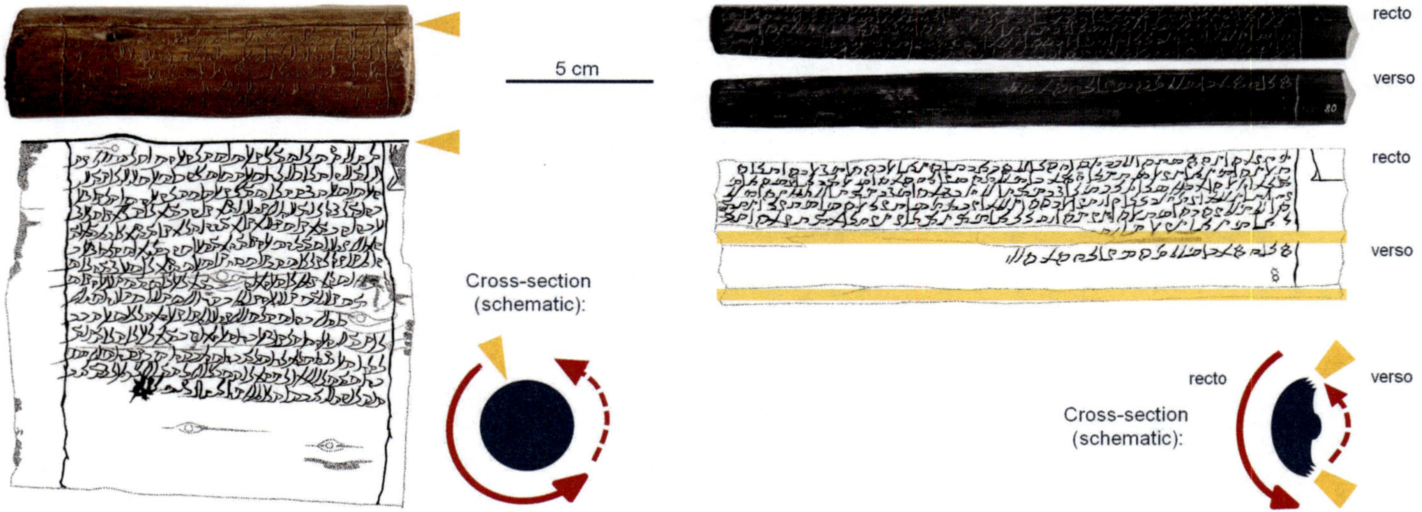

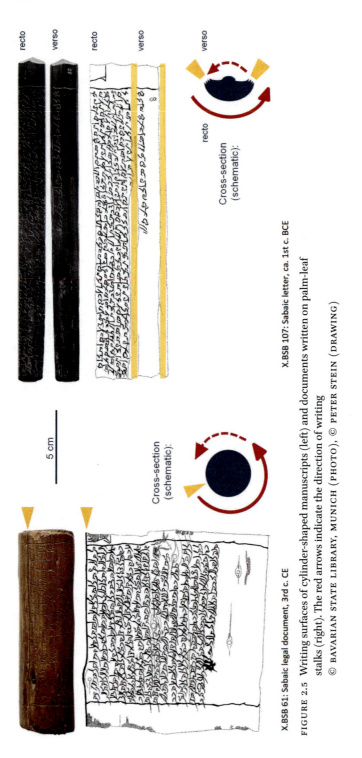

X.BSB 61: Sabaic legal document, 3rd c. CE

X.BSB 107: Sabaic letter, ca. 1st c. BCE

FIGURE 2.5 Writing surfaces of cylinder-shaped manuscripts (left) and documents written on palm-leaf stalks (right). The red arrows indicate the direction of writing
© BAVARIAN STATE LIBRARY, MUNICH (PHOTO), © PETER STEIN (DRAWING)

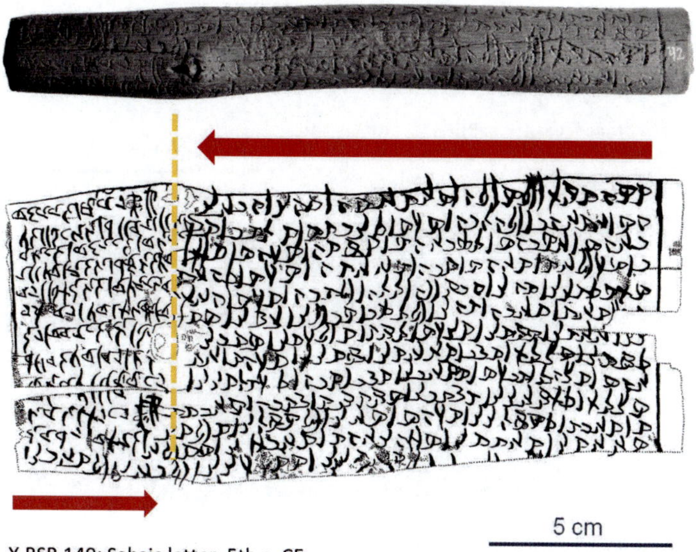

FIGURE 2.6 Manuscript with broad left margin that has been completely filled with text
© BAVARIAN STATE LIBRARY, MUNICH (PHOTO), © PETER STEIN (DRAWING)

its underside when growing on the tree) is always written on first, and is thus called recto in Figure 2.5. The smaller (or upper) side (verso) is only used when the length of the text requires it. The general orientation of palm-leaf stalks is always so that the broader end (originally closer to the trunk) is on the right-hand side. Writing thus starts in the upper right corner of the broader end of the recto. All other features are basically the same as with the round sticks: we have margins that may be separated by vertical lines and bear the symbol mentioned above.

Now, what happened if the space prepared like this did not suffice? If the scribe has left enough blank space at the margins, he could use it to continue the text—normally by turning the stick by 180° and starting from the upper right corner again. In our example in Figure 2.6, the main text field, consisting of 13 lines, covers about three-fourths of the entire length of the stick. The left margin contains, upside-down, another 11 lines in evidently smaller script that are a continuation of the text.

A final observation: Quite a large number of documents bear an eye or notch—always applied to the left margin of the stick (Fig. 2.7). One could argue that these eyes were made to tie several sticks of related matters together. Since this feature is restricted to documents on legal affairs, however, they could also

X.BSB 27: Sabaic acquittance, ca. 4th c. BCE
5 cm
X.BSB 121: Sabaic letter on legal affairs, about 200 CE

FIGURE 2.7 Two wooden documents with eyes for holding a string or perhaps even a seal

have served to hold a string with a seal. Although no traces of such have been detected so far, the procedure of sealing documents with wax and a stamp is explicitly reported in some of the texts.[26]

5 *Zbr*—*ʿlm*—*Ḥqq*: Documenting Processes in the Texts

Having studied the material aspects of Ancient South Arabian manuscript writing, we are now going to ask what information the texts themselves provide about the process of writing on a wooden support. This shall be done by proceeding along the three Sabaic terms quoted in the heading above, which refer to writing as such (*zbr*), authenticating (*ʿlm*), and invalidating (*ḥqq*) a written document.

To start with the first: a noun */zabūr/ (or however it may have been pronounced), which could resemble the respective term in the Arabic sources we spoke about, is thus far attested only once, in a Late Sabaic letter from the 5th century CE:

26 Cf. Ryckmans et al. 1994: 28–29; Stein 2010a: 32.

w-s(7)ṭrw ḏn zbrn
X.BSB 155/6 f.

They have written this *zbr*.[27]

That the noun *zbr* must refer to the present document is evident from the parallel usage of other words that are etymologically clear, as in the following example from a letter of the Middle Sabaic period (1st–2nd centuries CE):

l-ʾsʿd śśʿn ʿm-n ʾwsʿṯt w-hʾ f-qdmy ḏn sṭrn sṭr l-k mṯbt sṭr sṭrk
YM 11749 = TYA 14/1

To ʾAsʿad Šaśʿān from ʾAwsʿaṯt. As for him (i.e., the sender)—before this (present) writing he has already sent to you the answer to the writing you had written (before).

The expression *ḏn sṭrn*, "this writing," designates the particular letter in the hand of its addressee, as *ḏn zbrn* does with the Late Sabaic text. In identifying the term *zabūr* from the Arabic sources with the noun in this Sabaic letter (which is, of course, not necessarily true), we would have to translate the Arabic term neither as "script" nor as a writing instrument (as suggested by Noja, cf. above, near note 9), but rather as something "written," which also would match the (Arabic) pattern of *zabūr* as a passive participle (*faʿūl*).

Much more broadly attested than the noun is the corresponding verb. Although the common verb for "write," *sṭr*,[28] is used together with the noun *zbr* in the passage quoted above, the verb *zbr* occurs slightly farther, at the end of the same text:

w-(8)zbr ḏ-gdnm [signature]
X.BSB 155/7 f.

The man of (the clan) Gadanum (= the sender) has written.

27 The word *zbr* occurs in a similar context also in line 3 of that letter.

28 *sṭr* appears to be the most common word for "writing," attested in all Ancient South Arabian languages and used both for manuscript writing and for monumental inscriptions (Beeston et al. 1982: 129; Arbach 1993: 83; Ricks 1989: 159–160; *Sabäisches Wörterbuch*: s.v.). Also the nominal derivative *sṭr*, "(piece of) writing," sometimes also "lines (of inscription)" in the plural *ʾsṭr*, is widespread in quite different contexts. Etymologically this root is connected with *šaṭāru*, the common word for "write" in Akkadian, but is found (as loan from there?) in Aramaic and Hebrew and, later, Arabic as well (cf. the references collected by al-Selwi 1987: 109–110).

This is in fact a stereotypical formula found at the end of numerous documents (mostly letters) from the Late Sabaic period, i.e., from the 4th–6th centuries CE.[29] It is remarkable that the verb always occurs before a proper name, followed by the individual signature of the particular person.[30] This characteristic arrangement makes clear that the subject of the verb must be the person who finally signed the document.[31] Moreover, since the verb *zbr* appears to be restricted to the quoted formula at the end of a written record,[32] one may argue that its actual meaning is better rendered by "to sign, subscribe" rather than simply by "to write," resulting in a meaning of "signed document" for the writing called *zabūr*. Etymologically, the word can be connected with a process of incising or carving, which fits its usage with the wooden sticks quite well.[33] Be this as it may, the South Arabian "model" of the Arabic term *zabūr* clearly points to a scribal process, be it writing or signing or both, that is represented by documents carved on wooden sticks and authenticated by the signatures of involved persons. These signatures will concern us in more detail in what follows.

A superficial glance at some of these signatures already reveals that they are of individual shape, clearly differing one from the other. In some cases, even individual letters can be figured out that are obviously taken from the name of the particular person (in Fig. 2.8 bottom left, for example, the letter *ḥ* stands out from the middle of the signature—and is in fact the first letter of the author's

29 Cf. Stein 2010a: 28 with note 79, and the reference in the following note.

30 For evidence, cf. the lexical index in Stein 2010a: 735. Occasionally also the phonetic variant with /ḏ/ (*ḏbr*) occurs (Stein 2010a: 722), which is reported in the Arabic lexicographical literature as well (al-Selwi 1987: 91; Lane 1863–1893: 955c). The background of this variation in Sabaic is a sound shift by which the two phonemes /ḏ/ and /z/ have fallen together (cf. Stein 2013a: 43–44).

31 The supposition that the passage could refer to the whole document ("The man of Gadanum has written (the foregoing)") rather than to the following signature, as proposed, e.g., by Maraqten 2014: 34–35, can probably be ruled out (cf. already the discussion by Stein 2010a: 421).

32 Thus far, no other context of the root *z-b-r* has been revealed. How the few instances of a verb *zbr* in monumental inscriptions (C 287 = N 58/1 and VL 24 = J 2353/8; cf. also Robin 2005–2006: 52 and 60 for two more, still unpublished examples) relate to this evidence remains uncertain because the semantic background of these inscriptions is far from clear.

33 Cf. the rendering "tailler" and "briser" given by Cohen et al. 1995: 677–678 for the root *z-b-r* in Arabic dialects and Ethiopic. In this function, the Sabaic word seems to have replaced the older *ḫṭṭ* of basically the same meaning (cf. Cohen et al. 1995: 979: "creuser," "tracer des lignes sur le sol," etc.) that is commonly used, besides the neutral *sṭr*, to express "writing" in Sabaic (and Minaic) texts from earlier periods (cf. Stein 2008: 780–781; Stein 2010a: 326 with commentary for examples from correspondence).

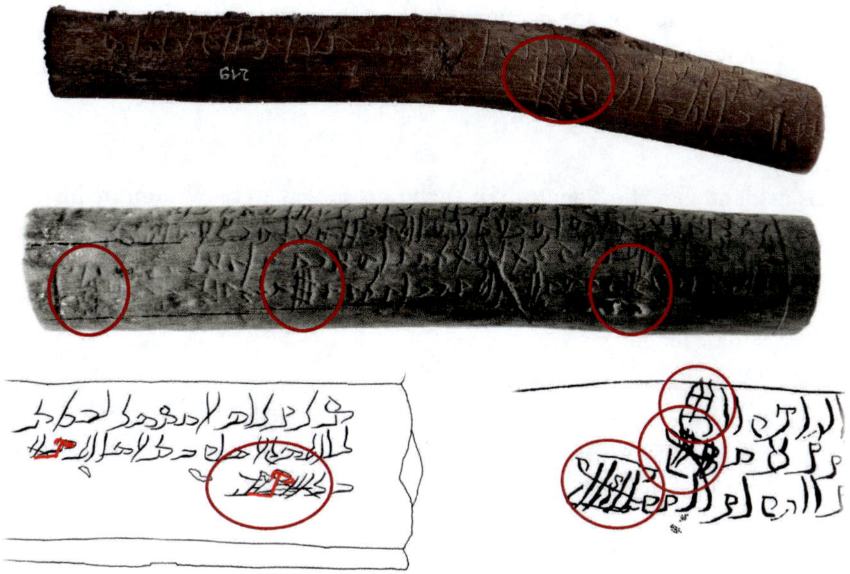

FIGURE 2.8 Examples of individual signatures on wooden documents. In the picture bottom left, the signature repeats the prominent first letter of the author's name mentioned immediately before

clan name immediately mentioned before; both highlighted in Fig. 2.8). It is obvious that these individual signs were made to specify the liability of the parties involved in the documented affair. This is of particular importance in legal and business documents. And indeed these documents reveal a specific terminology that exceeds the statements with the verb *zbr* we have seen before. A characteristic formula at the end of a legal document is the following, taken from a promissory note on a certain amount of money, laid down in the year 385 CE, from the Leiden collection:

> *wrḫ-hw ḏ-nsw[r]* (*10*) *ḏ-l-ḫrfn ḏ-l-ḫmst w-tsʿy w-ʾrbʿ mʾtm ʿlm* (*11*) *yd ʾlrm* (signature) *mḥmdm ḏ-ygr {b-smʿ}*[34] (signature) *b-smʿ slymm* (signature)
>
> L 25/9–11

34 The phrase *b-smʿ*, "under the testimony of," seems to be misplaced in this position. It probably belongs before the foregoing name of the first witness (as the translation proposes).

> Its (i.e., the present document's) month is Ḏū-Niswar of the year 495 (Ḥimyarite era). Signature by the hand of ʾIlrām (= the debtor) under the testimony of Muḥammadum of (the clan) Yagūr, (and) under the testimony of Sulaymum.

It is evident that the signature of each person was to be written by his own hand, as proved by the expression *ʿlm yd*, related to the debtor, as mentioned in line 2 of the document. Of course, this is not the only example.[35] More than 500 years earlier, we find quite similar expressions in legal documents written in the Minaic language:

> *w-kwnt ḏt šrḥtn b-wrḫ* (*12*) *ḏ-smʿ ḏ-ḫrf rfyḍm ḏ-mrn smʿm ḏ-yʿt*(*13*)*llm b-šrḥt*[*n*] *sṭr yd whyb*⟨*m*⟩ *ḏ-whbʾl* (signature) (*14*) *sṭr yd mtyʿm ḏ-frʿm* (signature) *sṭr yd mkrb*(*15*)*m ḏ-lḥgm b-šrḥtn* (signature)[36]
>
> Mon.script.sab. 624/11–15

> This warranty was set up in the month Ḏū-Samiʿ of the year of (the eponym) Rufayḍum of (the clan) Marrān. Witness who signs the warranty: handwriting of Wuhaybum of (the clan) Wahbʾil; handwriting of Mutayʿum of (the clan) Farʿum; handwriting of Mukarribum of (the clan) Laḥgum on the warranty.

In this formula, the noun *sṭr*, "writing," replaces the *ʿlm* of the Late Sabaic documents discussed before. It is thus beyond doubt that authenticating a legal deed has been done in writing, in that the involved persons and witnesses set their handwritten signatures to the particular document. As the quoted Minaic example shows, this authenticating process was expressed by a derivative of the verb *ʿlm*, "to know," which may be literally rendered as "to acknowledge, approve" (cf. Arabic *ʿallama*, "to put a mark").[37] We find the particular verb *tʿlm* again in a very expressive passage in the Middle Sabaic letter we have already quoted above:[38]

---

35 The same formula is attested in X.BSB 46 and 54, two promissory notes from the Munich collection, dated to the years 522 Ḥ = 412 CE and 579 Ḥ = 469 CE.

36 Transliteration without textcritical marks. The reading of the formula is basically supported by a number of parallels, such as Mon.script.sab. 508/11 f., 554/8–11 and 611/8 f. These documents were written between the 5th and 3rd century BCE.

37 In Sabaic, the verb is normally in T_2 stem, which corresponds morphologically to Arabic V *taʿallama*. In contrast to this, the Minaic cognate is a reduplicating stem T_3, on which see Stein 2011: 1058–1059.

38 Apart from this, the verb *tʿlm* occurs in numerous legal documents from Middle Sabaic

w-hʾ f-(2)rʾ hysr l-k ṯny mqbln w-tʿlm b-hmy w-hmy hkʔnk f-tʿlmn b-hmy w-hysrn l-hw ʾḥd mq(3)blm w-ʾḥd l-ygzyn b-ʿm-k[39]

YM 11749 = TYA 14/1–3

As for him (= the sender of the letter)—he has sent to you two copies (of a contract) and already signed them both. Now, when you have made a decision (?), sign both of them and send one copy back to him, and one shall remain with you.

Consequently, all three verbs, *zbr*, *sṭr*, and *tʿlm*, though of quite different etymology, are found to express that a written document is signed by hand. However, they are not completely interchangeable: while *zbr* and *sṭr* basically designate the practical aspect of incising the signature into the writing support, the verb *tʿlm* points to the immaterial sphere of acknowledging the bilateral process that exists behind the mere document.

Having analyzed these aspects of producing an effective document, it remains now to ask what happened when the affair had been settled and the respective document had become null and void. How did the South Arabians get a manuscript on wooden stick invalidated?

Apart from just tearing (i.e., breaking) it to pieces, the simplest way to visibly invalidate a document would be to cross it out—by scratching across the written text. And on numerous documents—interestingly, most of them concerning legal and business affairs—we find notches and scores, quite evenly distributed over the entire writing surface (Fig. 2.9). The regular shape of these scores can only be explained by deliberate destruction, not by random damage.[40] Moreover, even the written sources report on this practice of annulling documents, though not the wooden sticks themselves, but rather some monumental inscriptions.

It comes as no surprise that legal deeds of major importance, in particular receipts for the payment of financial obligations, were made public to demonstrate that the matter had been settled, and to rule out any further claims in that affair once and forever. These announcements were set up in monumen-

---

times in the same sense as in the stereotypical expression in the Minaic example quoted above (for evidence, cf. the index in Stein 2010a: 720).

39 For the reading and interpretation proposed here, cf. Stein 2006: 392 with note 40.

40 The dirt crust with which many of these scores are still covered is basically the same as that on the remaining surface of the sticks. This makes clear that the damage must have been inflicted on the sticks already in Antiquity, before they entered the soil they were unearthed from many centuries later.

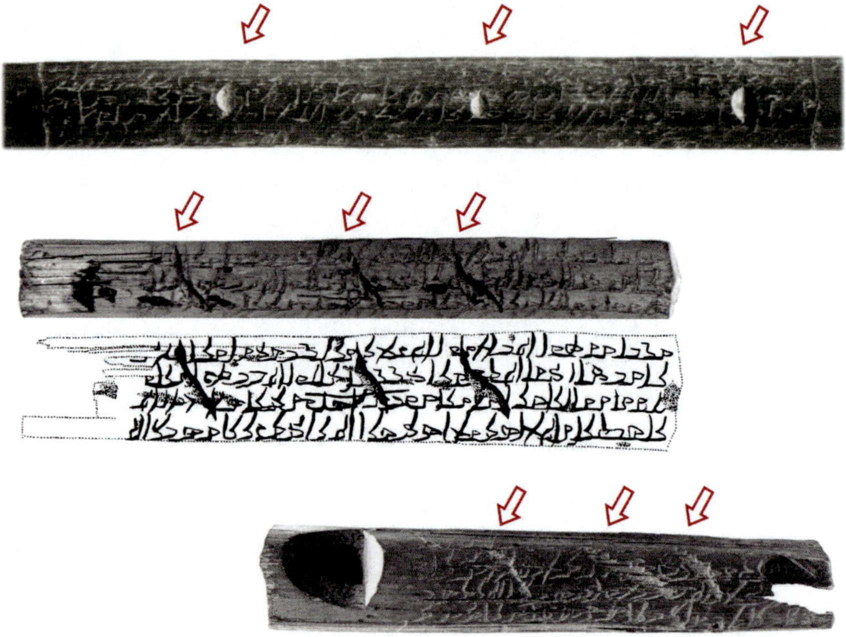

FIGURE 2.9 Annulment of wooden documents by carving and notching across the text
© BAVARIAN STATE LIBRARY, MUNICH (PHOTO), © PETER STEIN (DRAWING)

tal epigraphy and displayed at central places in the cities so as to gain broad public attention. One example of such a public announcement is the following, a monumental Sabaic inscription chiseled in a pillar at the entrance to the main temple in Ṣirwāḥ, an important religious center of the Sabaean kingdom not far from the capital Mārib, in the 3rd century BCE:

> *(1) w-hmẓʾ w-ṣdq ʾbkrb bn yqdm(2)ʾl bn ʿnnn l-ʾly st ʾqyn ṣrwḥ ʾ(3)[r]bʿ mʾn blṭm nʿmtm | m m m m | blṭ (4) fdy nšʾkrb ḏ-ḥbb ʾqyn ṣrwḥ (5) bn sʾl b-ʿly ʾbh-hw … … (8)* ***w-nfqm w-šṣṣm kl ẓhr w-ʿlmy b-hw stʿ****(9)****lm b-ʾlt blṭn ʾrbʿn mʾnhn bn ʿly*** *ʾ(10)****bkrb w-wld-hw*** *ʾ-hn-n ʿkr w-l yyfʿ(11)n bn byt ḏ-ḥbb w-ʾqyn ṣrwḥ w-nkrm w-(12)kwn ḏn mṣdqn b-kn twsyw b-ḏ nswr (13) qdmn gyl ḫrf yṯʿm bn ḥzfrm ḏ-rf(14)dn ṯkmtn w-hmṯl ḏn mṣdqn bn mṣ(15)dq b-hw tʿlm ḏ-ḥbb w-hlkʾmr bn š(16)hrʿly w-lḥyʿṯt bn krdn w-tbʿkr(17)b bn ʿnnn ḏ-ḏrʾn w-nšʾkrb bn drʿn*[41]
>
> Gl 1533 = J 2855

41 Cf. the interpretation of the text's central issue by Stein 2010a: 131–132. A thorough etymological clarification of the keywords on which the following analysis is based, however, could only later be achieved by Multhoff 2013 (cf. below, with note 43).

> (1) ʾAbukarib, son of Yaqdumʾil, (2) of (the clan) ʿInānān, has transferred and paid to the administrators of Ṣirwāḥ (3) four hundred excellent *blṭt*-coins (400), the coins (4) by which Našaʾkarib of (the clan) Ḥubāb, (representing) the administrators of Ṣirwāḥ, has redeemed (him) (5) from a demand (lasting already) on his fathers … … (8) **And every document and testimony that is signed (9) with respect to these four hundred *blṭt*-coins is invalid and 'broken' (away) from (10) ʾAbukarib and his offspring.**—Whenever wished, (the document) shall be delivered up (11) by the house of (the clan) Ḥubāb, the administrators of Ṣirwāḥ, or anybody else.—(12) This recording, when they guaranteed each other, took place in the first (of the two months named) Ḏū-Niswar (13) of the period of the first year of (the eponym) Yāṯiʿum of (the clan) Ḥazfarum Ḏū-Rafdān. (14) This document has been copied from the document (15) that (the following persons) have signed: the (representative) of Ḥubāb, Halikʾamar of (the clan) (16) Šahrʿalī, Luḥayʿaṯt of (the clan) Kardān, Tubbaʿkarib (17) of (the clan) ʿInānān Ḏū-Ḏarʾān, and Našaʾkarib of (the clan) Darʿān.

The passage of concern to us is in lines 8–10 (in bold type above): there it is explicitly stated that all documents which refer to the obligation that has just been settled are now considered invalid. However, if we look at older publications of this and other related texts, we will always find quite the contrary translated: that the particular documents are in fact binding and effective,[42] and not invalid, as we have translated here. The correct renderings of the terms in question, *nfq* and *šṣṣ*, have been detected by Anne Multhoff.[43] These two words belong to a group of adjectives that are regularly used, in varying compositions, in the particular formula of public announcements of settled obligations, just as is seen in the example quoted here.

These adjectives are (in alphabetical order) *bḏl*, *ḥqq*, *ḫdʿ*, *nfq*, *šṣṣ*, and *śḫl*.[44] A thorough analysis of their etymology reveals that they can be distributed into two semantic groups: one denoting the field of "settle, cancel, throw

42 Thus the rendering of the two terms in question here, *nfq* and *šṣṣ*, in the Sabaic dictionary by Beeston et al. 1982: 92 and 135.

43 Multhoff 2013. The etymologies quoted in the following notes are taken from there, where also the complete references are given. Besides the purely lexical arguments, there are also syntactic features that support this new interpretation, such as the phrase *w-ḏ-ʾl yhknn*, "and what is not to be produced any more," which likewise refers to the annulled documents such as the adjectives discussed here (cf. ibid., 109 f.).

44 Perhaps a form *ḫyb*, "forfeited, lost," has to be added as seventh term, cf. Multhoff 2013: 114 f. s.v. *ḫ(y)ḏ*.

away" (*bdl*,[45] *nfq*[46] and *śḫl*[47]), and the second denoting "destroy" and, even more precisely, "break to pieces" (*ḫdʿ*[48] and *šṣṣ*[49]). Interestingly, the word *ḥqq*, apparently related to the respective Arabic root *ḥ-q-q*, also belongs to this second category. Indeed, the well-known meaning of the common Arabic *ḥaqq* ("truth, rightness"), *ḥaqīqī* ("real, true"), etc. could suggest a positive function of the Sabaic word in the sense of "valid, effective." This allegedly clear parallel, however, in fact prevented earlier scholars from perceiving the truth behind the whole formula! An examination of the etymologies of the root *ḥ-q-q* in the Northwest Semitic languages reveals that it has a basic meaning "hew out, engrave," which only secondarily acquired the special function "issue a decree"—probably by carving it into a publicly displayed inscription. In our Sabaic formula *ḥqq* thus means not "true" but rather "crossed out," just as the material evidence of the wooden documents suggests. As reflected both in the textual evidence and in clearly visible traces on the manuscripts themselves, invalidating written records in South Arabia was executed by physical damage of the documents—by scratching, notching, and breaking them to pieces.[50]

6 Geniza or Rubbish Dump? The Character of the "Archive" in Naššān

Having reached this final stage in its life, what further was to be done with the document? A small piece of wood that has lost its function could simply be thrown away. If not put into the fire, the sticks would have been scattered around and, rotting in the soil, soon disappeared. The conditions of their discovery, however, point to another situation. Most of the sticks were apparently

---

45 Cf. Mehri *bəḏōl*, "abandon, throw over"; Arabic *baḏala*, "give freely, willingly," "not preserve or take care of (a garment)" (Lane 1863–1893: 174).

46 Cf. Arabic *nafiqa*, "come to an end, become exhausted"; Ethiopic *nafaqa*, "tear off, tear away, divide in two," may even point to our second category.

47 The corresponding verb in Sabaic and Minaic means "settle (a debt)" (cf. the evidence quoted by Multhoff 2013: 115 note 40).

48 The meaning "damage, demolish" of this root is already established in Sabaic (cf. Beeston et al. 1982: 58–59; *Sabäisches Wörterbuch*: s.v.).

49 Cf. Yemeni Arabic *ištaṣṣa*, "splinter."

50 A deliberate breaking of invalid documents is, of course, much less clearly provable than scratching their surface, since a piece of wood that came to light as broken fragment might have been randomly damaged by any other occasion. However, there are enough fragments in our hoard with only part of their original text preserved that could well be the result of such annulment by calculated destruction.

found not only at one and the same spot,[51] but also mixed up with a huge number of uninscribed pieces, which actually form half the stock of the Munich collection![52]

FIGURE 2.10 Originally uninscribed raw material prepared for writing but never used (Mon.script.sab. 39 and 301 from the Munich collection). The "texts" on them are modern additions
© BAVARIAN STATE LIBRARY, MUNICH

These sticks have the same appearance as the manuscripts proper: segments of palm-leaf stalks and other wood cut at both ends—apparently prepared for writing but then never used. They can be interpreted as raw material from the writing process that was put aside because there was no need for it at the moment. Since carving in wood becomes more and more difficult as its surface dries up, a scribe would always have used a new, freshly cut stick instead of one that already had rested with him for days or weeks. This explains why so many pieces without text have been unearthed together with the manuscripts. That most of them today bear some kind of script is a result of the general circumstances of their discovery: the hoard was excavated not by an archaeological mission, but rather by local people who were understandably more interested in material benefit than in scientific exploitation of their work. Consequently, numerous blank pieces were supplied with something that looks like ancient writing in order to sell better: many of them just by arbitrary scribbling, but some with carefully made, more or less successful copies of authentic inscriptions (Fig. 2.10).[53]

---

51 Cf. above, with note 12. The only known places where manuscripts have been unearthed outside Naššān are the settlement of Raybūn in Ḥaḍramawt (see most recently Frantsouzoff 1999) and the village of Maqwala southeast of Ṣanʿāʾ (the latter again in private excavations by local people, cf. preliminarily Maraqten 2014: 19 note 2; a publication on this hoard by Sarah Rijziger and the present author is in preparation).

52 In contrast to this, the collection of the Oosters Instituut in Leiden contains only 11 percent of such blank pieces.

53 A number of manuscripts from the Munich collection have been identified as models for these copies, but also at least one monumental inscription. Some specific aspects of this

But let us return to the original evidence. The hoard of manuscripts discovered in Naššān, one of the ancient cities in the Wādī al-Ǧawf in the north of Yemen, appears to represent the public archive of that city. Containing not only business documents and correspondence of quite different people, but also writing exercises and the blank material we just spoke about, it must be considered the remains of an office, a place where documents were composed and stored but also one where the skills of writing were obtained. The find-spot is reported to lie close to the ruins of a sanctuary, and the few but expressive records from oracular practice among the manuscripts likewise suggest a basic connection with the temple.[54] The only question that remains to be answered is whether our hoard is really the remainder of that archive, preserved within the ruins of the ancient office—or, rather, the contents of a dust hole nearby.

The extraordinarily good preservation of many pieces, yet the incredibly long span of about 1,500 years covered by the manuscripts (i.e., from the early 1st millennium BCE up to the 6th century CE),[55] basically seems to speak for a calculated, systematic storage of the documents reminiscent, for example, of the Jewish Genizas. What makes this likely association questionable, however, is the fact that so much unwritten material has been found side by side with the manuscripts. It is mainly the existence of the numerous blank pieces which suggests that the hoard is, rather, an assemblage of rubbish formed by material that was no longer of any use in the office and was thus thrown away—apparently always onto the same spot. Under favorable climatic conditions, the written documentation disposed of in this way not only accumulated over the entire span of Ancient South Arabian history,[56] but survived beneath the soil up to the present day. At any rate, manuscript writing in the Sabaic language was still alive in the first half of the 6th century, during the lifetime of Imruʾ al-Qays,

---

forgery, such as models, writing technique, and even the identification of different hands will be analyzed in the second part of the publication of the Munich collection, which is currently under preparation (cf. preliminarily Stein 2010a: 52–53; Stein 2015b: 205–207).

54 The information on the find-spot and the circumstances of its discovery is summarized by Jean-François Breton in Ryckmans et al. 1994: 2–4; cf. also Stein 2010a: 21–24. For discussion on the character of the archive, cf. Stein 2010a: 34–35.

55 The oldest known example, L 24 from the Oosters Instituut collection, has been radiocarbon dated to the 11th–10th centuries BCE. The so far youngest piece is the fragment of a legal deed, X.BSB 74, dated to the year 632 Ḥimyarite era, which corresponds to 522 CE (cf. Stein 2010a: 45–49; Drewes et al. 2013; a reevaluation of the chronology of the Ancient South Arabian script, including the manuscripts, is given by Stein 2013b).

56 As the palaeographical analysis of the manuscripts reveals, documentation covers the entire span without any significant gap. Cf. the palaeographical tables by Ryckmans 2001; Stein 2010a: 48–49; Stein 2013b.

the Arab poet quoted at the outset of this chapter. At least from a chronological point of view, the poet could very well have been an eyewitness to one or another inscribed stick preserved in our collections!

7 Conclusion

Having answered the question of *ʿasīb* and *zabūr* raised by Imruʾ al-Qaysʾ famous verse that opens this paper, let us have a final look at the poet and his conception of the mode of writing in Ancient Yemen. Why was it that the poet was "filled with sorrow," as he puts it, when reflecting upon traces of a dwelling-place as upon a piece of manuscript?[57] What was the *tertium comparationis* that linked the abandoned camp in his mind with the foreign script from Yemen? Did the almost obliterated traces of the camp remind him of effaced writings in a book, as a popular interpretation of this theme in Arabic love poetry (*nasīb*) suggests?[58] Probably not, since the incised script of the wooden sticks is, as we have seen, fairly impervious to being effaced. Was it simply the pictorial pattern of the remains of the camp, sometimes even compared with tattoos,[59] which brought that foreign script to his mind? Perhaps—but

57 As mentioned in note 4 above, prior to Krenkow's translation of the second half of the verse as "Like the writing of the Psalter on a Yamanite palm-leaf" (Krenkow 1927: 930), he translated the entire verse as "To whom belong the traces of a dwelling-place which I saw and which filled me with sorrow, resembling the hand-writing of a book upon South Arabian palm-bast?" (Krenkow 1922: 265).

58 In this sense, see, e.g., Jacobi 1971: 22–23, referring to the comparison of "verblaßte Tätowierung" (*ka-bāqi l-wašmi*) in the introductory verse of a poem by Ṭarafa.

59 Cf. for instance Labīd's poem, quoted already in note 16, on the camp of Mutāliʿ, the traces of which are compared not only to *zabūr* script but also to a body part that has been exposed to a woman applying tattoos to it (cf. the respective comments by ʿAbbās 1984: 139). A similar motive is quoted in line 9 of the same poet's *muʿallaqa* (cf. Jones 1996: 169, pointing at the "clear" appearance of the tattooing). Also Ṭarafa's verse quoted by Jacobi (see preceding note 58) might be understood in the same way—focusing not on the effacement but on the existence of the tattoo as such. Cf. also Lichtenstädter 1932: 31, referring to quite a number of metaphors, such as "Schriftstücke, deren Schrift mit dem *qalam* wieder aufgefrischt wurde," "vergoldete Schriftzüge," "Linien, die die Feder auf Lederstücke zieht," and others. In the same sense, see already Krenkow 1922: 264–265, referred to by Wagner 1987: 19 with note 27 (cf. note 4 above). A completely different interpretation of what the remaining traces could be has been proposed by Ahmad al-Jallad (Leiden) in personal communication. He thinks that the poets describe not material traces of the camp, but rather real script—in the form of inscriptions that had been left by the inhabitants of the site. Particularly the northern part of the Arabian Peninsula is densely crowded with inscriptions and graffiti in Ancient North Arabian dialects.

then why his sorrow about that script? Or could it be that the poet is grieved simply because he has not been able to read—the traces of the abandoned dwelling-place as well as the Yemeni script? To our mind, this seems the most plausible explanation: leaving no message of the missing behind, the camp before him has proved to be enigmatic, evoking questions just as the obscure foreign script did that he remembers right now![60]

Moreover, if we read the final *ʿasībi yamānī* in his verse as a construct, then the *nisba* would likely refer to a person. Unlike the attributive renderings "a Yemenite palm-leaf stalk" or "Yemenite script," this would imply that the particular script was not only restricted to correspondence originating from Yemen, but also accessible only to people from there. Thus our poet might once have seen in the hand of a Yemeni trader a writing that remained completely enigmatic to the poet himself. His sorrow about not being able to "read" the traces of the abandoned camp he saw as he passed by may have recalled this frustrating experience to him:[61]

> *li-man ṭalalun ʾabṣartuhū fa-šaǧānī / ka-ḫaṭṭi zabūrin fī ʿasībi yamānī*
>
> Who has left the traces I've seen, grieving me / like the script of a record on a palm-leaf stalk in the hands of a Yemeni?

Sigla of Quoted Texts

C 287 = N 58	CSAI
Gl 1533 = J 2855	CSAI
L	Drewes et al. 2016
Mon.script.sab.	(unpubl.)
VL 24 = J 2353	Jamme 1971: 86–88; cf. Robin 2014: 48 f.
X.BSB	Stein 2010a
YM (= TYA)	Ryckmans et al. 1994

60 This interpretation had already been proposed, though not explicitly for the poem in question, by Krenkow 1922: 265–266. Cf. also the respective gloss in the edition: "its traces have been effaced and disappeared so that one can see of it only something like a secret book" (*ka-ḫaṭṭi zabūrin ay qad darasa wa-ḫafiyat ʾāṯāruhū fa-lā yurā minhu ʾillā miṯlu l-kitābi fī l-ḫafāʾ*); Imruʾ al-Qays 1990: 85.

61 For the following translation of the verse, cf. also Maraqten 1998: 304.

Bibliography

ʿAbbās, ʾIḥsān. 1984. *Šarḥ dīwān Labīd b. Rabīʿa al-ʿĀmirī*. At-Turāṯ al-ʿArabī, vol. 8. 2nd ed. Kuwait: Maṭbaʿat ḥukūmat al-Kuwayt.

Arbach, Mounir. 1993. *Lexique Madhābien comparé aux lexiques sabéen, qatabanite et ḥaḍramawtique*. PhD thesis, Aix-en-Provence.

Beeston, Alfred F.L., Mahmoud A. Ghul, Walter W. Müller, and Jacques Ryckmans. 1982. *Sabaic Dictionary (English–French–Arabic)*. Publications of the University of Sanaa, YAR. Louvain-la-Neuve: Peeters/Beyrouth: Librairie du Liban.

Cohen, David, François Bron, and Antoine Lonnet. 1995. *Dictionnaire des racines sémitiques ou attestées dans les langues sémitiques*. Leuven: Peeters.

Conti Rossini, Karolus [Carlo]. 1931. *Chrestomathia arabica meridionalis epigraphica edita et glossario instructa*. Roma: Istituto per l'Oriente.

CSAI: *Corpus of South Arabian Inscriptions*. Web source: http://dasi.cnr.it.

Drewes, Abraham J., Thomas F.G. Higham, Michael C.A. Macdonald, and Christopher Bronk Ramsey. 2013. "Some Absolute Dates for the Development of the South Arabian Minuscule Script". In *Arabian Archaeology and Epigraphy* 24: 196–207.

Drewes, Abraham J., and Jacques Ryckmans. 2016. *Les inscriptions sudarabes sur bois dans la collection de l'Oosters Instituut conservée dans la bibliothèque universitaire de Leiden*. Texte révisé et adapté par Peter Stein, ed. Peter Stein and Harry Stroomer. Wiesbaden: Harrassowitz.

Frantsouzoff, Serguej A. 1999. "Hadramitic Documents Written on Palm-Leaf Stalks." In *Proceedings of the Seminar for Arabian Studies* 29: 55–65.

Grohmann, Adolf. 1967. *Arabische Paläographie, I. Teil*. Denkschriften der Österreichischen Akademie der Wissenschaften: Philosophisch-historische Klasse, vol. 94,1. Wien: Böhlau.

Horovitz, Josef, and Reuven Firestone. 2002. "Zabūr." In *Encyclopaedia of Islam, Second Edition*. Leiden: Brill, vol. 9: 372–373.

Imruʾ al-Qays. 1990. *Dīwān Imruʾ al-Qays*, ed. Muhammad ʾA.F. ʾIbrāhīm. Ḏaḫāʾir al-ʿArab, vol. 24. 5th ed. Cairo: Dār al-Maʿārif.

Jacobi, Renate. 1971. *Studien zur Poetik der altarabischen Poesie*. Veröffentlichungen der Orientalischen Kommission der Akademie der Wissenschaften und der Literatur Mainz, vol. 24. Wiesbaden: Harrassowitz.

Jamme, A. 1971. *Miscellanées d'ancient arabe II*. Washington, DC (privately published).

Jeffery, Arthur. 1938/2007. *The Foreign Vocabulary of the Qurʾān*. Baroda: Oriental Institute. / Texts and Studies on the Qurʾān, vol. 3. Leiden: Brill.

Jones, Alan. 1996. *Early Arabic Poetry, Vol. 2: Select Odes*. Reading: Ithaca Press.

Krenkow, Fritz. 1922. "The Use of Writing for the Preservation of Ancient Arabic Poetry." In *A Volume of Oriental Studies Presented to E. G. Browne on his 60th Birthday (7 Febru-*

ary 1922), ed. Thomas W. Arnold and Reynold A. Nicholson. Cambridge: Cambridge University Press, 261–268.

Krenkow, Fritz. 1927. "Khaṭṭ." In *The Encyclopaedia of Islam*. Leiden: Brill, vol. 2: 930.

Lane, Edward W. 1863–1893. *An Arabic–English Lexicon*. 8 vols. London: Williams and Norgate.

Lichtenstädter, Ilse. 1932. "Das Nasīb in der altarabischen Qaṣīde." In *Islamica* 5: 17–96.

Lundin, Avraam G. 1989. "Nadpisi vnutrennego Chadramauta (obščaja charakteristika)." In *Vestnik Drevnej Istorii* 2: 142–148.

Maraqten, Mohammed. 1998. "Writing Materials in Pre-Islamic Arabia." In *Journal of Semitic Studies* 43: 287–310.

Maraqten, Mohammed. 2014. *Altsüdarabische Texte auf Holzstäbchen: Epigraphische und kulturhistorische Untersuchungen*. Beiruter Texte und Studien, vol. 103. Beirut: Orient-Institut.

Müller, Walter W. 1994. "L'écriture zabūr du Yémen pré-islamique dans la tradition arabe." In Jacques Ryckmans, Walter W. Müller, and Yusuf M. Abdallah, *Textes du Yémen antique inscrits sur bois*. Publications de l'Institut Orientaliste de Louvain, vol. 43. Louvain-la-Neuve: Peeters, 35–39.

Multhoff, Anne. 2013. "'Und es sei aufgelöst und aufgehoben:' Zur Annullierung juristischer Urkunden im vorislamischen Südarabien." In *Entre Carthage et l'Arabie heureuse: mélanges offerts à François Bron*, ed. Françoise Briquel-Chatonnet, Catherine Fauveaud, and Iwona Gajda. Orient et Méditerranée, vol. 12. Paris: de Boccard, 105–117.

Noja, Sergio. 1988. "Une petite retouche à une traduction courante d''Imrū al-Qays." In *Rivista degli Studi Orientali* 62: 1–5.

Ricks, Stephen D. 1989. *Lexicon of Inscriptional Qatabanian*. Studia Pohl, vol. 14. Rome: Pontificio Istituto Biblico.

Robin, Christian J. 2005–2006. "Les banū Haṣbaḥ, princes de la commune de Maḍḥā^m^." In *Arabia* 3: 31–110; 324–327.

Robin, Christian J. 2014. "Le roi ḥimyarite Tha'rān Yuhan'im (avant 325–v. 375). Stabilisation politique et réforme religieuse." In *Jerusalem Studies in Arabic and Islam* 41: 1–95.

Rückert, Friedrich. 1843. *Amrilkais, der Dichter und König: sein Leben dargestellt in seinen Liedern*. Stuttgart: Cotta.

Ryckmans, Jacques. 1984. "Alphabets, Scripts and Languages in Pre-Islamic Arabian Epigraphical Evidence." In *Studies in the History of Arabia. Proceedings of the Second International Symposium on Studies in the History of Arabia, 13th–19th April 1979, Vol. II: Pre-Islamic Arabia*. Riyadh: Riyadh University Press, 73–86.

Ryckmans, Jacques. 1986. "Une écriture minuscule sud-arabe antique récemment découverte." In *Scripta Signa Vocis: Studies about Scripts, Scriptures, Scribes and Lan-*

guages in the Near East Presented to J[ohannes] H. Hospers by his Pupils, Colleagues and Friends, ed. Herman L.J. Vanstiphout et al. Groningen: Forsten, 185–199.

Ryckmans, Jacques. 2001. "Origin and Evolution of South Arabian Minuscule Writing on Wood (1)." In *Arabian Archaeology and Epigraphy* 12: 223–235.

Ryckmans, Jacques, Walter W. Müller, and Yusuf M. Abdallah. 1994. *Textes du Yémen antique inscrits sur bois*. Publications de l'Institut Orientaliste de Louvain, vol. 43. Louvain-la-Neuve: Peeters.

Sabäisches Wörterbuch. Friedrich-Schiller-Universität Jena. http://sabaweb.uni-jena.de.

al-Selwi, Ibrahim. 1987. *Jemenitische Wörter in den Werken von al-Hamdānī und Našwān und ihre Parallelen in den semitischen Sprachen*. Marburger Studien zur Afrika- und Asienkunde, Serie B: Asien, vol. 10. Berlin: Reimer.

Sima, Alexander. 2000. *Tiere, Pflanzen, Steine und Metalle in den altsüdarabischen Inschriften: eine lexikalische und realienkundliche Untersuchung*. Veröffentlichungen der Orientalischen Kommission der Akademie der Wissenschaften und der Literatur Mainz, vol. 46. Wiesbaden: Harrassowitz.

Stein, Peter. 2006. "Sabäische Briefe." In *Briefe. Texte aus der Umwelt des Alten Testaments. Neue Folge*, vol. 3, ed. Bernd Janowski, Gernot Wilhelm, et al. Gütersloh: Gütersloher Verlagshaus, 385–398.

Stein, Peter. 2008. "Correspondence by Letter and Epistolary Formulae in Ancient South Arabia." In *Documentary Letters from the Middle East: The Evidence in Greek, Coptic, South Arabian, Pehlevi, and Arabic (1st–15th c CE)*, ed. Eva Mira Grob and Andreas Kaplony (= *Asiatische Studien/Études Asiatiques*, vol. 62, 2008), 771–802.

Stein, Peter. 2010a. *Die altsüdarabischen Minuskelinschriften auf Holzstäbchen aus der Bayerischen Staatsbibliothek in München, vol. 1: Die Inschriften der mittel- und spätsabäischen Periode*. Epigraphische Forschungen auf der Arabischen Halbinsel, vol. 5. Tübingen: Wasmuth.

Stein, Peter. 2010b. "Literacy in Pre-Islamic Arabia: An Analysis of the Epigraphic Evidence." In *The Qurʾān in Context: Historical and Literary Investigations into the Qurʾānic Milieu*, ed. Angelika Neuwirth, Nicolai Sinai, and Michael Marx. Texts and Studies on the Qurʾān, vol. 6. Leiden: Brill, 255–280.

Stein, Peter. 2011. "Ancient South Arabian." In *The Semitic Languages: An International Handbook*, ed. Stefan Weninger et al. Handbücher zur Sprach- und Kommunikationswissenschaft, vol. 36. Berlin: De Gruyter, 1042–1073.

Stein, Peter. 2013a. *Lehrbuch der sabäischen Sprache, 1. Teil: Grammatik*. Subsidia et Instrumenta Linguarum Orientis, vol. 4,1. Wiesbaden: Harrassowitz.

Stein, Peter. 2013b. "Palaeography of the Ancient South Arabian Script: New Evidence for an Absolute Chronology." In *Arabian Archaeology and Epigraphy* 24: 186–195.

Stein, Peter. 2015a. "Beschriftete Holzstäbchen aus dem Jemen: Zum Alltagsschrifttum im vorislamischen Südarabien." Review article of Maraqten 2014. In *Orientalia* 84: 75–98.

Stein, Peter. 2015b. "Die altsüdarabischen Minuskelinschriften auf Holzstäbchen in der Sammlung des Oosters Instituut in Leiden." In *South Arabia and Its Neighbours: Phenomena of Intercultural Contacts. 14ème Rencontres Sabéennes*, ed. Iris Gerlach. Archäologische Berichte aus dem Yemen, vol. 14. Wiesbaden: Reichert, 193–211.

Stein, Peter. 2016. "Ein Beschwerdebrief aus dem antiken Südarabien." In *Ethnographische Streifzüge. Festschrift für Walter Raunig zum 80. Geburtstag*, ed. Claudius Müller and Markus Mergenthaler. Dettelbach: Röll, 25–33.

Stein, Peter. Forthcoming. "A New Aspect of Writing in Ancient South Arabia." In *Eretz-Israel: Archaeological, Historical and Geographical Studies* 34 (= Ada Yardeni Volume, ed. Shmuel Aḥituv, Hannah Cotton, and Moshe Morgenstern. Jerusalem: Israel Exploration Society).

Wagner, Ewald. 1987. *Grundzüge der klassischen arabischen Dichtung, Vol. 1: Die altarabische Dichtung*. Grundzüge, vol. 68. Darmstadt: Wissenschaftliche Buchgesellschaft.

Yule, Paul. 2013. *Late Antique Arabia—Ẓafār, Capital of Ḥimyar: Rehabilitation of a "Decadent" Society. Excavations of the Ruprecht-Karls-Universität Heidelberg 1998–2010 in the Highlands of Yemen*. Abhandlungen der Deutschen Orient-Gesellschaft, vol. 29. Wiesbaden: Harrassowitz.

PART 2

Papyri and Documents from the Early Islamic Period

CHAPTER 3

Coptic Fragments in the National Library of Egypt (Dār al-Kutub)

Anne Boud'hors, Maher A. Eissa and Naïm Vanthieghem

1 Introduction

The Papyrus Collection of the National Library and Archives of Egypt (*Dār al-Kutub wa-l-Wathā'iq al-Qawmīya*), founded in 1870, originally contained 3,739 documents: 2,627 papyri, 1,050 papers, 58 parchments, 3 ceramic tiles, and 1 piece of textile. Later, the collection was enlarged through the addition of Arabic papyri that were newly found in Egyptian towns and villages, as well as by the transfer of numerous pieces from the Egyptian Museum to the National Library of Egypt in exchange for Ancient Egyptian material (Hieroglyphic, Demotic, and some Coptic).

An Egyptian team has been studying and publishing the Arabic and Greek collections for a few years. In 2013, this team asked Maher Eissa to join them because they had discovered a few Coptic papyri. After doing some research in the entire collection, Eissa found that the National Library of Egypt actually possessed quite a large number of Coptic pieces. Although the assignation of a document to the category "Coptic" is not always obvious, since many texts are bilingual (Greek and Coptic, Coptic and Arabic), one can reckon the number of Coptic texts to be about 200.

Until recent times these Coptic texts had never been the subject of study or publication. In the past few years, however, attention has been drawn to some of them. The published catalogue of the Arabic papyri (Mughāwiri et al. 2008) contains the pictures of and basic information on three Coptic pieces (inv. 1735 / ID 473; inv. 768/ ID 4562–4563; and inv. 1732 recto / ID 5193),[1] while Delattre et al. 2012 contains the publication of one of these pieces, a bilingual Arabic-Coptic letter (inv. 1735 / ID 473).

The extensive study of the Coptic collection of Dār al-Kutub started in 2013, with a two-year Egyptian-French project directed by Anne Boud'hors and

1 The inventory number (inv.) refers to the object and the identification number (ID) to the text, since a single object can contain more than one text.

 | DOI:10.1163/9789004443877_004

Maher Eissa.[2] The aim of the project was to prepare a descriptive catalogue of the collection and to publish the texts gradually. In this chapter, we would like to give some information about their material, contents, provenances, and dates. In addition, we will provide the edition and translation of two letters and an Arabic document. Pursuing the study of the collection will depend on further funding opportunities.

2 Some Features of the Collection

Most of the Coptic texts are documentary, written on papyrus or paper, and belong to a late period, that is to say, after the Arab conquest. Most of them come from Hermoupolis/al-Ushmūnayn; one seems to come from Aphrodito/Ishqaw; and at least one from the Fayyum, as shown by a letter written in Fayumic dialect on the back of an Arabic document (inv. 1232 / ID 1490a). They belong to several genres:

(1) Some are legal documents, partly fragmentary, which are assignable to the 8th century:

> Inv. 2/ ID 3115 is a fragment of three lines containing the beginning of a document identified as a *enguetike homologia*, or "guarantee-declaration," a genre that is especially well known from 8th-century Aphrodito. In this kind of document, "either the presence, custody, or the appearance of persons therein named is guaranteed by the authors."[3] All the Coptic attestations are from Aphrodito, except for three.[4] Besides, the Greek invocation formula at the beginning of the text is of type 2G,[5] typical of the Antaiopolite nome, which is the region of Aphrodito: Ἐν ὀνόματι τοῦ πατρὸς καὶ υἱοῦ καὶ ἁγίου πν[εύματος τῆς ἁγίας (καὶ)] | ζωοποιοῦ καὶ ὁμοουσίου ἐν μονά[δ]ι [τριάδος] (ll. 1–2), "In the name of the Father and the Son and the Holy Spirit of the vitalizing and consubstantial Trinity in Unity."

---

2 The project was partly supported by "Imhotep," a program implemented in Egypt by the Academy of Scientific Research and Technology (ASRT) of the Ministry of Scientific Research, and in France by the Ministeries of Foreign Affairs and National Education.

3 Henry I. Bell, Introduction to P.Lond.IV 1494, note a. In the present article, all the references to papyrological tools are quoted according to the *Checklist of Editions of Greek, Latin, Demotic and Coptic Papyri, Ostraca and Tablets* (available on line: http://library.duke.edu/rubenstein/scriptorium/papyrus/texts/clist_papyri.html).

4 See Förster 2002: 223–224.

5 See Bagnall/Worp 2004: 100.

Inv. 16 / ID 3234 contains the end of a receipt (*apodeixis*) for the payment of a rent (*misthosis*); the formula ϵⲧⲃⲉ ⲡⲉⲕⲱⲣϫ ⲛⲁⲓ | ⲁⲓⲥⲙⲛ ⲧⲓⲁⲡⲟⲇⲓⲝⲓⲥ (ll. 2–3) is typical of similar documents coming from the region of Hermopolis/al-Ushmūnayn.

(2) Others are administrative documents that can be dated to the 8th and 9th centuries:

Inv. 6 / ID 3124 is an entagion issued in the name of Šabīb, son of Šahm, pagarch of the Hermopolite nome, to a taxpayer called Shenoute, son Panouoi, for the payment of 1/3 1/24 nomisma for the taxes of the 10th indiction. This pagarch is known by two other Coptic entagia: P.Lond. Copt. I 1050 and P.Mich.inv. 3384.[6]

Inv. tarikh 1741 / ID 3890 is a late Coptic tax receipt dated to the hegira year 273 (886/887) and hence is one of the latest examples of tax receipts written in Coptic. The receipt was issued for a tenant farmer whom Aḥmad, son of ʿAbd Allāh, was hiring from Ḥasan in a place named Tmoung'ani.[7]

(3) The collection contains many accounts and lists connected with the Arab administration and written in Greek, Coptic, and Arabic. Most are probably to be dated to the 8th century, some to the 9th, and deal with taxation and requisition. They are generally difficult to interpret because they are written with many abbreviations and numbers. Here are some examples:

Inv. 826 / ID 973 consists of two accounts written on papyrus in Coptic and beginning with the word ⲡⲗⲟⲅ(ⲟⲥ). Although some Coptic letters can be identified, the script, which can be assigned to the 9th or 10th century, is scarcely legible. There is an empty space between the two parts, a feature to be observed also in other documents of the collection.

Inv. 6 / ID 3220 contains two accounts, or one account in two parts, concerning several large amounts of wine (the measure used is the *diploun*). The script is a late majuscule typical of the 9th century.[8] The document

6 The Cairo entagion will be published soon by Alain Delattre and Naïm Vanthieghem.
7 Berkes / Vanthieghem 2019.
8 For this type of majuscule, see P.Brux.Bawit: 127–129.

possibly was cut from a previous document written in Arabic because on the right side the remains are visible of a line in Arabic written perpendicularly.

(4) At least one document seems to be a school exercise. The papyrus inv. 2368 / ID 3031, which was written at the top a reused Arabic document, consists of multiplication tables for the numbers 8, 9, and 10. This piece is quite close to P.Unterricht.Kopt. 307, a papyrus from the Fayyum, or P.Unterricht.Kopt. 309, where the same kind of tables are written on a paper quire.

(5) Some fragments are late Coptic letters written from the 9th century onward. They have been generally neglected because of their scarcely legible writing, their often no longer standardized orthography and syntax, and their frequent bilingualism. Some of the formulae show the influence of Arabic epistolography, a trend that tends to become clearer as more late letters are published.[9] Alain Delattre et al. (2012) published two remarkable late letters in which Arabic and Coptic are used, one of which belongs to the collection of Dār al-Kutub (see below). Here are some additional pieces of the same kind:

Inv. 1260 / ID 1527 begins with the Basmala and an Arabic line of greetings, then come eight lines of a Coptic text in which hardly any word can be identified. The script is reminiscent of certain plates of Crum's P.Lond.Copt. (1905), for instance P.Lond.Copt. I 1214 (pl. 15), a vertical piece of papyrus without known provenance: "Letter of over 16 lines on the recto and 11 on the verso. I am unable to read more than a few disconnected words."

Inv. 17 / ID 3150 is a Coptic papyrus letter written vertically with a Coptic account on the other side. The upper part is missing. Although the script is very cursive, it is not as illegible as in the previous text.

The two paper letters we are editing here are further examples of this category.

9 Already at the end of the 19th century, Jakob Krall had studied the patterns of Coptic letters in the Vienna Papyrussammlung (Krall 1889). Most of the letters in this collection are late, and several are on paper. As far as we know, their major part is still unpublished, except for CPR XXXI 13–14. The approach to these texts has been renewed, and very useful guidelines have been given by Richter (Richter 2008).

3 No. 1: Letter from Philotheos to Anoup by Anne Boud'hors

P.Cair.Eg.Lib.inv. 29 verso / ID 3251
Fig. 3.1
9.7 high × 12.3 cm wide
10th–11th centuries
Possibly from al-Ushmūnayn

A Coptic paper letter has been written on the back of an Arabic letter. The Arabic text was cut and is thus incomplete (see No. 2 below). The Coptic letter is not entirely preserved and there are clear traces of cutting in its lower part. The paper has been folded several times and the horizontal folds are still quite visible on the Coptic side.[10] Finally, the paper is damaged in the middle of the right half. It must have been already damaged when the Coptic letter was written because the scribe obviously avoided writing in this area. The similarities in formulary as well as some grammatical features point to a Middle Egyptian provenance. The document might even come from al-Ushmūnayn, like many other similar letters from the Vienna collection surveyed by Krall in the 19th century.[11]

The script is bilinear, slightly sloping, and generally not cursive, except for some ligatures that are quite unusual in Coptic texts: ⲧ+ⲉ (l. 1), ⲛ+ϩ (l. 2), ϩ+ⲁ (l. 2). The letter ⲛ has two different forms, the usual one (although sometimes close to ⲏ, see end of l. 1) and a kind of u (see, for instance, l. 1 ⲛ in ⲡⲛⲟⲩⲧⲉ and u in ⲣⲁⲛ). ⲏ has the shape of an "h." CPR XXI 14 displays similar palaeographic features.

The language is Sahidic, with some variations due to the late period or the influence of the northern dialects: ⲟ is written for ⲟⲩ in ⲛⲟϥ, ϫⲓⲛⲟϥ (l. 4), ⲁⲛⲟⲡ (verso); the particle of the genitive ⲛ- can be replaced by ⲉ- (l. 1, 2, 3); there is no superlineation; the conjunctive ⲧⲉϥⲧⲓ (l. 2) is the expected form of Fayoumic and Bohairic (the interpretation of the form ⲧⲉⲕ- in l. 3 is more delicate, see commentary below). Another unusual feature is the abbreviation of the Greek loanword ⲗⲟⲓⲡⲟⲛ as ⲗⲟ̄ⲛ̄. I am not aware of any other attestation of it in the Coptic and Greek papyri.

This letter reveals the influence of Arabic in several respects. The beginning, with no prescript but several initial blessings, is remarkable.[12] The same can

10 On the use of paper in Egypt, cf. Delattre et al. 2012: 179.
11 Krall 1889: 21; 28.
12 Grob 2010: 39–40: "Arabic letters on papyrus open with the Basmala as invocation. In

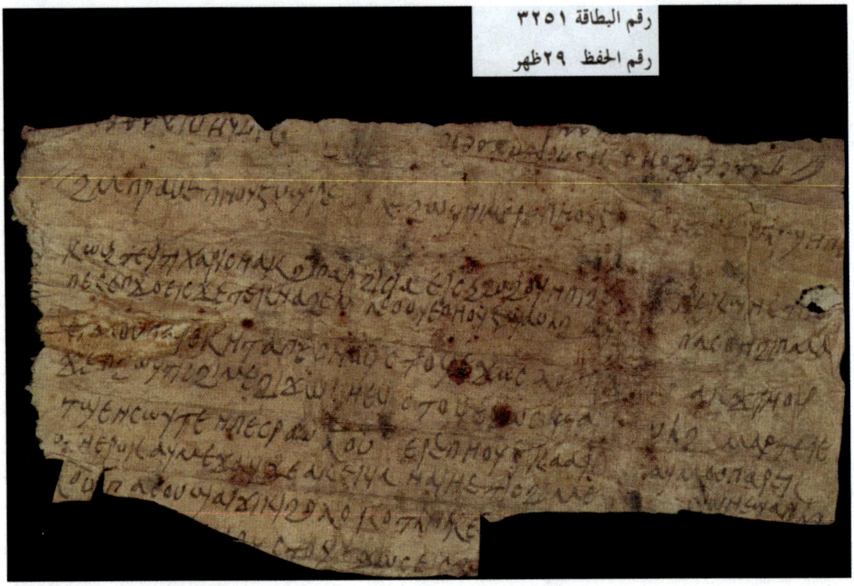

FIGURE 3.1 P.Cair.EgLib.inv. 29 verso / ID 3251
© EGYPTIAN NATIONAL LIBRARY, CAIRO

be said for the final blessing of the address. Finally, the text provides a new occurrence of the Arabic name Mubārak (ⲙⲟⲩⲡⲁⲣⲉⲕ, ll. 4 and 6). By contrast, the names of the sender and the addressee remain clearly Coptic: ⲁⲛⲟⲡ is for ⲁⲛⲟⲩⲡ, common in Middle Egypt, and ⲡⲓⲗⲁⲑⲉ must be a form of ⲫⲓⲗⲟⲑⲉⲟⲥ. Although the sign // at the beginning of the letter points out a certain religious neutrality,[13] the protagonists are likely to be Christians.

As is often the case, the content of the letter remains obscure, due to the incomplete state of the piece, as well as to the many particles, slide-in blessings, and inserted speeches that slow down or cloud the narration.

---

the early letters the Basmala is then followed by an internal address naming the sender and addressee. However, no internal address is given in private and business letters after the turn of the 3rd / 9th century. Sender and addressee remain unknown if no exterior address is preserved. This singles out Arabic epistolography from the contemporary epistolary traditions of the surrounding cultures." Even though the lack of prescript (or internal address) is not unknown in the Coptic letters of the 7th–8th centuries, the combination of this absence with the initial blessings appears only at this late period.

13 Richter 2003.

1 // ϩⲙ ⲡⲣⲁⲛ ⲉⲡⲛⲟⲩⲧⲉ ⲛϣⲟⲣ-vac.-ⲉⲡ ⲉϩⲱϥ ⲛⲓⲙ ⲉⲣⲉⲡⲛⲟⲩⲧⲉ vac. ϩⲁ̣ⲣⲉ̣ϩ ⲛ̣ⲉ̣ϩ̣ⲟ̣ⲟ̣ⲩ̣ ⲧ̣ⲏ̣ⲣⲟⲩ ⲛ̣ⲡⲉ-

2 ⲕⲱⲛϩ ⲧⲉϥⲧⲓ ⲭⲁⲣⲓⲥ ⲛⲁⲕ ϩⲓ ⲡⲁⲣϩⲓⲥⲓⲁ ⲉⲓⲥ ϩ̣ⲁ̣ϩ ⲉϩⲟ⟨ⲟ⟩ⲩ ⲛⲡⲓϩⲉ̣ vac. ⲉ̣ⲡ̣ⲉⲕϣ̣ⲓⲛⲉ ⲧ̣ⲓ̣ϩ̣ⲉ̣ⲗ̣-

3 ⲡⲉϫ̣ⲉ ⟨ⲉ⟩ⲡϫⲟⲉⲓⲥ ϫⲉ ⲧⲉⲕⲛⲁϩⲉⲙ ⲡⲉⲟⲟⲩ ⲉⲡⲛⲟⲩⲧⲉ ϣⲁ ⲛⲏϩ ⲁ̣ⲩ̣? vac. ⲡⲁⲥⲟⲛ̣ ϩⲓ ⲡⲙⲁ

4 ⲑⲩ̣ ⲙⲟⲩⲡⲁⲣⲉⲕ ⲛⲧⲁⲡⲉⲥⲛⲟϥ ⲥⲧⲟϥ ⲉϫⲱⲥ ⲗⲟ(ⲓⲡⲟ)ⲛ. vac. ⲁⲕϫⲓⲛ̣ⲟϥ

5 ϫⲉ ⲡϩⲱϥ ⲧⲓⲥϩⲓⲙⲉ ϩⲓϫⲱⲓ ⲏ ⲉϥⲥⲧⲟϥ ⲉϫⲱⲥ ϣⲁ vac. ⲛⲏϩ ⲙⲁⲣⲧⲉⲓⲉ

6 ⲧϣⲉⲛⲥⲱⲩ ⲧⲉ ⲛⲡⲉⲥⲣⲁⲛ ⲗⲟ(ⲓⲡⲟ)ⲛ ⲉⲣⲉⲡⲛⲟⲩⲧⲉ ⲕⲁⲁⲕ vac. ⲁⲩ ⲙⲟⲩⲡⲁⲣⲉⲕ

7 ϣⲓⲛⲉⲣⲟⲕ ⲁⲩ ⲙⲉϫⲁϥ ϫⲉ ⲁⲕⲉⲕⲓⲁ ⲛⲁⲓ ⲏ ⲉⲧⲓⲥϩⲓⲙⲉ vac. ...ⲛⲉ ϣⲁ ⲛⲏϩ

8 ⲗⲟ(ⲓⲡⲟ)ⲛ ⲡⲁⲥⲟⲛ ϣⲁⲓϫⲓ ⲕⲓϩⲟⲗⲟⲕⲟⲧⲏⲛ ⲕⲉ.[

9 [ ].ⲛ̣ⲟ̣ϥ ⲥⲧⲟϥ ⲉϫⲱⲥ ⲉⲓⲥ.[

Head to foot on the top of the letter

// ⲧⲁⲁⲥ ⲉⲡ\ⲁ/ⲥⲟⲛ ⲁⲛⲟⲡ ⲉⲣⲉⲡϫⲟⲉⲓⲥ ϩⲓⲧⲏⲛ ⲡⲓⲗⲁⲑⲉ.
ⲕⲁⲁϥ̣

2 χάρις, παρρησία 2/3 ἐλπίζειν 3 i.e. ϣⲁ ⲉⲛⲉϩ, i.e. ⲁⲩⲱ (?) 4 θυγάτηρ (?), i.e. ⲛⲧⲁⲡⲉⲥⲛⲟⲩⲃ, λοιπόν, i.e. ⲁⲕϫⲛⲟⲩϥ (?) 5 ἤ, i.e. ϣⲁ ⲉⲛⲉϩ 6 λοιπόν, i.e. ⲁⲩⲱ 7 i.e. ϣⲓⲛⲉ ⲉⲣⲟⲕ ⲁⲩⲱ ⲡⲉϫⲁϥ, ἐγγυᾶν, ἤ, i.e. ϣⲁ ⲉⲛⲉϩ 8 λοιπόν, i.e. ⲕⲉ (?) ὁλοκόττινος 9 i.e. ⲛⲟⲩⲃ

Translation

(1) // In the name of God. Before everything, may God protect all the days of you(2)r life and give you grace and confidence! Behold, for many days I have not heared from you. I hope (3) by the Lord that you are doing well. Glory to God forever! And, brother, concerning (4) the daughter of Mubārak, whose money has been returned to her, indeed you asked: (5) "Is the case of this woman upon me or has it been returned to her forever? Marteie (6) Tshensoou is her name." Then God preserve you! And Mubārak (7) greets you. And he said: "Did you make a guarantee for me or for this woman ... forever?" (8) Indeed, brother, I shall receive another *solidus* ... [...] (9) [...] money has been returned to her. Behold [...]

(Address) To be given to my brother Anop, God preserve him, from Pilathe.

Commentary

1–2 Similar formulae are quoted by Krall 1889: 28, 45: P.Vind.inv. K 17305: ⲉⲣⲉⲡϫⲟⲉⲓⲥ ϩⲁⲣⲉϩ ⲉⲛⲉϩⲟⲟⲩ ⲧⲏⲣⲟⲩ ⲉⲡⲉⲕⲱⲛϩ (Krall 1889: 45); P.Vind.inv. K 17306: ⲉⲣⲉⲡⲟ̅ⲥ̅ ⲕⲁⲁⲕ ⲧⲉϥⲧⲓ ⲭⲁⲣⲓⲥ ⲛⲁⲕ ϩⲓ ⲡⲁⲣϩⲏⲉⲓⲥⲓⲁ ⲛⲛⲉϩⲟ ⲧⲏⲣⲟⲩ ⲙⲡⲉⲕⲱϩⲉ ⲛⲉⲥⲁⲃⲟⲗ ⲉⲡⲉⲧⲑⲟⲟⲩ ⲛⲓⲙ (p. 28); see also CPR XXXI 14. They obviously are translations from well-known Arabic formulae.

It is interesting to note that the word παρρησία is already used in the Coptic letters from Kellis (4th century), although in a different wording (cf. P.Kellis V 5 20.7, 22.10).

2–3 Cf. Krall 1889: 28–29. P.Vind.inv. K 17003: ⲉⲣⲉⲡϫⲟⲉⲓⲥ ⲕⲁⲁⲕ ⲉϥⲣⲟⲉⲓⲥ ⲉⲣⲟⲕ ⲉⲥⲁⲃⲟⲗ ⲉⲡⲉⲑⲟⲟⲩ ⲛⲓⲙ ⲉⲓⲥ ⲟⲩⲙⲏⲏⲙ[sic]ⲏϣⲉ ⲛϩⲟⲟⲩ ⲙⲡⲓⲥⲱⲧⲙ ⲉⲡⲉⲕϣⲓⲛⲉ. ⲁⲗⲗⲁ ϯϩⲉⲗⲡⲓⲍⲉ ⲉⲡϫⲟⲉⲓⲥ ϫⲉ ⲕⲛⲁϩⲙ. ⲡⲉⲟⲟⲩ ⲉⲡⲛⲟⲩⲧⲉ ϣⲁⲉⲛⲉϩ; P.Vind.inv. paper without number (Krall 1889: 46): ⲁⲓϫⲓ ⲛⲡⲉⲕⲥϩⲁⲓ ⲁⲓⲟϣϥ ⲁⲓⲉⲓⲙⲉ ⲉⲡⲉⲧ⟨ⲛ⟩ ϣⲓⲛⲉ ϫⲉ ⲧⲉⲧⲛⲁϩⲙ ⲡⲉϩⲙⲟⲧ ⲉⲡⲛⲟⲩⲧ(ⲉ) ϣⲏⲡ. Here ⲧⲉⲕⲛⲁϩⲉⲙ cannot be a conjunctive, since the verbal form is a stative. According to the parallels, it must be analyzed as a 1st Present (durative conjugation), with a pronominal subject ⲧⲉⲕ- instead of ⲕ-. The verb ⲛⲟⲩϩⲙ is not attested in Coptic letters before the Arab conquest. In late letters it becomes usual, under the influence of Arabic epistolography; ⲉⲓⲛⲁϩⲙ, "I am doing well," can also be found (cf. Krall 1889: 45, paper 17305).

3 The scribe seems to use ⲁⲩ instead of ⲁⲩⲱ (again in ll. 7 and 8). Crum 1939: 19a gives three attestations of this form, one of them (P.Ryl.Copt. 243) being a late document on paper (a list with many words transcribed from Arabic).

4 ⲙⲟⲩⲡⲁⲣⲉⲕ is an Arabic masculine name (Mubārak); see Legendre 2014. It is attested three times in P.Stras.Copt. 67, a late account on paper from the Fayoum.

ⲡⲉⲥⲛⲟϥ can be analyzed in two ways, either as "the blood" or as "her (gold) money." The second analysis sounds better, since there is a woman involved in the following ⲉϫⲱⲥ. Who, then, is this woman? She should have been mentioned before. The only possibility is found in the two letters that appear before the name of Mubārak: I propose to read ⲑⲩ̣ as an abbreviation of the Greek θυγάτηρ. There is a single further attestation of this word in a Coptic text, even though uncertain, in SBKopt. III 1440 5, a list from Deir el-Naqlūn (Fayoum) dated to the 10th–11th centuries (ⲙⲟⲩⲛ ⲑⲉ ϭⲓⲁⲡⲟⲩⲗ). Another possibility would be ⲑⲓ̣(ⲙⲉ), "the wife (of)."

For this sense of ⲥⲧⲟ, see Richter 2002: 282.

5 ⲉϥⲥⲧⲟϥ seems to be a case of violation of the Stern-Jernstedt rule, unless ⲉ- can be analyzed as something else as a converter, but I do not see what it could be.

6 ⲛ- before ⲡⲉⲥⲣⲁⲛ is not expected in a nominal sentence.

7 ⲙⲉϫⲁϥ: Crum 1939: 285a quotes several examples of this form, especially P.Lond.Copt. I 1118, a late letter on papyrus from Ashmounein.

9 A repetition of what was said on l. 4?

Address Krall 1889: 38 had already noticed the particular formulation of the late letters: "Bei den Papieren wird es üblich, Zusätze, die uns aus den Anfangsformeln geläufig sind, der Adresse beizufügen." See, for instance, P.Vind.inv. K 17305 (Krall 1889: 46): ⲧⲁⲁⲥ ⲉⲡⲁⲥⲟⲛ ⲙⲉⲣⲕⲟⲩⲣⲉ ⲉⲣⲉⲡϫⲟⲉⲓⲥ ⲕⲁⲁϥ ... It is worth noting that the verb ⲕⲱ is frequently used with the meaning "to preserve" at this late period, in contrast to the previous centuries. O.Frange 89 (8th century), where the verb has the same meaning, is one of the first examples I know.

4 No. 2: Letter from Apouseri by Maher Eissa (Coptic) and Naïm Vanthieghem (Arabic)

P.Cair.Eg.Lib. inv. 30 recto-verso / ID 3252–3253
Figs. 3.2–3
9.4 high × 14.5 cm wide
11th century
Middle Egypt

The color of the paper is lighter than in the previous letter (see No. 1 above); many traces of folding are visible, especially on the back of the Coptic text (5 verticals and 2 horizontal folds). The Coptic was written in the lower margin of an Arabic letter of which two lines are preserved, one on recto and the other on verso one head to foot under the Coptic letter. The line written in Arabic on the upper part on recto reads *ʿālī al-raʾyi fī dhālika in shāʾa llāhu* ("[to him/you] belongs the exalted opinon in this [matter], if God wills"), while the other one might be read *bāʿitha ilayhi bi-l-manfaʿa al-madhkūra in shaʾa llāhu* ("[she] will send to him the aforementioned profit, if God wills"), and another one head to foot under the Coptic letter. Due to the cursivity and poor condition of the Arabic remains, nothing can be read except, on the back, the formula *in shāʾa allāh*, "God willing."

The Coptic script is a clumsy kind of sloping majuscule typical of manuscripts of the 11th century. The letter ϫ has a remarkable shape. The syllabic superlineation is replaced by a ⲉ (ϩⲉⲙ, ⲉⲛ, ⲉⲙ, -ⲉⲡ in ϣⲏⲣⲉⲡ). The letter ⲓ nevertheless bears a diacritic sign whose shape varies from a dot to a more or less

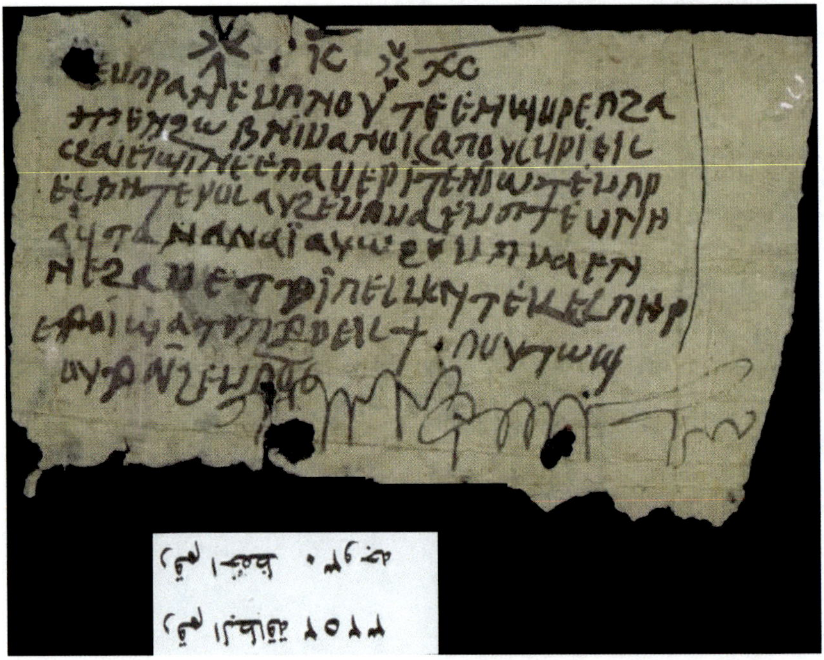

FIGURE 3.2 P.Cair.EgLib.inv. 30 recto / ID 3252
© EGYPTIAN NATIONAL LIBRARY, CAIRO

curved dash (and a dieresis on l. 6). On l. 9 the Bohairic (and Fayoumic) *nomen sacrum*, "the Lord," is used, as it often happens in late Sahidic texts.

In contrast to the previous letter (No. 1 above), this Coptic letter is clearly marked as Christian by the invocation of Jesus Christ on line 1. Such an invocation is frequent in the heads of manuscripts and at the beginning of letters on ostraca. The letter is perhaps addressed to a priest.

※ ⲓ̅ⲥ̅ ※ ⲭ̅ⲥ̅
ϩⲉⲙ ⲡⲣⲁⲛ ⲉⲙⲡⲛⲟⲩⲧⲉ ⲉⲛϣⲏⲣⲉⲡ ϩⲁ
ⲑⲏ ⲉⲛϩⲱⲃ ⲛⲓ̈ⲙ ⲁⲛⲟⲕ ⲁⲡⲟⲩⲥⲏⲣⲓ̈ ⲉⲓ{ⲥ}-
ⲥϩⲁⲓ̈ ⲉⲓϣⲓ̈ⲛⲉ ⲉⲡⲁⲙⲉⲣⲓ̈ⲧ ⲉⲛⲓ̈ⲱⲧ ⲉⲙⲡⲣ-
ⲉⲥⲃⲏⲧⲉⲣⲟⲥ ⲁⲩ ϩⲉⲙ ⲡⲙⲁ ⲉⲙⲡⲧⲉϥⲛⲏ
ⲁϥⲧⲁⲛ̣ⲁ ⲛⲁⲓ̈ ⲁⲩⲱ ϩⲉⲙ ⲡⲙⲁ ⲉⲛ-
ⲛⲉϩⲁⲙ ⲉⲧϫⲓ̈ ⲡⲉⲥⲙⲟ̣ⲩ ⲧⲉⲕⲉⲥⲡⲏⲣ
ⲉϫⲟⲓ̈ ϣⲁⲧⲉⲡϫⲟⲉⲓⲥ ϯ ⲡⲟⲩⲧⲱϣ
ⲟⲩϫⲁⲓ̈ ϩⲉⲙ ⲡⲟⲥ

4/5 πρεσβύτερος, i.e. ⲁⲩⲱ (?)

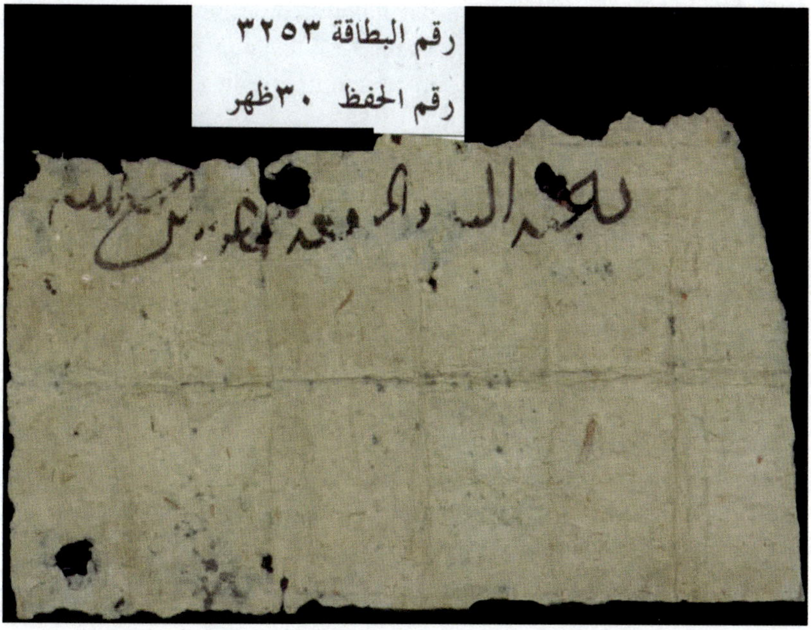

FIGURE 3.3 P.Cair.EgLib.inv. 30 verso / ID 3253

Translation

(1) Jesus Christ. (2) In the name of God first, be(3)fore everything. I, Apouseri, am (4) writing to and greeting my beloved father (and) pr(5)iest (or Presbyteros?). And concerning the cattle, (6) he ... me. And concerning (7) the craftsmen who receive the blessing, the other ... (8) is upon me until the Lord provide for them. (9) Hail in the Lord!

Commentary

3 ⲁⲡⲟⲩⲥⲏⲣⲓ. This personal name, which renders the Arabic Abū Sarī, has not been registered in Legendre 2014. However. there are three further attestations: P.HermitageCopt. 51.1–2 (a late later on paper containing several Arabic loanwords); SBKopt. III 1448.8; 14; 16 (an account on paper with Coptic and Arabic personal names); and SBKopt. III 1440.25 (another account on paper of the same kind from Naqlūn).

4–5 According to Coptic syntax, ⲡⲣⲉⲥⲃⲩⲧⲉⲣⲟⲥ must be interpreted as "priest." Nevertheless, given the late date of the text and its non-standard nature, the proper name Presbyteros should not be completely excluded.

Besides, another analysis of what follows could be ⲁⲩϩⲉ ⲙⲡⲙⲁ, “they found the place,” although this is much less likely given the general organization of the text, and less correct grammatically (the verb ϩⲉ is constructed with the preposition ⲉ-).

6 We cannot catch the meaning of the sentence ⲁϥⲧⲁⲛⲁ ⲛⲁï. Even though some construction involving the verb ⲁⲛⲁï, “to be pleasing,” would be appealing in the context (“concerning the cattle, it made me satisfied”), I do not see how to analyze the sequence accordingly.

7 Again the interpretation is not certain. Another possibility would be -ⲛⲉϩⲁⲙⲉⲧ ϫⲓ ⲡⲉⲥⲙⲟⲩ, the meaning of the whole sentence being “concerning the copper money, receive the blessing,” but the expression ϣⲁⲧⲉⲡ-ϫⲟⲉⲓⲥ ϯ ⲡⲟⲩⲧⲱϣ on l. 8, where ⲡⲟⲩ- seems to refer to the plural ⲛⲉϩⲁⲙ, is more appropriate to people.

8 ϯ ⲧⲱϣ: cf. Crum 1939: 451b: “give orders, take decision, provide.” This expression seems to be frequent in the texts from Lower Egypt (Bohairic texts and manuscripts copied in the Fayoum).

5 No. 3: An Arabic Letter by Naïm Vanthieghem

P.Cair.Eg.Lib.inv.29 recto / ID 3250
Fig. 3.4
9.7 high × 12.3 cm wide
4th–5th/10th–11th centuries
Unknown provenance

Light brown paper. Only the left margin is preserved; the extent of the loss at the top and right is difficult to assess. At the bottom, the last line that remains might also be the last line of the document. Based on the traces that are still visible, one can assume that the document was folded at least five times. The writing, executed by a professional hand, is quite cursive and recalls 4th–5th/10–11th century hands. The scribe, who was apparently writing with a thick pen, uses diacritical dots sparingly and only twice puts a horizontal stroke above the letter *sīn* to differentiate it from its homograph *shīn*. The document has been cut to write a Coptic letter on the back (see No. 1 above). There is no clue in the Arabic text as to the provenance of the text.

The document is a letter whose ins and outs are, given the state of preservation of the text, not easy to establish. After the usual greetings and wishes for good health (l. 1), there is a reference to commercial matters: the sender mentions donkeys (ll. 2, 3, and 5) as well as amounts of money (ll. 3 and 4). The letter ends with a usual epistolary formula (l. 5) with which the sender of the letter asks the addressee to give him news and to write to him if he needs anything. The last preserved line of the text contains a Ḥasbala, which could mark the end of the letter.

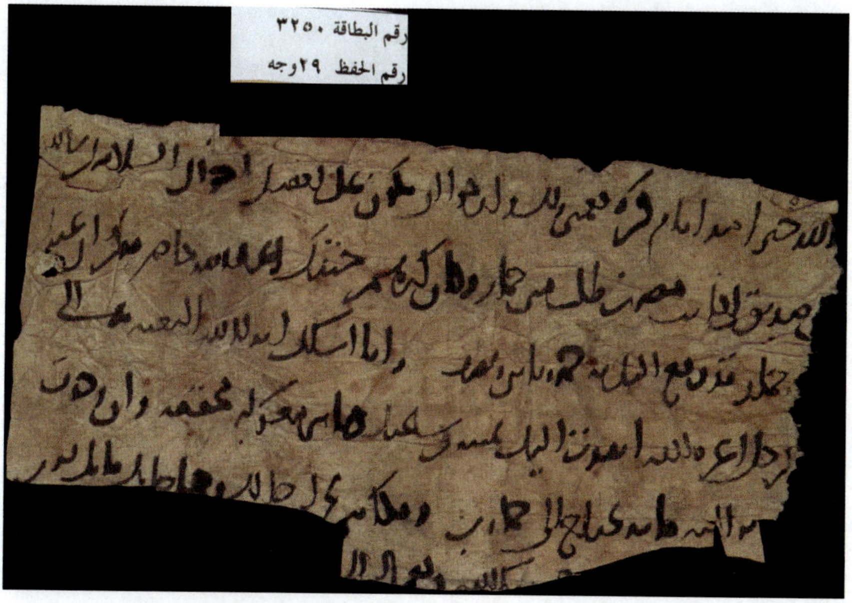

FIGURE 3.4 P.Cair.EgLib.inv. 29 recto / ID 3250

١ [... جزاك] الله خيرا منذ ايام كثيرة فغمني ذلك وارجوا ان تكون على افضل احوال السلامة ان شا الله

٢ [... فا]ن صديق لي كاتب مصري طلب مني حمار وكان كرهـ(ـهـ)ـم ختنك اعزك الله حاضر منك ان عندك

٣ [...] حمار قد دفع اليك به خمسة دنانير ونصف (*vacat*) وانا اسلك ايدك الله البقية α الى

٤ [... ا]لرجل اعزه الله انفذت اليك ثمنية من ساعتك دنانير مغسولة محققة وان رجوت

٥ [... كما كتبت] به اليه فانه يحتاج الى حمارين وتكاتبني بخبرك [و]حالك وحاجاتك فانك تسرني

٦ [بذلك ان شا الله ...]حسبنا الله ونعم الوكـ[ـيـ]ـل

---

١ ىكون—٢ صديق—حتنک—٣ قد—٤ اںعدت اليک—محققه—رحوت—٥ حمارىن

Translation

... (1) ...—may God reward you well!—for many days and it has saddened me. I wish you to do well, God willing ... (2) ... a friend of mine, an Egyptian scribe, asked me for a donkey, but your son-in-law—may God strengthen you being close to you—was not in favor of it. If you have ... (3) ... a donkey through which he paid you five and a half dinars. I ask you—God help you!—the remaining 1 [dinar] for ... (4) ... the man—may God strengthen him! I have sent you eight washed dinars of good quality immediately. And if you want ... (5) ... [as I] have written to him. For he needs two donkeys. Write to me about your news, your condition and your needs. You will please me very much, (6) [God willing]! ... God is sufficient for us, and how much! ...

Commentary

1 [*djazāka*] *llāhu khayran*: The same slide-in blessing is also attested in P.David-WeillLouvre 26.9; P.Cair.Arab. 317.4; P.Marchands II 11.3.
mundhu ayyām kathīra fa-ghammanī dhālika: The sequence cannot be linked directly to what immediately precedes it: it is difficult to see how a prospective formula could fit with the slide-in blessing. The syntagm *mundhu ayyām kathīra* can only refer to what preceded the slide-in blessing. In view of the complaint *fa-ghammanī ḏālika*, "and it saddened me," which follows immediately, it is possible that, in the gap, the scribe reproached his correspondent for not having written to him, as in P.Ryl.Arab. I VI 18.4 *mā samiʿtu laka khabar mundhu kathīr*, "I haven't heard from you in a long time." Or in P.Ryl.Arab. II 10.6 *fa-lam asmaʿ laka khabar mundhu ayyām*, "I haven't heard from you in days."
fa-ardjū an takūn ʿalā afḍal aḥwāl al-salāma: To my knowledge, there is no parallel formula in the documents published so far, except perhaps in *wa-ʿalā an takūn ʿalā afḍal aḥwāl* [...] (P.Heid.Arab. III 8.1).

3 The blank space that precedes the words *wa-anā as'aluka* recalls the blank space left between the narrative part of petitions (*expositio*), where the petitioner presents the events that prompted him to write a petition, and

the part where the petitioner presents the petition itself (*petitio*). On the use of blank spaces in the papyri, see, among others, Grob 2010: 189–191.

4 *thamāniya … danānīr maghsūla muḥaqqaqa*: The term *dīnār maghsūl*, "washed dinars," is common in Arabic documents (see Rāġib 2006: 42, § 110). In contrast, there are only rare mentions of *dīnār muḥaqqaq*, "dinar of good quality" in published material (cf. P.GenizahCambr. 12.11; P.GenizahCambr. 25.16 and P.MariageSeparation 45b.5); the participle *muḥaqqaq* also appears in the unpublished P.Cair.EgLib.inv. 1741.4 (cf. Grohmann 1954: 200 n. 9).

min sāʿatika: This syntagm, whose reading seems certain, has strangely been inserted between the number *thamāniya* and the word *dīnār*, which in principle form a tonic unity.

5 *wa-tukātibanī bi-khabarika [wa-]ḥālika wa-ḥādjātika*: One could also imagine that the scribe wrote *bi-kitābī* instead of the formula *bi-kitābika bi-khabarika …* (on this formula, see among others P.Jahn 14.11 and P.Marchands V/1 16r.9). Note that instead of *wa-ḥādjātika*, one finds rather the plural *ḥawāʾidjika* in letters (see, among others, P.GrohmannWirtsch. 2r.14 and P.Marchands II 42.5). On this formula common in Arabic papyri, see Diem's commentary on P. Heid. Arab. II 7.6 and Grob 2010: 69–70.

5–6 *fa-innaka tasurrunī* (6) [*bi-dhālika in shāʾa llāhu*]: For the reconstruction, see, for instance, P. Heid.Arab. II 18.12 and P.Merchants V/1 20.25. See also Diem's commentary on P. Berl Arab. II, p. 281.

6 *ḥasbunā llāhu wa-niʿma l-wakīl*: The Ḥasbala, common in legal documents, where it was generally used to fill in the empty spaces so as to prevent any addition inside the text (Rāġib 2006: 4, § 10), is not very frequent in letters (Grob 2010: 76 and n. 136).

Bibliography

Bagnall, Roger S., and Klaas A. Worp. 2004. *Chronological Systems of Byzantine Egypt*. 2nd ed. Leiden: Brill.

Bell, H[arold] I[dris]. 1911. *The Aphrodito Papyri: With an Appendix of Coptic Papyri Edited by W[alter] E. Crum*. Greek Papyri in the British Museum. Catalogue, with Texts, vol. 4. London: British Museum.

Berkes, Lajos and Naïm Vanthieghem. 2019. "A Late Coptic Tax Receipt from the Egyptian National Library (P. Cair. Nat. Library Inv. 3890)." In *Journal of Coptic Studies* 21: 13–17.

Crum, Walter E. 1905. *Catalogue of the Coptic Manuscripts in the British Museum*. London: British Museum.

Crum, Walter E. 1939. *A Coptic Dictionary*. Oxford: Clarendon Press.

Delattre, Alain et al. 2012. "Écrire en arabe et en copte: le cas de deux lettres bilingues." In *Chronique d'Égypte* 87: 170–188.

Förster, Hans. 2002. *Wörterbuch der griechischen Wörter in den koptischen dokumentarischen Texten*. Texte und Untersuchungen zur Geschichte der altchristlichen Literatur, vol. 148. Berlin/New York: de Gruyter.

Grob, Eva Mira. 2010. *Documentary Arabic Private and Business Letters on Papyrus: Form and Function, Content and Context*. Archiv für Papyrusforschung und verwandte Gebiete, Beiheft, vol. 29. Berlin/New York: de Gruyter.

Grohmann, Adolf. 1954. *Einführung und Chrestomathie zur arabischen Papyruskunde, vol. 1: Einführung*. Monografie Archivu Orientálního, vol. 13,1. Prague: Státní pedagogické nakladatelství.

Krall, Jakob. 1889. "Koptische Briefe." In *Mitteilungen aus der Sammlung der Papyrus Erzherzog Rainer* 5: 21–58.

Legendre, Marie 2014. "Perméabilité linguistique et anthroponymique entre copte et arabe: l'exemple de comptes en caractères coptes du Fayoum fatimide." In *Coptica Argentoratensia: textes et documents. Troisième université d'été de papyrologie copte (Strasbourg, 18–25 julliet 2010)* (*P.Stras.Copt.*), ed. Anne Boud'hors et al. Collections de l'Université de Strasbourg, Études d'archéologie et d'histoire ancienne, Cahiers de la Bibliothèque copte, vol. 19. Paris: de Boccard, 325–440.

Morelli, Federico. 2001. *Documenti greci per la fiscalità e la amministrazione dell'Egitto arabo*. Corpus Papyrorum Raineri, vol. 22. Griechische Texte, vol. 15. Vienna: Hollinek.

Morelli, Federico. 2010. *L'archivio di Senouthios Anystes e testi connessi: lettere e documenti per la costruzione di una capitale*. Corpus Papyrorum Raineri, vol. 30. Vienna: Hollinek.

Mughāwiri, Saʿīd, et al. [Meghawry, Said, et al.]. 2008. *al-Bardīyāt al-ʿarabīya bi-Dār al-Kutub al-Miṣrīya. Arabic Papyri, National Library of Egypt*. Cairo: National Library of Egypt.

Rāġib, Yūsuf. 2006. *Actes de vente d'esclaves et d'animaux d'Egypte médiévale*, vol. 2. Cahiers des Annales Islamologiques, vol. 28. Publications de l'Institut Français d'Archéologie Orientale, vol. 955. Cairo: Institut Français d'Archéologie Orientale.

Richter, Tonio Sebastian. 2003. "Spätkoptische Rechtsurkunden neu bearbeitet. (III): P.Lond.Copt. I 487, Arabische Pacht in koptischem Gewand." In *Journal of Juristic Papyrology* 33: 213–230.

Richter, Tonio Sebastian. 2008. *Rechtssemantik und forensische Rhetorik: Untersuchungen zu Wortschatz, Stil und Grammatik der Sprache koptischer Rechtsurkunden*. 2nd ed. Philippika, vol. 20. Wiesbaden: Harrassowitz.

Richter, Tonio Sebastian. 2008. "Coptic Letters." In *Documentary Letters from the Middle East: The Evidence in Greek, Coptic, South Arabian, Pehlevi, and Arabic (1st–15th c. CE)*, ed. Eva Mira Grob and Andreas Kaplony. Bern: Lang 2008 (= *Asiatische Studien* 62,3: 671–906), 739–770.

CHAPTER 4

The Second Source of Islam: Reconsidering Ḥadīth Papyri

Ursula Bsees

Although[1] the Qur'ān, the Holy Book of Islam, regulates many aspects of daily life,[2] it does not give accurate information on some topics, such as how to perform prayer or pilgrimage rites. These and many more issues are covered by the Tradition (*sunna*) of the Prophet Muḥammad, whose accounts have been preserved in many works on Ḥadīth (accounts of prophetic tradition). They are based on chains of transmitters (*isnād*, plur. *asānīd*) that are traced back to the Prophet Muḥammad and other relevant persons of Early Islam. Ḥadīth Science quickly became a separate branch of the Islamic sciences, although it is closely intertwined with its other disciplines, such as Transmitters' Prosopography (*'ilm al-ridjāl*) and Genealogy (*'ilm al-nasab*). The development of Ḥadīth Science was spurred by the growing Islamic community's need for a fundament for Islamic Law and consequently for jurisdiction.[3] Due to the delicacy of the material, which after all recounts the exemplary practice of the Prophet, Ḥadīth Science has seen continuous discussions about the authenticity of its contents. Some accounts have been classified as right, strong, and authentic (*ṣaḥīḥ*) and others as weak and unauthentic (*ḍa'īf*),[4] mostly based on the chains of transmitters.

The oldest original sources available for Ḥadīth Science are Arabic papyri. In spite of this fact, most studies on its earliest stages have neglected original source material. The extensive examination that the early Ḥadīth have received has hitherto been based almost exclusively on literary sources written later than the 3rd/9th century.

---

1 I express my sincere thanks to Prof. Christopher Melchert for his remarks on an earlier version of this paper. All remaining shortcomings are of course my own.

2 E.g., the detailed description of how a heritage must be split up among the inheritors in Sūrat al-Nisā' (Q 4).

3 For a general discussion of Ḥadīth Science, see Motzki 2004.

4 There are other degrees of reliability concerning Ḥadīth accounts that are omitted here for the sake of brevity and comprehensibility.

© KONINKLIJKE BRILL NV, LEIDEN, 2021 | DOI:10.1163/9789004443877_005

1 The Field of Literary Papyri

A discussion of Ḥadīth on papyrus almost automatically triggers a discussion about the attention—or lack of attention—that Arabic literary papyri have received so far. Only four monographs on literary papyri have been published (David-Weill 1939–1948, Abbott 1967; Khoury 1972; Khoury 1986). Malczycki's PhD thesis (2006) has been published only online, other publications on Ḥadīth papyri exist in scattered articles,[5] and none of them draws on a sufficient material basis.

Literary papyri have in general been almost completely neglected, especially compared to the work done on documentary papyri.[6] We are still dependent on the groundbreaking work of Nadia Abbott (1897–1981), who edited 14 papyri from the realm of Ḥadīth texts, adding a rich commentary on the tradition of Ḥadīth Science and on the transmission of texts in Early Islamic times.

It is not the scarceness of material that has kept scholars from working on Ḥadīth documents, but first and foremost the great interest in the history of Egypt after the Islamic conquest and, second, the difficulties in dealing with this kind of document. Like all literary papyri, Ḥadīth texts are individually composed and do not fit into any formulaic structure that could help reconstruct missing parts in damaged texts—and almost all are damaged. If a text has no parallels in one of the famous Ḥadīth collections, then it is very difficult to determine not only from which author it originates but also what the complete text *is*. What, then, are we to do with the text? As long as we have only scattered papyrus sheets with no archaeological context,[7] some of them badly damaged, and no archives of literary texts, a complete text can hardly be established. And even if one succeeds in this, the papyrus version most likely differs from the modern editions available to us. And why should not there be different versions of texts so often copied and so widely spread?[8] Thus the work with

5 All these articles by Khoury, Malczycki, Sijpesteijn, and others can be found on the APD Bibliography, https://www.apd.gwi.uni-muenchen.de/apd/bibliography.jsp (last access 05 October 2020).

6 All major editions (P.Cair.Arab.; P.Vind.Arab.; P.Berl.Arab.; P.Heid.Arab.; P.Marchands; CPR volumes) that deal with Arabic papyri contain documentary texts only.

7 Clarysse 1983 has shown that establishing a connection between the two worlds of documentary and literary papyri is possible if they are found in a shared archaeological context. Together with the examination of documentary and literary archives, establishing the *Sitz im Leben* of some Greek literary papyri is a manageable task. However, the lack of archives and the small number of published Arabic papyri make the situation quite different concerning our texts.

8 For a discussion of the transmission history and variants of Arabic poetry on papyrus, see Muehlhaeusler 2014.

literary papyri also proves to be of little reward, especially when compared to work with documentary papyri.

However, not only documents are direct witnesses of their times. Literary papyri can tell us just as much about Early Islamic Egypt as documentary papyri. Studying the literary output of a society we have met hitherto mostly in letters, legal acts, and tax documents will add a new facet to our perception of its intellectual and ideological background and of the personalities and concepts that shaped them both.

There is rich evidence for a significant amount of literary papyri, and especially Ḥadīth texts, still to be discovered, as browsing through the microfilms of the Austrian National Library Papyrus collection showed. This chapter deals with a selection of the Ḥadīth papyri that can be found in the Vienna collection.

2 Ḥadīth Papyri Revisited

For this chapter, we will use an approach that differs from traditional ways of analyzing Ḥadīth texts: neither the authenticity of a given *isnād* (chain of transmitters, pl.: *asānīd*) and the *matn* (content or text of a Ḥadīth report) and tracing the chains of transmitters (applied in traditional Islamic scholarship), nor the analysis of the *asānīd* in order to establish ideological and scholarly networks and transmission lines (applied in modern Western Ḥadīth scholarship) plays a very important role. This is, after all, primarily a papyrological study, and not only does its interest lie in other aspects of the texts, but an *isnād-cum-matn* analysis would be of little representative value as long as there is no sufficient text corpus of Ḥadīth papyri established.[9] A comprehensive study of the *asānīd* and the probability of their authenticity is also beyond our scope in time and effort. Here we will content ourselves with some remarks on the most important transmitters mentioned in the papyri.

Our analysis of papyri from the Austrian National Library papyrus collection, all chosen because of one or another interesting aspect they display, leads less into the realm of Ḥadīth studies than in the direction of a multilayered description of a possible background of both the scribe and the text itself. What interests us in this study is not so much whether the transmitters mentioned could have given authentic accounts as the *Sitz im Leben* (setting in life) that the texts had in the past, e.g., by whom and for what purpose they were used.

9 Critical approaches to Ḥadīth analyses are found in Motzki et al. 2010.

The editions have been written using the Leyden bracket system, with uncertain parts put inbetween half brackets ⸢ ⸣. Three dots mark an unknown number of missing letters. All Qur'anic passages in their English version have been taken from Arberry 1964.

3 No. 1: Ḥadīth from ʿAwn b. Abī Djuḥayfa

P.Vind.inv. A.P. 6666v
9.4 high × 12.3 cm wide
3rd/9th century

Recto has a business letter dealing with agricultural produce in a cursive, casual hand almost typical for the 3rd/9th century. Verso has a text in an archaizing hand, sometimes dotted. The archaization can be seen in the effort to achieve a very angular kind of style, a style the scribe cannot keep up through all of the text. It can be seen in the angular *lām* in *qāla*, in the way he writes *kāf*, and also in the drawn-out form he uses for *ṣād*. From line 6 downward, his hand gradually becomes rounder and more relaxed again. The papyrus is torn on all sides, so it is impossible to tell how much is missing from the margins. It visibly contains two traditions whose *asānīd* both go back to ʿAwn b. Abī Djuḥayfa and his father. The first ḥadīth about exaggerated piety has been transmitted by Bukhārī (*Ṣaḥīḥ*), Tirmidhī (*Sunan*), Abū Yaʿlā (*Musnad*) and several others, the ḥadīth about having forgotten to pray or having slept during prayer time can be completed from the parallels in Abū Yaʿlā's *Musnad* or Ibn Abī Shayba's *Muṣannaf*. Only the *matn* of the second ḥadīth has been taken over word by word in the edition, since the transmitters mentioned in the lost *isnād* were not necessarily the same as in the modern printed version of the mentioned works. Reconstruction is much more difficult for the first ḥadīth, since there are several versions of the text that differ considerably from each other.

١ [... صلـ]ـى [الـ]ـله [عـ]ـليه وسـ[ـلم ...]

٢ [...] قال قال قالـ«ـت» ان [...]

٣ [...] ر⸢ان⸣ فقال ما أنا بطا[عم ...]

٤ [... ا]ن لجسدك [عليـ]ـك حقا صم وافطر صلي ونـ[ـم وأ]عـ[ـط كل ذي حق حقه
...]

FIGURE 4.1 P.Vind.inv. A.P. 6666 verso
© AUSTRIAN NATIONAL LIBRARY, VIENNA

٥ [...أبـ]ـو الدردا ليقوم قال فحبسه سَلمان حتى إذا كبر الفجر ˹قال˺ [...]

٦ [...] أبو الدردا إلى رسول الله فاحيوه قال فقال له مثل ما قال له [سلمان ...]

٧ [... حدثنا فلان بن فلان عن عبد الجبار] ˹ابن˺ العباس الهمداني عن عون بن أبي جحيفة عن [أبيـ]ـه قال كا[ن رسول الله صلى الله عليه وسلم في سفره الذي]

٨ [ناموا فيه حتى طلعت] الشمس فقال إنكم كنتم أمـ[ـواتا فـ]ـعود ˹الله˺ [إليكم أرواحكم فمن نام عن صلاة فليصلها]

٩ [اذا استيقظ ومـ]ـن نسى فليصلي إذا ذ[كر[10] ...]

١٠ [...] ˹معه عن {أبي} أبيه قال ˹بما˺ [...]

١١ [...] ن ا... ..... [...]

---

٣ انا—بكا—٤ حقا—وافطر صلي—نم—٥ ليقوم—فجسه—سَلمان—الفحر—٦ فاحيوه—فقال—٧ كان—٨ الشمس— كنتم—٩ اذا ذكر—١٠ ابى

Translation

1 .... and give [him peace (?) ...]

2 ... he said: He said: She (?) said that ...

3 .... so he said: I am not eat[ing ....]

4 [... y]our body has a right over you. Fast, break your fast, pray and slee[p, and gi]ve [those with right their right ...]

5 [... Ab]ū l-Dardā' to stand up (for prayer). He said: "So Salmān held him back until the call to *fadjr*-prayer," he said (?) ...

6 [...] Abū l-Dardā' to the Messenger of God, so they greeted him. He said: "So he told him like what [Salmān] had told him [...]

7 [... so-and-so b. so-and-so reported to us from ʿAbd al-Djabbār] Ibn al-ʿAbbās al-Hamdānī from ʿAwn b. Abī Djuḥayfa from his father, he said: "T[he Messenger of God—may God bless him and give him peace—was on the journey in which]

8 [they slept until the sun] rose, so he said: "You were d[ead and] God (?) gave [you back your souls, so anyone who sleeps and misses a prayer should pray it]

9 [when he wakes up and any]one who forgets should pray when he re[members]

10 [...]*maʿa* (?) from his father, he said: By what (?) [...]

11 ...

---

10 Ibn Abī Shayba 1425/2004, vol. 1: 477 (2/63 Indian edition); Abū Yaʿlā 1410/1990, vol. 2: 192.

Commentary

4 The scribe retains the long final vowel in imperative and apocopate forms of verba tertiae infirmae instead of shortening it: In l. 4 the imperative *ṣallī* and in l. 9 *fa-l-yuṣallī*. The imperative of verba mediae infirmae is correctly formed (l. 4 *ṣum*).

5 *fa-ḥabasahu*: There seems to be something like a big *ḍamma* above the *sīn* of *ḥabasahu*. It could have been meant as a *muhmal* sign for differentiation between undotted letters.

10 It looks as if the scribe has written *abī* and afterward added *–hi* after *yā'*.

The first ḥadīth can be found in several slightly different versions, though none of them seems to bear sufficient similarity to the papyrus text for reconstruction. It mentions Abū l-Dardā''s exaggerated piety and the prophet's advice to balance acts of worship with fulfilling the body's needs.[11]

The second text speaks about what to do when one forgets to pray, which is either pray when one remembers or pray when waking up after having slept. Parallels passages are found in Ibn Abī Shayba's *Muṣannaf*[12] and Abū Ya'lā's *Musnad*,[13] and an *isnād* is given as "Ibn al-'Abbās al-Hamdānī from 'Awn b. Abī Djuḥayfa from his father." The *isnād* can be completed from both Ibn Abī Shayba and Abū Ya'lā. However, we cannot say with certainty that the papyrus originally carried the names that are now lost.

Although the *Musnad* is too late to have been laid down on papyrus, it seems to bear more similarities with our P.Vind.inv. A.P. 6666v. 'Awn b. Abī Djuḥayfa al-Suwā'ī (m. before 120 AH) was a Kūfan *muḥaddith*, as was 'Abd al-Djabbār b. al-'Abbās al-Hamdānī, one of the acknowledged transmitters from 'Awn b. Abī Djuḥayfa.[14]

Interestingly, both ḥadīth texts seem to reassure believers that being overzealous in *'ibāda* is not necessary for good religious practice. Considering the pietistic tone that ḥadīth papyri often show, this approach seems more lenient and practical. It is hard to tell if the compiler of these traditions is intentionally trying to form a collection of aḥādīth that offer a more feasible take on

11 Tirmidhī 1996, vol. 4: 212 (2413); al-'Asqalānī/Bukhārī 2000/1421, vol. 10: 256 (6139); Abū Ya'lā 1410/1990; vol. 2: 193–194 (898); al-Arna'ūṭ/Ibn Ḥibbān 1988/1408 vol. 2: 23–24 (320); Bayhaqī 1424/2003, vol. 4:457–8/276 (7344); Ṭabarānī 1404/1983, vol. 22: 112–113 (285).

12 Ibn Abī Shayba 1425/2004, vol. 1: 477 (2/63 Indian edition).

13 Abū Ya'lā 1410/1990, vol. 2: 192.

14 al-Mizzī 1413/1992, vol. 16: 385.

daily religious practice than the texts calling for repeated prayer, *duʿāʾ* and fear of judgment. He might as well have intended to collect traditions from ʿAwn b. Abī Djuḥayfa, therefore the question if the compilation was originally meant to be *musnad*- or *muṣannaf*-style cannot be answered with this fragment.

Yet, why was a Ḥadīth work written on the back of a letter? Perhaps we must part with the picture of literary texts existing in codices and try another approach connected to how knowledge was transmitted at the time papyrus was used as writing material. Let us suppose that people present at a lecture wrote down what they were especially interested in. Possibly, we are looking at a student's note, written on the back of a business letter of medium-quality papyrus (verso is coarser than recto). Abbott assumes that rather casual or badly executed hands would belong to students "whose handwriting was not yet stabilized" and who had to take notes hurriedly at crowded lectures.[15] A student's hand would naturally try to imitate an angular, beautiful style known to him from impressive Qurʾān exemplars or perhaps from inscriptions. Maybe he even had to hand his text in for correction.

When we talk about a Ḥadīth student, about someone who had mastered writing to a degree that he could deliberately archaize his style, we must bear in mind that we are dealing with a text written by someone receiving higher education in religious matters and therefore belonging to a quite small stratum of 9th-century Egyptian society. Judging from the letter on recto, this person might have been a Ḥadīth scholar or a Ḥadīth student who also engaged in trade, or a family member of a trader who used the back of his relative's letter after it was no longer needed. Although it is tempting to do so, trying to establish a connection between the texts on recto and verso may not be necessary. It is possible that the papyrus was first used as a letter and then sold by a trader in used papyrus. A student in need of writing material may have purchased the papyrus from the trader, perhaps some timeafter it had first been written upon. It is doubtful that a sheet of this style would have been presented to a scholar for an *idjāza* (authorization), although we cannot completely exclude this. It seems to originate from a lower level of scholarly activity, maybe written by a young student who had to compile some Ḥadīth accounts from a lecture he heard, or by someone noting down accounts he found interesting for his own personal use.

15 Abbott 1967: 89.

4 No. 2: Different Traditions Relating to Prayer, Ritual Purity and Behavior in a Mosque

P.Vind.inv. A.P. 10128
17.0 high × 10.6 cm wide
2nd–3rd/8th–9th centuries

The light brown papyrus has writing on recto and verso by the same hand. Parts of the papyrus are torn off on all sides except at the lower margin, which is nonetheless quite irregularly cut. Presumably, the lower margin already looked this way when the papyrus was written upon, since there is quite a bit of space under the text, undoubtedly left by the scribe for aesthetic reasons. The papyrus has been damaged and has several holes, but the text on recto has suffered more than the one on verso. A part of about 11 lines, approximately in the second third of the text, has been almost completely rubbed off. The hand is casual and well used to writing. Ink circles mark the beginning of a new Ḥadīth. The text deals with matters relating to prayer, including traditions on ritual purity, on prayer times and on prayer during travel, as well as on correct behaviour during congregational prayer. The papyrus' fragmentary status does not allow for a complete reconstruction of most traditions. Naturally, the subject of prayer occurs extensively in practically all canonical and extra-canonical books of ḥadīth.

recto

١ [...]
٢ [...] حت من أهلك حتى ترجع الـ[ـيهم[16] ...]
٣ [...] ˹ين˺ قال وإن أقمت عشرا فقال ˹بن˺ عبا [س ...]
٤ [...] ركعتين حتى ترجع إليهم ○ أبو[...]
٥ [...] عيد قال فقمت لأصلي فتـــرين.. [...]
٦ [«فـ»ـ]ـصل إن شئت ○ أبو إسحق عن الحار[ث ...]
٧ [...] صلاة الوسطى وعن أدبار السجود و[...]

16 Ibn Abī Shayba 1425/2004 has a similar ḥadīth, transmitted by ʿAbd Allāh Ibn Masʿūd and Abū Isḥāq (ibid. vol. 3: 488, ḥadīth 8239; Indian edition 2/447).

٨ [...] صلوة العصر وهي التي فرط فيها سـ[ـليمان[17] [...]

٩ [...] ⌜ركـ⌝ـعتان ⌜قبل⌝ صلوة الفجر ○ أبو إ[سحق...]

١٠ [...] أبي مسعود إنه قال إذا قرأ الرجل ا[...]

١١ [...] «ركع» [....] [...] ⌜صنع⌝ قا[ل] ذلك ⌜بحر⌝ [....] «و»ان[...]

١٢ [...عن سعيد] بن ⌜جبير⌝ قرأ سورة ص [وهو على المنبـ]ـر فنزل [فسجد ثم عاد إلى مجلسه...][18]

١٣ [...] في التنخم ⌜قا[ل]⌝ ا[«بو»...............].] ر [...]

١٤ [...] ست ا[±26] [...]

١٥ [...] بوصل[±30] [...]

١٦ [...] [±25] قال [....] ..محر[...]

١٧ [...][...........] «ل» .... كـ . «من» ... ⌜ابو⌝ [...]

١٨ [...] [±15] احل صحـ .«وابو» احمـ⌝[ـد...]

١٩ [...] [±16] ما يحل منها وعن «ال»ـ[...]

٢٠ [... قـ]ـال مـ[ـنـ]ـ[ـا [..] ن بشيء في يد[...]

٢١ [...]رسول الله أما الصلو[ة...]

٢٢ [...] .... ⌜ول⌝ وليس لك ما حـ[...]

---

٣ عشرا

17 Ibn Abī Shayba 1425/2004, vol. 3: 583 (ḥadīth 8692, Indian edition 2/504).

18 Ibn Abī Shayba 1425/2004, vol. 2: 406 (ḥadīth 4386 & 4387, 2/17 Indian edition).

FIGURE 4.2 P.Vind.inv. A.P. 10128 recto
© AUSTRIAN NATIONAL LIBRARY, VIENNA

FIGURE 4.3 P.Vind.inv. A.P. 10128 verso
© AUSTRIAN NATIONAL LIBRARY, VIENNA

verso

١ [...ـمصا ○ أبو إسحق عن...]

٢ [...] ⸢يجزيك⸣ ○ أبو إسحق عن الحارث [عن ...]

٣ [...] . ملك ⸢يجزيك⸣ ○ نافع عن أبي عـ[...]

٤ [...] ـفمه قراءته ○ عمر بن محمد ا[...]

٥ [... ا]لقراءة خلف الإمام فقال ابن ⸢عـ⸣[...]

٦ [...] ـه قال عمر بن محمد وأخبرني الاعـ[...]

٧ [... فـ]ـقال رسول الله من ذا الذي سر .. على [وإذا قرئ]

٨ [القرآن فاستمعـ]ـوا له وأنصتوا لعلكم تـ[ـرحمـ]ـون ○ أبو [...]

٩ [...] ⸢كـ⸣ـبر لهم فأراد أهله أن ـهرنفو[ا [...]

١٠ [...] قا]ل إنما [...] من أهل البيت ○ أبو إ[سحق...]

١١ [...] كان ..⸢ـلهم⸣ كان يؤذينا وكان [...]

١٢ [...]ـ]⸢ـسـ⸣ـر بن على فسألته عن ذلك فقال حـ[...]

١٣ [...] عن علي قال سألته عن الا[سـ]ـتنشاق فقا[ل...]

١٤ [...] ـحت ○ أبو إسحق عن رجل عن حذيفة قا[ل...]

١٥ [...مكـ]ـانك وإذا استـ⸢ـو⸣يت قائما فاسـ[ـتو...]

١٦ [...] سجدت فاسى ⸢حتا سجدا⸣ عـ[...]

١٧ [...] عن أبي عمر قال قال رسول الله عليه [الصلوة والسلام ...]

١٨ [...] ـعل الإمام ليتام به فإذا كـ[...]

١٩ [...] ولا سبقوه في الصلوة ○ [...]

٢٠ [... سا]فرت في شهر رمضان فإن[...]

٢١ [...] فالصوم أفضل ○ أبو إسحق [عـ]ـن الحـ«ـمـ»[...]

---

١٤ [...] ـحبت—١٨ ليتام

Translation

recto

1 […]
2 […].. your family until you return to the[m …]
3 […]*īn*, he said: "Even if you stay ten (years)," and he said: "From … […]
4 […] two prostrations until you return to them." ○ Abū […]
5 […]*ʿīd* said: 'So I stood up for prayer and … […]
6 [… then] pray if you like." ○ Abū Isḥāq from al-Ḥārith […]
7 […] the middle prayer and at the end of the *sudjūd* and […]
8 […] the afternoon prayer, and it is the one which Su[laymān neglected …]
9 […] two prostrations before the *fadjr* prayer. ○ Abū I[sḥāq …]
10 [… from] Abū Masʿūd, that he said: "If a man recites .[….]'
11 […] … […] … he sa[id]: "This is … […] and that (?) […]
12 […from Saʿīd] b. Djubayr: He recited Sūrat Ṣād [while on the minba]r, then he came down, [prostrated himself and returned to his place …]13 […] on coughing, A[bū ………….] sa[id ……….] .. […]
14 […]
15 […] to bring something […]
16 […] he said […]
17 […]
18 […] … … and Abū Aḥma[d (?) …]
19 […] what of it is allowed and on … […]
20 […] … [h]e said: "We [h]ave a … of something in the hand of … […]
21 […] …. the Messenger of God [said (?)]: "What concerns the praye[r …]
22 […] … and you have nothing that …

verso

1 […] … ○ [Abū Isḥā]q from …… […]
2 […] he rewards you." ○ Abū Isḥāq from al-Ḥārith […]
3 […] … he rewards you." ○ Nāfiʿ from Abū ʿ[…]
4 […] his recitation." ○ ʿUmar b. Muḥammad […]
5 [… t]he recitation after the Imam, so Ibn ʿ[…] said […]
6 […] ʿUmar b. Muḥammad said: al-Aʿ[radj?] related to me […]
7 [… so] the Messenger of God said: "Who is it … over [… *And when the Koran is recited,*]
8 [*give your ear to*] *it and be silent; haply you will find mercy.*"[19] ○ Abū […]

19 Sūrat al-Aʿrāf, Q 7:204.

9 […] he … for them. His family wanted to … […]
10 [… h]e said: "But indeed, […] from the Prophet's family" ○ Abū I[sḥāq …]
11 […] he was … them, he was harming us and he was ..[…]
12 […]sr (?) b. ʿAlī, so I asked him about it and he said "…[…]'
13 […] from ʿAlī, he said: "I asked him about cleaning t[he nost]rils, so he sa[id …]
14 […] …" ○ Abū Isḥāq from a man from Ḥudhayfa, he sa[id …]
15 [… your] place, and if you stand up straight then straight[en up …]
16 […] you made the *sudjūd*, then … until the two of them made the *sudjūd* (?) … […]
17 […] from Abū ʿUmar, he said: "The Messenger of God—bles[sing and peace upon him …]
18 […].. the Imam in order to go (?) with him, and if …[…]
19 […] and they did not overtake him in prayer." ○ […]
20 [… if you trav]el in the month of Ramaḍān, then … […]
21 […] then fasting is better." ○ Abū Isḥāq [fr]om al-Ḥm[…]

Commentary

r 3 *min* could also be read instead of *ibn*.
r7–9 The scribe writes صلاة in recto 7, but then goes on writing صلوة on recto 8 and 9. This practice could hint at him copying from different written sources. Had he copied from memory or from an oral lecture, he would certainly have written the same word in the same way on consecutive lines.

The texts deal with prayer while travelling and with prayer etiquette in general. At least one tradition can be traced to the *Muṣannaf* of Ibn Abī Shayba, which has the account with the closest similarity to the papyrus. Though the *matn* of ḥadīth 4387 seems to correspond closely to our text, [Saʿīd] b. Djubayr can be clearly read, meaning that for the *isnād*, ḥadīth 4386 would be more appropriate. Abū Isḥāq is mentioned several times at the beginning of new traditions. This could be Abū Isḥāq ʿAmr b. ʿAbd Allāh as-Sabīʿī (32–127/653–744), a Kūfan *muḥaddith*, who transmitted from Ḥudhayfa b. al-Yamān via Ṣila b. Zufar al-ʿAbsī (also from Kūfa).[20] This assumption is backed by the phrase "Abū Isḥāq from a man from Ḥudhayfa" (v14), which corresponds to the chain of transmit-

20 Khoury 1986: 142–143.

ters just mentioned. Instead of Ṣila b. Zufar, we only find "a man" (*radjul*) in the papyrus text. This replacement could either be due to a name no longer readable on the manuscript the scribe copied from, or due to a scribe who wrote down what a scholar taught from memory. If he forgot one of the names, he could insert "a man" in order to avoid distortions of the number of members in the chain of transmitters. The same can be said for a scribe copying a partially damaged or unreadable text and attempting to fill the gap by inserting at least something in order to clarify that there has been still another transmitter in between Abū Isḥāq and Ḥudhayfa.

Al-Ḥārith, from whom Abū Isḥāq transmitted the second tradition on verso, could be Abū ʿAbd al-Karīm al-Ḥārith b. Yazīd al-Ḥaḍramī al-Miṣrī (m. 130/747–748).[21]

ʿUmar b. Muḥammad (verso 4 and 6) could be ʿUmar b. Muḥammad b. Zayd b. ʿAbd Allāh b. ʿUmar b. al-Khaṭṭāb. He transmitted traditions from ʿAbd Allāh b. Yasār al-Aʿradj,[22] a fact that is mirrored in verso 6 of the papyrus, if the partially lost name beginning with al-Aʿ… indeed means al-Aʿradj. Moreover, another tradition on verso 3 begins with Nāfiʿ (m. 117/735), from whom ʿUmar b. Muḥammad transmitted as well.[23]

Though attempts at the reconstruction of the fragmentary text have only proven partially successful so far, the general structure of the collection appears to be clear: One part of the traditions is transmitted via *asānīd* beginning with Abū Isḥāq, then al-Ḥārith or other transmitters; whereas the other part comes from Nāfiʿ *ʿan* Ibn ʿUmar. It seems that many aḥādīth on prayer during travel were transmitted via that *isnād*. Considering the many parallels the papyrus bears to Ibn Abī Shayba's *Muṣannaf*, which generally has abundant occurrences of the transmitters just mentioned, we might wonder if it was part of his material that was taught in Egypt as such, maybe still during his lifetime.

5 No. 3: On the Superiority of ʿAlī

P.Vind.inv. A.P. 10129v
25.0 high × 12.4 cm wide
2nd–3rd/8th–9th centuries

21 Khoury 1986: 110.
22 al-Mizzī 1413/1992, vol. 21: 500.
23 al-Mizzī 1413/1992, vol. 21: 500.

Recto carries faint traces of probably two lines of writing. Their position in the middle of the sheet, combined with the fact that the main text is on verso, could mean that they are what remains of an earlier title page for the text that begins on the other side. This is confirmed by the partially readable *Kitāb al-*… in the first line, as well as the *nafaʿa llāhu bihi* that can be seen in the second line. It is preceded by what looks like the author's name that looks like *al-Djā*…. The rest of the ink has been rubbed off. Verso has a text starting with the Basmala. We do not know how much of the papyrus is missing on the left side, but we can assume an average of five to eight words that must be added. Simple circles are used as paragraph marks. Even a marginal note written by the same hand occurs, possibly the repetition of a misspelled word to ensure complete legibility of the text, which can be seen similarly in P.Heid.inv. Arab. 50–53, the papyrus scroll published by Khoury where some words are repeated on the margin with the same little half-circle separating them from the main text as in P.Vind.inv. A.P. 10129.[24] That means that the marginal note *al-umma* beside l. 15 repeats a now lost word from the left half of the papyrus. If what remains of the text was part of a larger corpus, then the marginal note could also have helped the writer in finding passages he was looking for. Marginal notes for this purpose can be seen in P.Mich.inv. 5608 (published in P.AbbottLiteraryPapyri II 13) and P.Cam.inv. Michaelides D 953. Both papyri originally belonged to the same text.

The writing becomes gradually smaller, maybe due to a lack of space. Some remarkable features of the writing are the hooks to the left on final *lām* (although not carried out on all occasions), the long *ṣād*-form, and the *ṭāʾ-alif* (l. 14) and *ẓāʾ-lām* (l. 18) ligatures, as well as the long, horizontal curve to the left after *mīm*.

Lines 7 to 18 of the text appear almost literally in the modern print edition of Furāt al-Kūfī's (m. 381 AH) *Tafsīr*, in the chapter on Sūrat Āl ʿImrān.[25] The part on the chosen people from Sūrat Āl ʿImrān was much later integrated into *Biḥār al-Anwār* by Madjlisī, the largest Ḥadīth collection of the Shīʿa.[26] *Tafsīr Furāt* has two slightly different versions of the account, both going back to Abū Dhārr al-Ghaffārī. Additions of text lost on the papyrus were made from both accounts, depending on the estimated numbers of words necessary for filling the gaps. However, neither account from *Tafsīr Furāt* is completely compatible with the papyrus text, which points to a complex transmission history the text shares with other literary works on papyrus.

---

24 Khoury 1986: 310, l. 83, and in several other places on the papyrus. The same phenomenon also appears in the Wahb b. Munabbih papyrus also published by Khoury: P.Heid.inv. Arab. 23, GD 2.19; PB 4.10 and several other places.

25 Furāt al-Kūfī 1416/1995: 81–82 (in the chapter treating Sūrat Āl ʿImrān).

26 al-Madjlisī 1388/1430 AH, vol. 7: 98.

FIGURE 4.4 P.Vind.inv. A.P. 10129 verso

١ بسم الله الرحمن الرحـ[ـيـ]ـم [...]

٢ محمد وأحمد بن عبد الله[...]

٣ عليه السلم وعلى أهل بيتـ[ـه] كـ[...]

٤ قال من [و]ليتم قالوا أبو [بـ]ـكر[...]

٥ اما والله لو وليتموها عليا[...]

٦ أرحلكم وما اختلف فيكم[...]

٧ يبايعوا فيه لأبي بكر فوقف عـ[ـ ... إن الله]

٨ اصطفى آدم ونوحا وآل [إبرهيم وآل عمران على العالمين]

٩ ذرية [بـ]ـعضها من بعض والد[ـه سميع عليم فأهل بيت نبيكم هم الآل من]

١٠ آل إبرهيم والصـ[ـفـ]ـو[ة] والسلـ[ـا]له مـ[ـن إسماعيل والعترة الهادية من محمد]

١١ وأخذوا الفضل من قومهم فهم [كـ«ـالسماء المرفوعة والأرض المدحية»]

١٢ والجبال المنصوبة والشمس الضاحـ[ـية «والنجوم الهادية والشجرة الزيتونة»]

١٣ المـ[ـبـ]ـاركة أضاء زيتهـ[ـا] وبورك «زبد»هـ[ـا فمحمد «وصي آدم ووارث علمه» علي بن أبي]

١٤ طالب اما والله لو قدمتم من قد[م الله و«خلفتم الولاية لمن خلفها النبي» والله لما]

١٥ عال [و]لي الله ولا طاش سهم من فرا[ئض الله ولا تنازعت هذه الأمة في شيء من]

١٦ امر دينها إلا كان [عـ]ـلم ذلك في كـ[ـتابه العزيز الذين آتيناهم الكتاب يتلونه حق تلاوته]

١٧ فذوقوا وبال ما فرطتم وما الله[...وسيعلم الذين]

١٨ ظلموا أي منقلب ينقلبون ○ وعنه[...]

١٩ لما كثر الاختلاف بين [أصحـ]ـاب محمد كـ[ـ....]

٢٠ على ..ـى الفتنة فـ«ـعـ»ـ..ـت ˹صلى˺ الا لو[...]

٢١ ا[..]حـ«ـر» قد قمت به [... ....]ـد˹رين˺ ما الا[...]

٢٢ والـ˹ـفجر˺ نخرجت [... ..] ˹ذلك˺. وقد[...]

٢٣ الفجر قد خلى ى أخذ [...] ربه ومضـ[ـ....]

---

١٢ الضاحية—١٣ زيتا—١٦ كان—١٧ وبال—١٨ سملون—١٩ الاحلاف—٢٣ ربه

Translation

1 In the name of God, the Compassionate, the Merciful.

2 Muḥammad and Aḥmad b. ʿAbd Allāh [...]

3 —Peace be upon him—and upon his famil[y] .[...]

4 He said: "Whom did you make the leader?" They said: "Abū Bakr [...]."

5 "But, by God, had you made ʿAlī its leader [...]."

6 "He would have made you leave (?) and whoever disagrees among you [...]"

7 pledging allegiance to Abū Bakr in it, ʿ[...] stood [...*God chose*]

8 *Adam and Noah and the House of* [*Abraham and the House of Imran above all beings,*]

9 *the seed of one another; Go*[*d hears, and knows.*[27] *Your prophet's family belongs to*]

10 *the House of Abraham and the b*[*e*]*s*[*t*] (*of them*) *and the chain of ancestors is fr*[*om Ismael and the leading progeny is from Muḥammad, may God bless him and grant him peace*]

11 *and they took the favour from their people, so they are* [*like the raised sky and like the praising* (*?*) *earth*]

12 *and the erected mountains and the shining s*[*un and the leading stars and the blessed olive*]

13 *tree, whose oil made light and whose essence was blessed.* [*Muḥammad is the mandatory of Adam and the inheritor of his knowledge is ʿAlī b. Abī*]

14 *Ṭālib, and, by God, if you had preferred whom Go*[*d preferred and left leadership to whom the prophet left it, by God, then*]

15 *God's close companion would never have deviated in any way and no arrow would ever have missed the religious duties tow*[*ards God and never would this community have fought about anything concerning*]

16 *a matter of their religion without God knowing this in* [*His mighty book* (?): *Those to whom We have given the Book and who recite it with true recitation*][28]

17 so taste the evil of what you have neglected and God is not [... *and those who*]

18 *do wrong shall surely know by what overturning they will be overturned.*[29] ○ Also from him [...]

---

27 Āl ʿImrān, Q 3:33–34.

28 al-Baqara, Q 2:121.

29 al-Shuʿarāʾ, Q 26:227.

when the dispute grew between [the Compa]nions of Muḥammad .[...]
on ... ... the civil war, so ... ... be it not that [...]
.[..].. I have fulfilled it [... ...].... not/what the ..[...]
and early morning time, so I went out [... ..] that (?) . and [...]
the early morning had already past (?) .. he took (?) [...] his Lord and ...[...]

Commentary

4 *Abū Bakr* is written instead of the accusative (*Abā Bakr*) demanded by *wallaytum*. The fossilized, unchangeable constructus form *Abū* is common in Arabic papyri.[30] This special treatment of the word *ab* becomes even clearer on the next line, where *ʿAlī* is in the correct form after the same verb (*ʿaliyyan*, acc.).

15 *wa-lā ṭāsha sahmun min farā*[*ʾiḍi llāh*]: *ṭāsha* ("to miss") is combined with *ʿan* in its standard form.

Although more than the left half of the papyrus is lost, there can be no doubt about its content: by the time that the papyrus was in use, Egypt saw a lively discussion about whether Abū Bakr or ʿAlī had priority in leading the Umma. This papyrus shows part of this discussion, a polemic position in favor of ʿAlī's caliphate that uses Qurʾanic verses for justification. It cannot be regarded as Ḥadīth in a stricter sense, but at the early stage we are dealing with here, Ḥadīth and other literary branches, especially historiography and biographical literature, often cannot be easily told from each other.[31]

Since *Tafsīr Furāt* probably was not written before the second half of the 4th/10th century, it cannot have been a source for our text, but it is rather the other way around. We might be looking at a text which, among many others, was later collected by Furāt al-Kūfī in his work. Going deeper into the transmission history of the account would go beyond the scope of this article.

30 Hopkins 1984: 156–157.

31 P.Vind.inv. A.P. 10129v certainly deserves a more elaborate treatment, which will be undertaken elsewhere.

6 No. 4: Supplication of the Prophet after His Nighttime Prayer and ʿAlī's Supplication for a Quick Answer

P.Vind.inv. A.P. 1603
10.0–11.5 high × 10.2–15.2 cm wide
3rd/9th century

This papyrus is special in several aspects.[32] First, it consists of eight pages of a booklet, of which seven carry recognizable writing. The eighth page seems to have contained writing, but this has been thoroughly washed off, resulting in a black layer of ink all over the page and only illegible traces of writing. One can still make out a knot out of papyrus fibers in a corner of an additional fragment, which was most probably part of the binding. Since the text starts in the middle of a prayer, at least one page from the original booklet is missing entirely now.

Some parts of the texts have been lost or rendered incomprehensible due to the scraped-off ink and a tear in the middle of the page. Two pages show illumination, although one of them has not been finished: obviously the scribe began to draw and then remembered that he wanted to add some more text, so he added the words in smaller script to fit them into the space left ("say this supplication and what you want after it"). Since different hands were involved in the composition of the texts, it looks as if a later hand wanted to imitate the beautiful illumination carried out by a prior hand. The half-finished drawing and the partially very casual writing do not suggest a very well thought-out and professional composition background (at least for one of the hands).

The texts have been written by two or three hands, four pages by one hand, two pages by another hand that also may have written the third page. One page contains some poetic expression of the fear of God and Judgment Day, although it might also contain allusions to romantic love (leaf 3 verso and leaf 4 verso). It is, however, most certainly not the work of a professional poet, since the rhyme scheme is not built well. A second part of the text bears parallels to some of the supplication-section in Tirmidhī's *Sunan* (leaf 1 recto and leaf 1 verso), while another part (leaf 3 recto and verso) shows a striking similarity to what is mentioned as ʿAlī's prayer for a quick answer in Kulaynī's *Uṣūl al-Kāfī*.[33]

---

32 I express my sincere thanks to the late Raif Georges Khoury, who had reserved this papyrus for publication but kindly ceded it to me. To my great sadness, he passed away before it could be published.

33 al-Kulaynī 1428/2007, vol. 2: 321. The papyrus Is widely compatible with, but not identical to, the wording in the print edition.

FIGURE 4.5 P.Vind.inv. A.P. 1603 recto
© AUSTRIAN NATIONAL LIBRARY, VIENNA

As expected, the text differs somewhat from the wording in Tirmidhī, and even passages that look identical to the Tirmidhī text are written in a different sequence on the papyrus. For the sake of comprehensibility, the edition follows the alignment of the Tirmidhī text as closely as possible without having to separate text units on one and the same sheet. Some slight syntactical weaknesses appear together with deviations from Tirmidhī's text, which could be a sign suggesting a scribe writing down the text from memory. Since the text starts in the middle of a sentence, there must be at least one preceding page missing from the original booklet.

Leaf 1 recto (Figure 4.5, upper right corner)

١ بها عملي وتبيض بها وجهي وتلهم بها

٢ رشدي وتعصمني بها من كل سوء مراد

٣ لي اللهم إني أسلك إيمانا صادقا

٤ ويقين ليس بعده كفر ورحمة أنال بها

٥ شرف كرامتك في الدنيا والآخرة اللهم

FIGURE 4.6 P.Vind.inv. A.P. 1603 verso

٦ إني أسلك الفوز عند القضاء ومنازل

٧ الشهداء وعيش السعداء والنصر علي

٨ الأعداء ومرافقة الأنبياء اللهم إني أسلك

٩ [إن قصر عمـ]ـلي وضعف رأيي وأنا فقير

١٠ [إلى رحمتك فأسلك يـ]ـا قـ[ـاضى الـ]ـأمور ويا شا[في]

١١ [الصدور كما تجير من في البحور أن]

١٢ [تجيرني من عذاب السعير ومن دعوة]

١٣ [الثبور ومن فتنة القبور ...]

---

١ عملي—وجهي—تلهم—٢ نعصمي—٥ في—٦ ابي—٧ عيش—والنصر علي

Leaf 1 verso (Figure 4.6, upper left corner)

١ نحب بحبك الناس ونعادي بعداوتك من

٢ خالفك اللهم إني أسلك الأمر الرشيد

٣ والحبل الشديد والأمن يوم الوعيد

٤ والجنة يوم الخلود مع المقربين الشهو[د]

٥ الركع السجود الموفون بالعهود إنك

٦ رحيم ودود وإنك تفعل ما تريد أنت ربـ[ـي]

٧ وإلاهي هذا الدعاء وعليك ˹الاستجابة˺

٨ وهذا الجهد وعليك التكلان لا حول

٩ ولا قوة الا بالله ○ اللـ˹ـهـ[ـم اجعل]˺

١٠ ˹لـ[ـي] نور[ا وأعطني نورا وأعظم]˺[34]

٢ اي—٣ والامن—٦ ربى—٧ والاهي

Leaf 2 recto (Figure 4.5, lower right corner) has been washed off and bears only unreadable traces of writing.

Leaf 2 verso (Figure 4.6, lower left corner)

١ إن الذى ˹اسمك سما...˺ ... ـسى

٢ علا في ملكه متوحدا ˹بعرشه˺

٣ الذين لا ˹مماد˺ فيما مضا˹د ..ـوا˺ رحمته

٤ النبي محمدا ˹صحم د عـعه كانعزاله

٥ وجهه ˹بـ˺ـرم يدي . بالمكارم وارتدا

٦ من أهل بيت ˹ينتمون˺ إلى العلا و˹رما˺

٧ [...] ـصا متوحدا ....

٤الي

Leaf 3 recto (Figure 4.6, upper right corner)

١ اللهم أنت العلي الأعلا ˹فد...ـب ر..ر في˺

٢ الأدنا وأنت عند من ذ[كـ]ـرك من الـ[ـرسل]

34 al-Tirmidhī 1996, vol. 5: 419–420.

٣ والأ[نـ]ـبياء اللهم إني نسلك باسمك المخزون

٤ المكـ[ـنون] النور البرهان المنير الذي هو

٥ نور بنور ⟨ونـ⟩ـور ⟨في نور⟩ ونور مع نور ونور فوق نو[ر]

٦ ونور تظاء معه كل ظلمة وتكسر بـ[ـه]

٧ قوة كل سلطان ولا يقوا عـ[ـدو ...]

٨ ولا [تقوم به سمـ]ـاء [و] يأمـ[ـن] به كـ[ـل خائف]

---

٢ من—٤ المنير—٥ بور—فى

Leaf 3 verso (Figure 4.5, upper left corner)

١ واستو[يـ]ـت به على كرسيك[35] باسمك

٢ العظيم الذي خلقته في كلك

٣ فاستقر فيك فلا نخرج منك إلى شيء

٤ أبدا أسلك بك وبه يالله يا

٥ رحمان˺ ○ ادعوا هذا الدعاء

٦ ثم وادعوا مثل ما شئت بعد

Drawing

---

٣ سي—٤ بالله

Leaf 4 recto (Figure 4.5, lower left corner, another hand)

١ يا ويح نفسي إذا قامت ˹ممن صنى˺

٢ ندعو «امن لو له» ودمعها ذرروا

٣ فالكتب قد نشرت والصحف

٤ قد فتحت والقبر قد حفر أو القوم

٥ قد حصروا فأين المفر من الجبار

---

35 al-Kulaynī 1428/2007: vol. 2:321.

٦ يومئذ كلا هنالك لا منجا

٧ ..... روا Drawing

---

٢ ندعوا—٣ نسرب

Leaf 4 verso (Figure 4.6, lower right corner, another hand)

١ ⌜خلق أبو يونس⌝ كم ذر الدمع

٢ ⌜سمموا⌝ من ⌜مقلبتك⌝ وكم

٣ ذا الحرر والسهر وا كم

٤ ليلة بينها من ذكر ⌜منقلبي⌝

٥ كأنما عرشه في

٦ مضجعي اروا ذكر الجهنم

٧ و[«ذكر»] التعب ان ⌜فتى⌝ .....

---

٤ ممعلي—٥ فِي

Translation

Leaf 1 recto

1 by it my work, and whiten by it my face, and inspire (me) by it
2 toward righteous behavior, and protect me by it from any evil wanted
3 toward me. Oh God, I ask You earnest faith
4 and creed after which there can be no unbelief, and mercy by which
5 I can attain the honor of Your graciousness in this world and in the afterlife. Oh God,
6 I ask from You victory at the Judgment, the resting place
7 of the Martyrs, the life of the blissful, victory over
8 enemies and the company of the Prophets. Oh God, I ask You
9 [if (?) my (good) work comes sho]rt, my reason is weak, I am needy
10 [of Your mercy. So I ask You, oh Judge of all ma]tters and oh Healer
11 [of all hearts; just as You protect those on the Oceans,]
12 [protect me from the pain of Hellfire, from being among the]
13 [dwellers therein and from the pain of the grave.]

Leaf 1 verso

1 (that we) love by Your love the people and confront with enmity whoever
2 works against you. Oh God, I ask from You a righteous order,
3 a tightly pulled rope, and safety on the Day of the Promise,
4 and Paradise on the Day of Eternity, together with the Close Ones (*maʿa l-muqarrabīn*), the Martyrs,
5 with those praying at all times, with those who fulfill their contracts. Indeed, You are
6 merciful and affectionate and You do what You want. You are my Lo[rd]
7 and my God. This is the supplication and the answer is up to You,
8 this is the effort and on You is (our) reliance. There is no might
9 and no strength except through God. ○ Oh Go[d, make]
10 [li]ght for [me] [and give me light and increase] the light

Leaf 2 recto

[...]

Leaf 2 verso

1 Verily, ... Your name (?) names (?) ... ...
2 exaltedness in His dominion in His oneness by His throne (?)
3 the religion. There is no ... in what is against .... His mercy
4 the Prophet Muḥammad, the master of (?) His ... . his solitude (?)
5 his face ... the hands of (?) .... with gracious deeds and he ...
6 from a family who belongs to exaltedness (?) and ...
7 .... He alone [...]

Leaf 3 recto

1 Oh God, You are high, the highest and .... concerning
2 the lowest and you are with anyone re[mem]bering you among the [Messengers]
3 and the Prophets. *Oh God, I ask You by Your name, the well-preserved,*
4 *the we[ll-kept], the light, the ultimate enlightened proof, which is*
5 *light through light and ⟨l⟩ight ⟨in light⟩ and light with light and light above ligh[t]*
6 *and a light by which every darkness is lighted up and by [which] You break*

7 *the power of every ruler and no ene[my] has strength* [...]
8 *and no [sk]y is set up [by it, and] it as[sures] anyone [afraid]*[36]

Leaf 3 verso

1 *And by it You are firmly established on Your throne* through Your exalted
2 name that You created in Your bountiful existence,
3 so it became firmly established in You. We do not ever leave you for anything
4 else. I ask You by You and by it, oh God, oh
5 Merciful ○ Say this supplication
6 and say something you like after it.

Leaf 4 recto

1 Oh my poor soul, when it stands up from (?) my ....
2 we supplicate unto Him who ... ... and its tears were spread
3 and the books shall be spread out and *the scrolls*
4 *shall be unrolled*,[37] the grave shall be dug or the people
5 shall be gathered closely together, so where is a place of refuge from the Omnipotent
6 that day; no, there is no secure place
7 ...

Leaf 4 verso

1 The (poetic) creation of Abū Yūnus (?): How many teardrops
2 were poisoned (?) by your deception (?) and how many
3 of ... and sleeplessness, and I ask, how many
4 nights are between it/her since I mentioned my fate (?)
5 as if His throne was on
6 my resting place .... the thought of hell
7 and the thought (?) of the strain, if (?) [...]

36 Text in italics corresponds to al-Kulaynī 1428/2007, vol. 2: 321.
37 al-Takwīr, Q 81:10.

Commentary

1r.3 *īmānan* has a little stroke under *mīm*.

1r.4 *yaqīn* misses the *alif tanwīn* for the accusative, which is carried out correctly in *īmānan ṣādiqan* (3).

1v.2–3 *asaluka l-amr al-rashīd wa-l-ḥabl al-shadīd* instead of *allāhumma dhā l-ḥabl al-shadīd wa-l-amr al-rashīd*.[38] This can only be a slip of the pen or a lack of understanding of the text, since God is the one holding the rope tightly. Wishing for a tight rope, as written here, does not make sense. There are other similar syntactical irregularities throughout the text.

1v.5 Instead of the correct genitive *al-mūfīna*, the scribe uses the nominative *al-mūfūna*. By using the hypercorrect form, he tries to avoid the dialectal tendency to end all forms of strong masculine plural with –*īna*.[39]

1v.7 *al-istidjāba* is doubtful, but the best reading parallel to *al-idjāba* in Tirmidhī.

3r.3 *ʾny nslk* can be read as *innī nasaluka*, "I ask You," i.e., a n-form for the first person singular, or as *innā nasaluka*, "We ask You," with *alīf maqṣūra* instead of *alif mamdūda*.

3r.5 It seems that the scribe has forgotten to write *wa-nūr* once, maybe also due to his writing down from memory.

3r.6 *tuḍāʾu* is written with *ẓāʾ* instead of *ḍād*, a phenomenon not uncommon in papyri, as in P.Heid.Arab. II 69r.39; P.Berl.Arab. II 35r.10; P.DiemKhalili 5.8; P.Loth 2r.8 = P.Berl.Arab. II 75r.8; and many times in P.Cair.Arab. 291 = P.DiemVulgarismus.

3v.5 *raḥmān* is written *plene*. This phenomenon is, although attested, quite rare.[40] Moreover, some doubt remains as to whether *raḥmān* is the correct reading, considering the little hook between *mīm* and *alif*. Maybe we should read *yā raḥmatān*, though *yā raḥmān* is more plausible from a textual point of view.

---

38 al-Tirmidhī 1996, vol. 5: 420.

39 Blau 1981: 31–32.

40 Attestations from Arabic Papyri until the 4th/10th century are P.Khurasan 32.12 and P.GrohmannUrkunden 4.4. Other attestations are from the 5th–6th/12th–13th centuries, i.e., much younger.

3v.6 The imperative singular of *daʿā* I should not have a final long vowel, nor the *alif*; however, the orthography is not uncommon.

4r.2 The words after *nadʿū* are uncertain; there is no feasible reading for them so far.

4v.1 Instead of *abū*, *ibn* could be read as well.

4v.2 *maqlaba* could be a non-standard form of *maqlab*, "fraud, deception."

Apart from a long prayer text attested in Tirmidhī, one page contains a poem about the fear of Judgment Day and death. There is also a page with a supplication found in the print edition of *Uṣūl al-Kāfī*. This suggests that at an earlier stage Sunni and Shīʿī materials were not transmitted separately and cut off from each other, as it appears nowadays, but most probably have common sources, as P.Vind.inv. A.P. 1603 shows. Again, the question is what purpose the codex (or, rather, the booklet) served. It seems to be a collection of recommended supplications, enriched by some pietistic rhymed prose. No *isnād* appears in it.

A further peculiarity is the number of different hands. If the texts were really gathered into a single booklet, then it might mirror a scholar's micro-library in which he collected handwritten texts from colleagues (or students?). A scholar could also have acquired a manuscript and then added the piece of (inexpert) poetry himself.

7 No. 5: Supplications for Cure and Subsistence

P.Vind.inv. A.P. 10126+10134[41]
13.7 high × 12.1 cm wide
2nd/8th century

The papyrus is scarcely dotted but is abundantly vocalized; it even uses a small "bird-wing" sign for *hamza*. On the verso, several dots appear on the papyrus, but they are not precisely placed over or under letters and seem to serve a purpose we are unaware of. The hand is very balanced and sophisticated, and the quality of the papyrus is quite good. It has circles as paragraph markers and some small corrections (two words on recto and one on verso are crossed

41 This papyrus, now one, was put together from two fragments by Mrs. Simone Suppan and me.

through). On the verso, the circles have a dot in the middle.[42] P.Vind.inv. A.P. 263 = PERF 731 = P.AbbottLiteraryPapyri I 2 has a quite similar script. This becomes especially clear in words such as *abī* and *ʿan*, which appear several times on both papyri. Other hints are the big, triangle-shaped final *hāʾ* and high, slim *alif*s and *lāms*. In the papyrus described by Abbott, the scribe used a less cursive hand, whereas in our document, the *rasm* slants considerably to the left, though most probably not as a sign of negligence but as an expression of his refined style, which is even more elegant than the straight book hand he employs in P.Vind.inv. A.P. 263. Abbott has identified the latter as part of the *Muwaṭṭaʾ* by Mālik b. Anas, yet hitherto no obvious connection between the two papyri (apart from some similarities in the handwriting) was established.

The wide margins on the top and on the right (recto) and left (verso) sides, respectively, suggest that this is a page of a codex of some sort, though it may have consisted of only a few leaves sewn together. The recto has traditions concerning supplication, probably in order to show what is recommended. Some of the *asānīd* are partially preserved. The text bears parallels to Ibn Abī l-Dunyā's *Kitāb al-yaqīn* and Nuʿaym b. Ḥammād's *Kitāb al-zuhd* (edited by Ibn al-Mubārak), or at least to passages transmitted by these authors (verso ll. 3–6 and 9–11). The *asānīd* on the papyrus seem to be identical with those of the printed books.[43]

recto

١ ±20 [ا]حد الحبَر بِكـ[...]

٢ لَـ...ن ±7 ـمـ.. [واهـ]ـدِنا وعافِنا و[ارزقنا ...عيسى بن]

٣ ⌜مريم⌝ دعا ±7 أ]صحابِهِ فقالُوا زِدنا فقالَ [... جرير]

٤ بن حازم الأزدي قالَ ⌜حدثَني⌝ المِقدامُ بنُ زائدهَ عَن [فلان ...]

٥ للـ..د ⌜الصمـ⌝ـن أصبَحنا لا نَملكُ ما نَرجوا ولا نَستَ[«ـحق»...]

٦ أفقرُ [«مِنـ»]«ـ»ـا ○ وأخبَرني عـ[ـبـ]ـدُ اللهِ بنُ لَهيعَهَ الحـ[ـضرمي]

٧ {فقالوا} قالو[ا] عيسى بنَ مريمَ فقالوا ادعُ لنَا فقَال لا إلهَ لـ[ـا ...]

٨ اعـ[...] وَاهدِنا وانصُرنا وارزُقْنا «دُ»[...]

٩ [... أ]يوبَ عَنِ النعمَن {وعمرو [...]}

42 For textual dividers, see the first section of the Conclusion below.

43 Ibn al-Mubārak 1425/2004: 453 (no. 85).

١٠ [... فلان] بن [مسـ]«ـعـ»ـودٍ وهوَ لا يَسَمَعُ فقـ˺ـو˹[...]

١١ [...] ودٍ وبنُ مَسعودٍ ˹وذلِكَ˺ لا يَسَمَعُ من «مثالِه النبي هذ[ا» ...]

١٢ ـسى نُعطَ .وهوَ [في ذلـ]ـكَ لا شيء [لـ]ـهُ فقَال بنُ [فلان ...]

---

٢ واهدِنا—٣ اصحابه—زِدنا—٤ راندهَ—٩ايوبَ

verso

١ [...] عبدِ اللهِ بنِ أبي ±16

٢ [...] بوارِ ˹الإثمِ˺ وأعوذُ بـ.... ... .ر والسُمعةِ ○

٣ [...عبيد الله بن أبي] جعفرٍ انَ رجلًا أصابَهُ مَرض [فمنعه من] الطَعامِ

٤ [والنوم فبينا هو ليلة ساهر سمع وجبة في حجرته فإذا هو يسمع] كَلامًا فوعاهُ فتكَلَمَ بِهِ فبرأَ مكانَهُ اللهُمَ

٥ [إني أعبدك ولك أصلي فاجعل الشفاء من جسدي واليقين في قلبي والنور في بصـ]ـري والشُكرَ في صدري وذِكرَكَ بـ[ـالليل و]ا[لنها]ر

٦ [في لساني أبدا ما أبقيتني وارزقني منك رزقا غير ممنوع ولا محظور[44] ... فلان] بن أبي {نفلل} أيوبَ عن [أ]بي عيسى عَن سعيدِ بنِ أبي

٧ [ايوب...] قَال اذنُهْ اذنُهْ قال ˹فدَنَوتُ˺ حتى أصابَتْ

٨ [...]..ا في الإيمانِ والمال والوَ[لاد ±8]ا

٩ [....]ـه ○ وأخبرني عنِ [...قال رسول الله صلى الله عليه وسلم]

١٠ [إن القلوب أوعية وبعـ]ـضها أوعَى مِن بعضٍ فادعوا الله [أيها الناس]

١١ [حين تدعون وأنتم موقنون بالإجابة فإن الله لا يستجيب] لعبد دعاه عن ظَهرِ قلبٍ غافلٍ ○[45] وأخبرني[...]

١٢ ... /دَخَلَ\ ...

---

44 Ibn Abī l-Dunyā 1993/1414: 30–31.

45 Ibn al-Mubārak 1425/2004: 453 (no. 85).

Translation

recto

1 [...S]omeone the report about ...
2 [...] ... [and gu]ide us and give us well-being [and provide us ... Jesus, the son of]
3 Mary made the supplication .... his disciples and they said: "Tell us more," so he said [... Djarīr]
4 b. Ḥāzim al-Azdī, he said: "al-Miqdām b. Zā'ida told me, from [so-and-so ...]
5 to the .... Companions, he does not possess what he wishes and does not des[erve (?) ...]
6 poorer than us (?)." ○ ʿA[b]d Allāh b. Lahīʿa al-Ḥa[ḍramī] reported to me [...]
7 {so they said} they sai[d]: "Jesus, the son of Mary," and they said: "Supplicate for us," so he said: "There is no God .[...]
8 .... and guide us and make us victorious and provide us .[...]
9 [... A]yyūb from al-Nuʿmān {and ʿAmr} [...]
10 [... So-and-So] b. Masʿūd and these [...] do not hear ...[...]
11 [...]ūd and Ibn Masʿūd and that (is): "The Prophet does not hear from the likes of him (?)... thi[s ...]
12 ... ... and he .... he has nothing (?)," so Ibn [...] said [...]

verso

1 ʿAbd Allāh b. Abī [................]
2 .... and I take refuge in ... . and (from) ill will." ○
3 [... *ʿUbayd Allāh b. Abī*] *Djaʿfar that a man was afflicted with illness and it kept him from eating*
4 [*and sleeping. One night when he was awake, he heard the sound of something falling in his room, then he heard*] *words, he understood it and spoke it and recovered immediately: "Oh God,*
5 [*I worship You and unto You I pray, so put the cure in my body and conviction in my heart, light in my eye*]*sight, thankfulness in my breast, and Your remembrance by* [*night and*] *b*[*y da*]*y*
6 [*on my tongue, as long as You let me live, and provide me with sustenance neither forbidden nor prohibited."* ... So-and-so] b. Abī {Bfll} Ayyūb from [A]bū ʿĪsā from Saʿīd b. Abī
7 [Ayyūb ...], he said: "His will, His will," he said: "I came closer (?) until [...] afflicted

8 [...] in faith, possessions and ch[ildren ...]

9 [...] him. And he reported to me from [... *The Messenger of God, may God bless him and grant him peace, said*]

10 [*Indeed, all hearts are aware and so*]*me are more aware than others, so supplicate to God,* [*oh people, when you supplicate, convinced that you will be*]

11 [*heard because God does not answer*] *a servant calling unto Him with an inattentive heart* ○ And he reported to me [...]

Commentary

r2r *aṣḥābihi* has two dots, one under *bāʾ* and one over *hāʾ*.

v12 *Kāf* after the three dots could also be read as *dāl*.

The text is almost completely vocalized, yet not in a way that aims to be instructive for the reader but in some kind of mannerism, vocalizing letters that definitely do not need it to be comprehensible. Not only vowel signs but also corrections on the recto seem to have been carried out in another hand using another, greyer kind of ink. The scribe may have made corrections himself, probably during the process of *idjāza* (authorization), or have handed the papyrus in for inspection to his teacher who then made the corrections. Vowel signs added after the completion of the text but obviously serving no instructional purpose may have been added as a sign to the scholar himself that he had received the *idjāza*. If he was traveling and carried several texts, he may also have developed a system that allowed him to quickly recognize which of the texts had already been proofread and approved. The vowel signs could have helped in this respect.

Two kinds of paragraph markers appear. One is a simple circle; the other is a circle with a dot inside. In P.Vind.inv. A.P. 263, a circle with a dot inside marks the beginning of a new chapter, as we know from the chapter headline preserved. The text before the headline ends in a circle with dot, which is repeated again at the beginning of the headline. At the end of it, a simple circle appears, most probably a paragraph or sub-chapter marker, whereas the dotted circle marks off a new chapter or a longer passage. In our document we find both, although the circle on recto could have had a dot inside. It is difficult to discern whether this is a dot or the end of the stroke making up the circle.

Some of the traditionists in the text can almost certainly be identified. For instance, if we add the name "Djarīr" to the end of line r3, we can reconstruct the name Djarīr b. Ḥāzim al-Azdī, his full name being Djarīr b. Ḥāzim b. Zayd Abū l-Naḍr al-Azdī al-ʿAtakī (88–167 or 170 / 706–783 or 786). Among the scholars who transmitted from him are Ibn al-Mubārak,[46] as well as many Baṣran scholars. ʿAbd Allāh b. Lahīʿa (r6) was a famous Egyptian traditionist. Khoury has dedicated a whole monograph to his biography, his scholarly activity, and his pupils.[47] The name on line v3, of which only "Djaʿfar" has survived, means in all probability Abū Bakr ʿUbayd Allāh b. Abī Djaʿfar al-Miṣrī, since ʿAbd Allāh b. Lahīʿa and Saʿīd b. Abī Ayyūb, both also mentioned in the *asānīd* of this papyrus, transmitted from him.[48] The name of Saʿīd b. Abī Ayyūb can be reconstructed on lines v6–7. His whole name is Saʿīd b. Abī Ayyūb Miqlāṣ Abū Yaḥyā al-Khuzāʿī al-Miṣrī (100–161/718–777). Ibn al-Mubārak transmitted from him.[49]

An interesting aspect of this papyrus is that it cites Jesus, the son of Mary, as author of some recommended supplication, an indication for the pietistic tone the text conveys, since Jesus and David are the prophets most closely associated with fearful piety in the Islamic tradition.

The text was, despite its beautiful hand, most probably not part of a "beautiful" Ḥadīth volume, as we can easily tell by the corrections the scribe made. If at all, it was a rough copy for a text before it reached its final flawless stage. We must ask ourselves if in Early Islamic times, Ḥadīth collections looked similar to ornamental Koran parchments. There is, however, evidence for manuscripts of ḥadīth collections written by order: The secretary of Marwān I. (reg. 684–685 CE) was ordered to write down the Ḥadīth of Abū Hurayra,[50] and al-Manṣūr (reg. 754–775 CE) is said to have had Ibn Isḥāq write down all of his historic accounts.[51] It is not impossible that at that time, before the canonization of not only the works of tradition, but also Islamic law, most works of Ḥadīth existed only in copies the scholars made and circulated mostly in the milieu of the scholars.

46 Ibn Ḥibbān 1400/1980, vol. 6: 144–145.

47 Khoury 1986.

48 al-Mizzī 1413/1983–1992, vol. 19: 19.

49 al-Mizzī 1413/1983–1992, vol. 10: 342–343.

50 Abbott 1967: 90.

51 Schoeler 1992: 15. Schoeler also lists further instances for early commissioned works (Schoeler 1992: 32).

8 Conclusion and General Remarks

8.1 *Textual Composition, Structuring, and Hands*

Literary papyri are often easily recognizable by the book hands in which they are written. Book hands share certain conspicuous features, among which their often angular style is most prominent. What the writers had in mind was most probably an archaization of their writing in order to achieve a style similar to Kūfī or Ḥidjāzī script. These were the styles associated with early, religiously relevant texts, first and foremost the Qurʾān, but also with inscriptions.

It is interesting to see that the practice of angular writing for religious and literary texts was followed in the majority of Ḥadīth papyri. We can conclude that this was an established custom that was taught to new students at some point in their curriculum. Two reasons for this are imaginable: the origins of this practice could lie in the respect due to texts with religious relevance like the Ḥadīth, and the practice made literary texts easily recognizable in case they were kept or in some way handled together with other written material.

Abbott argues that literary hands originated on the one hand from chancellery scripts and on the other hand from monumental scripts used for the Qurʾān.[52] Angular book hands widely used for literary papyri were, as Abbott states, derived from chancellery script, while more or less careless styles "represent the *naskhī* [cursive script] poorly executed in the manner of the book-seller-copyist."[53] One can also imagine that notes meant for personal use only, maybe hastily taken down during a lecture, were carried out with little care for their aesthetic value. The example of P.Vind.inv. 6666v has shown that the intent of using more or less angular hands for Ḥadīth was definitely there, but whether the writer could keep it up while writing the whole text was a different issue. If we suppose that this text's writer was used to *naskhī* in daily life, yet not advanced in his Ḥadīth studies, then his inability to carry out the whole text in an archaisized style can be explained.

Writers of literary texts were aware of writing conventions that exceeded mere matters of cursive or angular style. *Muhmal* vocalization signs marking letters without diacritical dots appear in some papyri, though not very frequently. Some texts are dotted, and we find the whole spectrum of diacritical signs, ranging from undotted texts to texts with a few, then many dots, until we find Ḥadīth papyri with full diacritical signs, as well as fully vocalized texts with markers for *hamza*. Admittedly, the sample of literary papyri at our disposal, as

---

52 Abbott 1967: 2–5. Cribiore 1996:7 says the same on Greek literary papyri, their book hands being likewise derived from chancellery style.

53 Abbott 1967: 4.

well as the corresponding research, are still not advanced enough to draw further conclusions, let alone to establish correlations between texts to explain why some writers preferred to use diacritical signs and others did not. However, we preliminarily might think of different schools of writing emphasizing different skills in their students' training. While some set higher store on the correct use of *muhmal* signs, other teachers in other regions or traditions may have paid more attention to the correct representation of *hamza*. The teachers' preferences could have been connected to their own main field of specialization and the conventions used therein.[54]

Apart from the *rasm* and diacritical signs, literary papyri show us early examples of how scribes marked and structured text. Most of these conventions are well known from later paper manuscripts, but papyri can show us the earliest surviving examples of the employed techniques. Such conventions include the insertion of headings or other ways of separating chapters or other text units from one another, marginal notes, and corrections. Some scribes separated textual units by leaving a space between paragraphs, some drew horizontal lines between chapters,[55] and others inserted traditional headings stating the following chapter's content.[56] In P.Vind.inv. A.P. 10136r, a new Ḥādīth beginning with the names of transmitters is marked by pulling the first name out into the right margin, thereby indenting the following lines. Repeated, apparently common principles and habits in one text genre, especially concerning the categorization of material, point to an agreement among scholars, a "common language" that was already established at that time. This observation that Brockopp has made for legal texts holds equally true for Ḥadīth papyri.[57]

What we see mostly on the papyri from an organizational point of view, are collections of Prophetic traditions in a thematic, *muṣannaf*-like (i.e., categorized) composition. Apart from thematic structures, there were other ways of gathering the text material, as can be seen in P.Berl.inv. P 11998, a Berlin papyrus that lists Aḥādīth transmitted by ʿAbd Allāh b. Lahīʿa from Yazīd b. Abī Ḥabīb, so clearly a *musnad*. The way a Ḥadīth was structured depended on the aspect the scholar teaching it would have emphasized most. If he wanted to teach the prevailing view on a certain topic (according to a specific school of Ḥadīth), he would have used texts enumerating various traditions on this special issue,

54 Legal treatises for example seem to have followed a distinct, angular style (see e.g. P.Vind .inv. A.P. 10132, P.Vind.inv. A.P. 9937).

55 Cf. P.Vind.inv. A.P. 10113v.

56 P.Berl.inv. P 11998 has "Aḥādīth by Ibn Lahīʿa via Yazīd b. Abī Ḥabīb" to the left of the initial Basmala.

57 Brockopp 2017: 132, Fn 100.

while someone intending to focus on the teachings of a certain *muḥaddith* (traditionist) would have preferred an overview of the latter's work. So far, there is no temporal sequence of *muṣannaf* or *musnad*-style texts traceable in papyri, especially as to which kind of categorization might have appeared earlier in time.

Another conspicuous feature of which literary papyri are easily recognizable are the little shapes used to separate textual units. In their simplest form, they appear as circles or drops, but there are also multiple circles, either repeated on the line or inside each other. These circles can also have dots inside.[58] We also find little *hāʾ*-s, a known abbreviation for *intahā* (meaning "finished" or the end of a quotation) widely used in later paper manuscripts.[59] As mentioned above, Abbott has two theories about the variety of shapes and their use as markers in literary papyri. She argues that these signs could have been subject to fashions, certain shapes being popular during certain periods of time. Her second thought concerns different shapes of textual markers as expressions for stages of the collation process of certain Ḥadīth texts or accounts. Complex signs could be an indication of double collation, in which a scholar relied on both oral and written transmission for his text.[60] Another possible reason for the variety of textual dividers might lie in the process of *idjāza*. Students and scholars of Ḥadīth might have marked texts or single traditions that they had already read back to their teacher(s) or that they were already allowed to pass on to others with signs distinguishing these accounts from other material whose *idjāza* they had not yet received.[61]

Marginal notes appear in literary papyri, albeit not very frequently. So far, two kinds of marginal notes can be distinguished: notes repeating illegible words in the main text, and notes commenting the main text. They are sometimes separated from the main text body by half-circles or lines reminiscent of elongated brackets.

Again, to our present state of knowledge, the mentioned techniques are individual examples. The identification of broader trends and conventions, and perhaps even schools of text treatment in literary papyri, still awaits future research.

---

58 Nice though fragmentary examples of this practice can be found in P.Vind.inv. A.P. 10101; P.Vind.inv. A.P. 10106; and P.Vind.inv. A.P. 10118r. P.Vind.inv. A.P. 10136 ends a tradition in a circular marker in a flower- or cloud-like pattern.

59 Abbott 1957–1972, vol. 2: 87.

60 Abbott 1957–1972, vol. 2: 88.

61 At this early stage of Islamic scholarship, we cannot assume a coherent, fully developed system of *idjāza* like it appears in later manuscripts. The term has been chosen for the sake of brevity.

8.2 *The* Sitz im Leben *and the* (*Scholarly*) *Background of the Papyri*

Given the existence of Ḥadīth papyri and the information we have on their origins, we must probably review our *a priori* assumptions about the surroundings in which high-ranking scholars acted. Many papyri come from outside of al-Fusṭāṭ, which points to scholarly activity in the Islamic sciences outside of al-Fusṭāṭ at a time before Egypt was Arabized, let alone Islamicized.[62] We do not know how comprehensive the texts were or how extensive the written material was that scholars consulted and cited. What we miss most is any archive of a scholar that could enlighten us on this point, or another established collection of texts that are evidentially connected to each other. Brockopp has underlined the importance of the Kairouan manuscripts because they, contrarily to our papyrus fragments, share a common background that allows for statements on aspects of their transmission history as well as on scribal and scholarly habits of their respective times.[63]

A topic that has stirred much discussion in the past is the question of oral and/or written transmission. In the papyri edited above, there is only one definite hint at how Aḥādīth were transmitted: The writer of P.Vind.inv. A.P. 10128 wrote *ṣalāt* once with *alif* (r7), yet on all other occasions with *wāw* (r8; r9; r21; v19). We might assume that he copied from different written sources (or from different sources among which were written texts), in which he found both variants. Had he taken notes during a lecture (or during another kind of dictation), he would have used only the variant he personally preferred.

In the process of learning and teaching, some sheets were only meant to be a short-lived support to help with memorizing a text. Some Ḥadīth papyri may have been drafts or rough copies, meant to be recopied later in a more beautiful script. Schoeler has argued convincingly that writing and publishing are two different processes.[64] Texts might be written, but not with the intent of presenting them as a "book" (in Brockopp's terminology), as a finished work produced in "a single redactional effort" continuously undertaken by one author,[65] as it was the case with most Ḥadīth papyri. Scholars may have used their texts only for a period of time, or they might have kept them with or without the intention of passing them on physically to their students after their death. They wrote but they did not publish, at least not their written material on papyrus.

Due to the circumstances in which most literary papyri have been found—as heaps of discarded material—it is very probable that most Ḥadīth papyri

62 Especially Ḥadīth papyri datable to the 2nd/8th century affirm this assumption.

63 Brockopp 2017: 119–121.

64 Schoeler 1992: 10; 12–13.

65 Brockopp 2017: 84.

are indeed discarded notes or preliminary copies that were of no use at a later stage of text production (if that stage ever came into being). Final versions, perhaps codices, may have undergone different treatment when they were no longer needed. Although the extreme care that was applied to the proper disposal of worn-out Qurʾān exemplars did not apply to works of tradition and other religious sciences, there may have been reluctance to throw them on the garbage heaps that were the final destination of so many papyri. Instead, they might, for instance, have been cut up to serve as lining and binding material for new books or used for other purposes. Another assumption would be to suppose a "material barrier," in the sense that papyrus was used for *musawwadāt* (drafts, rough copies) and unfinished texts or working copies, while ornamental Ḥadīth works were written on parchment, similar to the Qurʾān exemplars of early times. Apparently there was no objection to throwing out religiously relevant but more or less short-lived texts in the same way other material was discarded. The question of whether there was really no reluctance to discard these texts carelessly is not limited to Arabic papyri, however, but is generally dealt with under the rubric of "sacred trash."[66]

Although we can make some tentative statements about the nature and content of Ḥadīth papyri, we still lack a comprehensive study. Only such a study would enable us to differentiate between general qualities and special traits of the texts, as Fred Donner puts it: "in such cases there is no way to be sure which aspects of an account might represent the 'consensus' of the tradition's view, and which the […] distortions. Rather, it becomes necessary to compare an account with as many others on the same subject as possible in an effort to gain a glimpse of the growth of the collective tradition on that subject over time."[67]

However, even our short examination of some very few Ḥadīth papyri, chosen arbitrarily for certain peculiar aspects, brings new insights. These include that it is difficult to say if *musnad* or *muṣannaf*-style text structures were preferred by scholars. In theory, early texts were preferably grouped thematically, like the *Muwaṭṭaʾ*.[68] Not only due to the papyri's fragmentary status is it often hard to tell what classification their writers had in mind. Many texts group traditions together that all start with the same *isnād* or at least with one common transmitter, but then they also show thematic coherence at the same time. A clear statement about the intended structure can be obtained from P.Berl.inv. P. 11998, which has a headline that identifies the contents as Ḥadīth by ʿAbd

66 Luigendijk 2010: 217–254.

67 Donner 1998: 290.

68 Melchert 2006: 40.

Allāh b. Lahīʿa from Yazīd b. Abī Ḥabīb. The single Aḥādīth's thematic spectrum is wide enough to support the assumption of a *musnad*, which however does not contradict the early preference for *muṣannaf* style, since the papyrus can be palaeographically dated to the third/ninth century, by which time *musnad* composition was already established.[69] Another rather certain example for a *musnad* is the booklet to which both P.Mich.inv. 5608 and P.Camb.inv. Michaelides D 953 belonged. All *asānīd* start with ʿAlī b. Maʿbad, and notes about the contents have been added on the margins, which suggests that the main text lacked this structure. A *muṣannaf* type of text probably appears in P.Vind.inv. A.P. 10126+10134 (edited above as No. 5), which has Aḥādīth on *duʿāʾ* transmitted via several different *asānīd*.

Even in this very short study, we see that papyri can be joined or identified as having been written by the same scribe as other papyri. One can only imagine how many precious insights we could gain through a larger study of Ḥadīth papyri, considering the unexpected, promising results that even a very short study has brought. We are in dire need of a broad, systematic, quantitative, and comprehensive study to help us gain an overview of the topics and texts most frequently reproduced in the first three centuries of Ḥadīth Science.

Bibliography

Abbott, Nabia. 1967. *Studies in Arabic Literary Papyri, Vol. 2: Qur'ānic Commentary and Tradition.* Oriental Institute Publications, vol. 76. Chicago: University of Chicago Press.

Abū Yaʿlā Aḥmad b. ʿAlī al-Mawṣilī. 1410/1990. *Musnad Abī Yaʿlā*, ed. Ḥusayn Salīm Asad, vol. 2, 13 vols. 2nd edition. Damascus: al-Ma'mūn.

Arberry, Arthur J. 1964. *The Koran Interpreted.* Oxford/London/New York: Oxford University Press.

Al-Arnā'ūṭ, Shuʿayb; Ibn Ḥibbān, Abū Ḥātim Muḥammad b. Ahmad. 1988/1408–1991/1412. *al-Iḥsān fī Ṣaḥīḥ Ibn Ḥibbān*. vol. 2, 18 vols. Bayrūt: Mu'assasat al-Risāla.

Al-ʿAsqalānī, Ibn Ḥadjar Aḥmad b. ʿAlī. 2000/1421. *Fatḥ al-Bārī. Sharḥ Ṣaḥīḥ al-Bukhārī*, ed. Muḥammad Fu'ād ʿAbd al-Bāqī, vol. 10 13 vols. al-Riyāḍ: Dār al-Salām.

Al-Bayhaqī, Abū Bakr Aḥmad b. al-Ḥusayn. 1424/2003. *al-Sunan al-kubrā*, ed. Muḥammad ʿAbd al-Qādir ʿAṭā. vol. 4, 10 vols. 3rd. edition. Bayrūt: Dār al-kutub al-ʿilmiyya.

Blau, Joshua. 1981. *The Emergence and Linguistic Background of Judaeo-Arabic: A Study of the Origins of Middle Arabic.* 2nd edition. Jerusalem: Ben-Zvi Institute for the Study of Jewish Communities in the East.

69 Melchert 2005: 50, Fn. 88.

Brockopp, Jonathan. 2017. *Muhammad's Heirs: The Rise of Muslim Scholarly Communities, 622–950*. Cambridge Studies in Islamic Civilization. Cambridge: Cambridge University Press.

Clarysse, Willy. 1983. "Literary Papyri in Documentary 'Archives.'" In *Egypt and the Hellenistic World: Proceedings of the International Colloquium, Leuven, 24./26. May 1982*, ed. Edmond van't Dack et al. Studia Hellenistica, vol. 27. Leuven: Orientaliste, 43–61.

Cribiore, Raffaella. 1996. *Writing, Teachers and Students in Graeco-Roman Egypt*. American Studies in Papyrology, vol. 36. Atlanta: Scholars Press.

Donner, Fred McGraw 1998. *Narratives of Islamic Origins: The Beginnings of Islamic Historical Writing*. Studies in Late Antiquity and Early Islam, vol. 14. Princeton: Darwin.

Furāt b. Ibrāhīm al-Kūfī, Abū l-Qāsim. 1416/1995. *Tafsīr Furāt al-Kūfī*, ed. Muḥammad al-Kāẓim. 2nd edition. Tehran: Wezāret-e farhang-o-ershād-e eslāmī.

Hopkins, Simon. 1984. *Studies in the Grammar of Early Arabic: Based upon Papyri Datable to before 300 A.H./912 A.D.* Oxford: Oxford University Press.

Ibn Abī l-Dunyā, Abū Bakr ʿAbd Allāh b. Muḥammad. 1414/1993. *Kitāb al-yaqīn*, ed. Muṣṭafā ʿAbd al-Qādir ʿAṭā. Bayrūt: Muʿassasat al-kutub al-thaqāfiyya.

Ibn Abī Shayba, Abū Bakr. 1425/2004 *Kitāb al-muṣannaf fī l-aḥādīth wa-l-āthār*, ed. Ḥamad b. ʿAbd Allāh Djumʿa and Muḥammad b. Ibrāhīm al-Luḥaydān, vol. 1. 16 vols. al-Riyāḍ: Maktabat al-rushd.

Ibn Ḥibbān, Abū Ḥātim Muḥammad b. Aḥmad. 1393/1973–1403/1983. *Kitāb al-thiqāt*. ed. Muḥammad ʿAbd al-Muʿīd Khān, vol. 6. 9 vols. Hyderabad: Dā'irat al-maʿārif al-ʿuthmāniyya.

Khoury, Raif Georges. 1972. *Wahb b. Munabbih*. Codices Arabici Antiqui, vol. 1. 2 vols. Wiesbaden: Harrassowitz.

Khoury, Raif Georges 1988. *ʿAbd Allāh b. Lahīʿa (97–174/715–790): juge et grand maître de l'école égyptienne. Avec édition critique de l'unique rouleau de papyrus arabe conservé à Heidelberg*. Codices Arabici Antiqui, vol. 4. Wiesbaden: Harrassowitz.

al-Kulaynī, Ṯiqat al-Islām Muḥammad b. Yaʿqūb. 1428/2007. *Uṣūl al-Kāfī*, vol. 2. 4 vols. Bayrūt: Manshūrāt al-fadjr.

Luigendijk, A. 2010. "Sacred Scriptures as Trash: Biblical Papyri from Oxyrhynchus." In *Vigiliae Christianae* 64: 217–254.

al-Madjlisī, Muḥammad Bāqir. 1430. *Biḥār al-anwār al-djāmiʿa li-durar al-a'imma al-aṭhār*, vol. 7, 35 vols. Qom: Mu'assasat iḥyā' al-kutub al-islāmiyya.

Malczycki, W. Matt. 2006. "Literary Papyri from the University of Utah Arabic Papyrus and Paper Collection." Unpublished PhD thesis, University of Utah 2006. (https://collections.lib.utah.edu/details?id=194166, accessed 23.08.2017 12:06)

al-Mizzī, Abū l-Ḥadjdjādj Yūsuf b. ʿAbd al-Raḥmān. 1403–1413/1983–1992. *Tahdhīb al-kamāl fī asmā' al-ridjāl*, ed. Bashshār ʿAwwād Maʿrūf, 35 vols. Beirut: Mu'assasat al-risāla.

Melchert, Christopher. 2005. “The *Musnad* of Aḥmad ibn Ḥanbal. How it Was Composed and What Distinguishes it from the Six Books.” In Der Islam 69: 1–43.

Melchert, Christopher. 2006. *Aḥmad b. Ḥanbal*. Makers of the Muslim World, vol. 9. Oxford: Oneworld.

Motzki, Harald (ed.). 2004. *Ḥadīth: Origins and Developments*. The Formation of the Classical Islamic World, vol. 28. Aldershot: Ashgate.

Motzki, Harald, et al. (ed.). 2010. *Analysing Muslim Traditions: Studies in Legal, Exegetical and Maghāzī Ḥadīṯ*. Islamic History and Civilization, vol. 78. Leiden: Brill.

Ibn al-Mubārak, ʿAbd Allāh al-Marwazī. 1425/2005. *Kitāb al-zuhd wa-yalīhi Kitāb al-raqāʾiq*, ed. Ḥabīb al-Raḥmān al-Aʿẓamī. Beirut: Dār al-kutub al-ʿilmiyya.

Muehlhaeusler, M. 2014. “Fragments of Arabic Poetry on Papyrus: Questions of Textual Genesis, Attribution, and Representation.” In *Journal of the American Oriental Society* 134: 673–687.

Schoeler, Gregor. 1992. “Schreiben und Veröffentlichen: Zur Verwendung und Funktion der Schrift in den ersten islamischen Jahrhunderten.” In *Der Islam* 69: 1–43.

Al-Ṭabarānī, Abū l-Qāsim Sulaymān b. Aḥmad. 1404/1983. *al-Muʿdjam al-Kabīr*, ed. Ḥamdī ʿAbd al-Madjīd al-Salafī. vol. 22, 25 vols. al-Qāhira: Maktabat Ibn Taymiyya.

al-Tirmidhī, Muḥammad b. ʿĪsā. 1996. *al-Djāmiʿ al-kabīr: Sunan al-Tirmidhī*, ed. Bashshār ʿAwād Maʿrūf, vol. 5, 6 vols. Beirut: Dār al-gharb al-islāmī.

CHAPTER 5

Using Papyri to Determine the Purchasing Power of a Dinar in Early Islamic Egypt

W. Matt Malczycki

1 Introduction

There have always been examples of historians using papyri in their work. Shelomo Goitein's work with the Cairo Geniza (1967) is the gold standard, although Goitein worked mainly with Geniza documents rather than Arabic papyri. Eliyahu Ashtor's work (1969; 1976; 1983; 1986) incorporated some papyri, but on a limited scale. In the 1980s Kosei Morimoto (1981) used papyri extensively, as did Jørgen Simonsen (1988). Much more recently, Gladys Frantz-Murphy (2001) and Petra Sijpesteijn (2013) have combined philology and history to make arguments that greatly enhance our understanding of the administration of Early Islamic Egypt. There are also several theses and dissertations waiting to be turned into books that take a similar approach.

So, today there are many scholars using Arabic papyri in the service of history, and the voices of the critics grow ever fainter. Nevertheless, papyrologists need to do everything they can to maintain this momentum and to continue to make Arabic papyrology relevant, useful, and perhaps even interesting to the up-and-coming generation of historians. With that in mind, this chapter talks about something that everyone can relate to: getting paid.

Early Muslim historians often mention dinars when they talk about the revenues of provinces, the value of booty taken in raids, or the gifts emirs lavished on favored poets and concubines. The amounts reported are usually in the dozens, hundreds, or thousands of dinars. In the papyrological record, too, dinars appear frequently both as a currency and as units of account. The papyrological record, however, describes a much more modest economy than the one that the literary sources depict. Whereas the literary sources name caliphs who spent in the millions of dinars, the papyri refer to farmers, craftsmen, and merchants who counted their wealth in single dinars and fractions of dinars. This paper is about these folks, not the sultans and emirs.

Statements to the effect that a dinar could pay the annual rent on a *faddān* of land or the annual lease on an urban shop are common among Arabic papyrologists. Close examination of footnotes and bibliographies shows that

 | DOI:10.1163/9789004443877_006

the source of many of these statements is page 44 of Adolf Grohmann's *From the World of Arabic Papyri* (Grohmann 1952a). Since Grohmann's day, hundreds of additional papyri have been published. These new publications do not contradict Grohmann. In fact, they basically reaffirm his statements about land and real estate prices. What these papyri don't clearly reveal is the ability of the common folk to pay these rents and leases or to feed and clothe themselves. The texts also say little about working conditions and day-to-day work life.

2 Wages

Among the most interesting papyri for the topic of wages[1] are P.Cair.Arab. 377 and P.Cair.Arab. 378. Both of these are fragments of account books from agricultural estates. The first one, P.Cair.Arab. 377, has a date: 288 Hidjri, which is 901 of the Common Era. Grohmann dates the other text, P. Cair.Arab. 378, to the 2nd or 3rd/8th or 9th centuries. The text does not contain a year, but it does name a month, Rabīʿ I. Normally, just having the name of the month would be nearly useless information, but this text references the clover (*barsīm*) harvest several times. The text also refers to threshing clover. Clover is planted usually between September and November, and then cut for fodder several times a season. After the last cutting, the plants are allowed to grow until they flower and produce seeds. The mature plants are harvested and the seeds kept for planting the following year. Whereas clover is cut and harvested multiple times a season, the threshing occurs only once a year, usually at the end of spring, often in May. So, finding years in which the Islamic month of Rabīʿ I corresponded to the Gregorian month of May might narrow down the possible dates. The most likely candidates fall between five ranges: the years 181–183/797–799, 213–215/828–830, 246–248/860–862, 281–283/894–896, 314–316/926–928. Given the similarity in language between the undated P.Cair.Arab. 378 and the dated P.Cair.Arab. 377, we should probably favor one of the later dates, either Rabīʿ I 282/May 895 or Rabīʿ I 316/May 928. Unfortunately, Grohmann 1952b does not provide an image

1 Maya Shatzmiller has a very useful website for beginning economic research about the medieval Middle East. Her site, *Measuring the Medieval Islamic Economy* (http://www.medievalislamiceconomy.uwo.ca/), provides information on wages, cost of living, rents, taxes, and consumer goods. It incorporates some figures from Grohmann's *Arabic Papyri in the Egyptian Library* and a few references drawn from the *Arabic Papyrology Database* (http://www.naher-osten.lmu.de/apd), but, for the papyrus era, it draws most heavily on Ashtor 1969. Ashtor uses papyri, but not extensively by modern standards. To get a closer look at wages and work life, one has to turn to individual papyri.

for this papyrus. If we did have the image, we could analyze it in light of Eva Grob's 2010 book, and thereby reach a more definitive conclusion.

The men mentioned in P.Cair.Arab. 377 were agricultural workers of various types. We find among them overseers (*khawlī*, plur. *khawla*), journeymen (*adjīr*, plur. *udjarā'*), watchmen (*ḥāris*, plur. *ḥawāris*), and farmers (*muzāri'*, plur. *muzāri'īn*). It seems that each overseer was in charge of a crew of three to five men. The estate owner or manager paid the overseers according to the number of bundles of wheat their crews harvested. The pay rate was 1 dinar for every twenty bundles. The journeymen earned from one-half to 1 full dinar for working the harvest, but the overseers earned more than three times that amount.

This particular papyrus mentions three overseers by name: 'Abbād b. Luqmān, Djibrīl b. Yūsuf, and 'Ubayd Allāh b. Aḥmad. All three of the overseers appear to have been Muslim, although Djībrīl b. Yūsuf could have been Muslim, Christian, or even Jewish. The journeymen were split between Muslims and Copts. In fact, each of the crews consisted of both Muslims and Christians working side by side.

In addition to harvesting, the crews worked on canal maintenance. It seems that working on the canal paid better than working the harvest. The pay may also have been more equitably split among the overseers and the journeymen, as each of the men earned at least 1 dinar. One of them earned slightly more—1 9/24 dinars (1.375 dinars) per month—which was the same amount paid to the overseer.

Guard work could pay well. The best-paid guard earned 2 dinars for watching sugarcane. The other guards earned 1 to 1 1/4 dinars (1 to 1.25 dinars) per month. Guarding palm groves earned a similar amount of pay. Working as the bird guard (*ḥirāsat al-ṭayr*) paid little but may have offered more work more often. Grohmann translates *ḥirāsat al-ṭayr* as "watching against the birds," but it seems that the phrase could also mean "guarding the birds," as in guarding chickens, ducks, or pigeons, all of which are favorite targets of cats, dogs, and other predators. Regardless of whether the *ḥāris al-ṭayr* guarded birds or guarded against birds, his monthly wages were less than those of the harvesters and canal workers. The bird guard made 15/24 dinar (0.625 dinar) per month, which is about half what the other men were paid. That said, the account ledger provides an interesting detail about the job security of the bird guard. Whereas the ledger lists monthly or seasonal wages for all the other workers, it lists both a monthly and a yearly wage for the bird guard. The bird guard was paid 6 1/8 dinars (6.125 dinars) per year. The fact that the ledger gives both wages suggests that the bird guard enjoyed more permanent employment than the others, albeit at lower pay.

It appears that, although the overseers were responsible for paying the journeymen, the estate manager kept track not only of the amount paid out to the overseer, but the amount that the overseer was supposed to pay to each man on his work crew. It's impossible to know if the estate manager kept records this way simply out of obsessiveness or because he wanted to hold the overseers accountable for paying their men the wages they had earned. Everyone who worked on the estate was provided with *rizq* (maintenance) in addition to pay, which we can take to mean that the estate fed the workers on those days that they worked.

P.Cair.Arab. 378 references journeymen and watchmen, but it also mentions porters (*ḥammāl*, plur. *ḥammāla*) and sailors (*nūtī*, plur. *nawātī*). It also says that men were paid for working the harvest and the threshing, although it does not provide a specific name for those occupations. The names of the men show an even balance of Muslims and Christians. The crops mentioned in this papyrus are clover and barley rather than wheat. The text refers to payments made for various periods of employment. Some of the payouts are for a month's work, while other payouts are for an entire harvesting season or even an entire year.

The wages and food allowances in this text are similar to P.Cair.Arab. 377. Cutting clover and barley earned a man about 1 1/2 dinars (1.50 dinars) per month of harvest, which is similar to the wages paid for working the wheat harvest in the previous text. Guard duty paid a little better than harvesting, cutting, and threshing. A man could make 3 dinars per month guarding the crops and the village. Some of the guards worked both as guards and as harvesters. As was the case in the other text, the estate provided food for the workers while they were on the job.

But regarding maintenance, P. Cair.Arab. 378 has some interesting features. Whereas in P.Cair.Arab. 377 the estate paid for *rizq* of overseers and their crews while they were working, the estate in P.Cair 378 seems to have hired some of the men full time. The text lists payments for individuals rather than for overseers and their journeymen. Some of these maintenance payments were substantial: the estate spent 5 dinars per month on the maintenance of one man. It is not clear whether these 5 dinars were solely for the maintenance of one man and perhaps his family or whether the money went to the maintenance of the man and his underlings. If it was the former, then it seems that, between wages and maintenance, some of the overseers lived fairly comfortably.

One category of workers that appears in P.Cair.Arab. 378 but not in the other papyrus is transporters, or shippers. A porter named Nuṣayr earned 1 dinar for hauling the harvest from the village. An overseer and his journeyman were paid

2 1/4 dinars (2.25 dinars) per month for transporting 100 artabas of barley. Most interestingly, we have sailors transporting barley. Unfortunately, we don't know how much they were paid, but we do know that they conveyed grain to al-Fusṭāṭ, presumably by boat or barge.

These two papyri contain the most information about wages, but there are others that mention wages for other agricultural jobs. For example, P.Cair.Arab. 384 shows that an estate paid men between 1 and 2 dinars for preparing fields for planting. P.Chrest.Khoury I 61 gives a wage for bean harvest of 1/12 dinar (0.083 dinar) per month, and CPR XXVI 15 lists a wage for sugarcane harvest of 1 dinar per month.[2]

P.Cair.Arab. 386 is one of the few papyri that mentions nonagricultural work. It does not contain a date, but Grohmann suggests it was composed in the 3rd/9th century. It lists payments in both dinars and dirhams, which poses a problem for historical analysis. In this papyrus, stonecutters (*naqqāṭīn*), masons (*bannāʾ*, plur. *bannāʾīn*), and journeymen (*raqqāṣ*, plur. *raqqāṣīn*) worked to repair a house in or near al-Ushmūnayn in the 3rd/9th century. The stonecutters earned a wage of 1/2 dinar (0.50 dinar) every day, although the text does not state the number of stonecutters. There were two masons on the job, and they earned 3 dirhams per day plus 1/2 dirham/day *rizq*. There were six and a half journeymen, and collectively they were paid only 1 1/2 dirhams in *rizq* (0.23 dirham each). P.Cair.Arab. 386 is one of those papyri that historians find quite maddening because it provides some data but also leaves many questions. First, without knowing how many stonecutters there were, it is impossible to compare their pay to that of the masons and journeymen. Second, the text does not provide any clues about the dirham-to-dinar exchange rate. In the 3rd/9th century the rate fluctuated between 13 1/8 dirhams to the dinar and 28 1/3 dirhams to the dinar. Although 24 to 1 seems to have been the average, there simply is no way to know for sure until more papyri are published.[3] Third, the text mentions a half journeyman. Grohmann thinks that this is a reference to a boy who would have been sent on errands, but it could also refer to a journeyman who worked only half the day. Finally, Grohmann's reading of the text leads him to conclude that the journeymen were not paid at all, but instead only received *rizq*. However, given that the agricultural overseers and journey-

2 Line 4 of P.Chrest.Khoury I 61 reads "he gave him for these two months one-sixth dinar, for each month two dirhams." There were wide fluctuations in the dirham-to-dinar exchange rate, but at least in this one text it is clear that 1/24 dinar = 1 dirham. This papyrus contains a date (227/841). For more on exchange rates, see Ashtor 1969: 76–77, and also Grohmann 1954: 191.

3 Ashtor 1979: 76–77; Grohmann 1954: 184–219.

men worked in crews, it seems likely that the same was true for construction workers. If the foremen of agricultural work crews were supposed to pay their men out of their shares, then perhaps the same was true of the construction workers.

Having examined the details, one can now step back to gain greater perspective. Taken together, the documents provide a sketch of work life in the Egyptian countryside. The men worked in teams, and the teams included men of both faith communities. Overseers made a slightly better wage than journeymen. The documents reveal that Christians and Muslims worked side by side in the fields and on the canals. There does seem to have been a preference for Muslim overseers—only one of the overseers in the documents examined here has a distinctly Christian name—but this is just as likely the consequence of fragmentary evidence as it is of what moderns might call religious discrimination. About half the men mentioned in the documents appear to have been Muslim and the other half Christian.

It took the average agricultural worker a month to earn 1 dinar. Planting and harvesting paid about the same. Transporting and shipping could bring in extra money. Serving guard duty was another way a man might make an extra dinar or two. If a man worked all year for the same wage, then he could expect about 12 dinars a year. But could a man work all year? The documents suggest that planting and harvesting time provided many opportunities for work and wage earning, but they don't say much about other times of year. It may have been the case that families had to stretch the money they made at harvesting and planting time to last all year. If so, then poverty must have been endemic in the countryside. Then again, it may have been the case that people did different kinds of work at different times of year. Even when there were no crops to tend, there must have been houses to repair and canals to maintain. Indeed, other papyri suggest that some men, perhaps most, were capable of many different kinds of work. Some of them worked in construction when they were not engaged in agricultural work. One can probably also assume that some of them engaged in crafts and small-scale manufacturing when they were not working in the fields. Perhaps it was not too difficult for a hard-working man to put some money aside for investments in land, property, and livestock. In other words, maybe there was more social mobility than scholars have previously granted.

3 Conclusion

Pamuk and Shatzmiller (2014) recently argued that the average Egyptian of the Early Islamic period had a standard of living that was above subsistence level.

Pamuk and Shatzmiller are probably right in saying that average people lived above the subsistence level. A working man could probably afford to feed himself and his family and still have a little left over. With brains and luck, he may have managed to acquire a small farm of his own or, if he already had his own farm, been able to build a small estate.

Now, one must admit that this is an optimistic interpretation of the papyri. Surely there were years in which there was less work to be had. Our literary sources make it clear that famine was not unknown. Both the literary sources and the papyri confirm that there were some years in which tax rates and the collection of taxes were higher. There were revolts and even civil wars. But it seems that the working people of Early Islamic Egypt enjoyed material security most of the time. They had work and they worked hard. They were able to take care of themselves and their families and perhaps even save money. One hopes that future historical analysis of new editions of papyri will confirm this cheerful assessment.

Bibliography

Abulafia, David. 1993. *Commerce and Conquest in the Mediterranean: 1100–1500*. Variorum Collected Studies Series, vol. 410. Aldershot: Ashgate-Variorum.

The Arabic Papyrology Database, ed. Andreas Kaplony et al. Ludwig-Maximilians-Universität München, Institute of Near and Middle Eastern Studies. http://www.naher-osten.lmu.de/apd, last accessed 14 September 2014.

Ashtor, Eliyah. 1969. *Histoire des prix et des salaires dans l'Orient médiéval*. Monnaie, Prix, Conjoncture, vol. 8. Paris: SEVPEN.

Ashtor, Eliyahu. 1976. *A Social and Economic History of the Near East*. Los Angeles: University of California Press.

Ashtor, Eliyahu. 1983. *Levant Trade in the Later Middle Ages*. Princeton: Princeton University Press.

Ashtor, Eliyahu. 1986. *East-West Trade in the Medieval Mediterranean*, ed. Benjamin Z. Kedar. Variorum Collected Studies Series, vol. 245. London: Variorum Reprints.

Frantz-Murphy, Gladys. 2001. *Arabic Agricultural Leases and Tax Receipts from Egypt, 148–427 A.H./765–1035*. Corpus Papyrorum Raineri, vol. 21. Vienna: Hollinek.

Goitein, S[hlomo] D. 1967. *A Mediterranean Society, Vol. 1: Economic Foundations*. Los Angeles: University of California Press.

Grob, Eva. 2010. *Documentary Arabic Private and Business Letters on Papyrus: Form and Function, Content and Context*. Archiv für Papyrusforschung und verwandte Gebiete, Beiheft 29. Berlin: De Gruyter.

Grohmann, Adolf. 1952a. *From the World of Arabic Papyri*. Cairo: al-Maaref.

Grohmann, Adolf. 1952b. *Arabic Papyri in the Egyptian Library, Vol. 4: Administrative Texts*. Cairo: Egyptian Library Press.

Grohmann, Adolf. 1954. *Einführung und Chrestomathie zur arabischen Papyruskunde*. Monografie Archivu Orientálního 13. Prague: Státní Pedagogické Nakladatelství.

Measuring the Medieval Islamic Economy, ed. Maya Shatzmiller et al. Western University Department of History. http://www.medievalislamiceconomy.uwo.ca, last accessed 4 October 2014.

Morimoto, Kosei. 1981. *The Fiscal Administration of Egypt in the Early Islamic Period*. Asian History Monographs, vol. 1. Kyoto: Dohosha.

Pamuk, Şevket, and Maya Shatzmiller. 2014. "Plagues, Wages, and Economic Change in the Islamic Near East 700–1500." In *The Journal of Economic History* 74: 196–229.

Scheidel, Walter. 2010. "Real Wages in Early Economies: Evidence for Living Standards from 1800 BCE to 1300 CE." In *Journal of the Economic and Social History of the Orient* 53: 425–462.

Sijpesteijn, Petra M. 2013. *Shaping a Muslim State*. Oxford Studies in Byzantium. Oxford: Oxford University Press.

Simonsen, Jørgen Baek. 1988. *Studies in the Genesis and Early Development of the Caliphal Taxation System with Special References to Circumstances in the Arab Peninsula, Egypt and Palestine*. Copenhagen: Akademisk Forlag.

Thung, Michael H. 2006. *Arabische juristische Urkunden aus der Papyrussamlung der Österreichischen Nationalbibliothek*. Corpus Papyrorum Raineri 26. München: Saur.

PART 3

Fāṭimid Documents from the Cairo Geniza and Other Places

CHAPTER 6

A 6th/12th Century Supplementary Deed of Sale for the Nubian Slave Woman Naʿīm (Gen. T-S 18 J 1.17v)

Craig Perry

In the spring of 508/1115,[1] the Jewish widow Sitt al-Munā sold her Nubian slave woman Naʿīm to a Christian scribe named ʿAbd al-Masīḥ for 20 dinars (see Fig. 6.1).[2] The acknowledgment (*iqrār*) that records this transaction is written on the verso of an Aramaic and Judaeo-Arabic bill of sale, on recto, for the same slave woman written seven years earlier (1420 Seleucid era/1180, see Fig. 6.2).[3] This earlier bill of sale records the purchase of Naʿīm by Sitt al-Munā from another Jewish woman, Sitt al-Aqrān—also for 20 dinars. The single leaf that contains these two records was preserved in the Cairo Geniza until Solomon Schechter removed it—along with a few hundred thousand other manuscripts—and deposited them in what is now the Taylor-Schechter Geniza Collection at Cambridge University Library.[4]

1 My research has been supported by the Fox Center for Humanistic Inquiry at Emory University, a Collaborative Research Grant from the National Endowment for the Humanities, and a Stulman Research Grant from the Leonard and Helen R. Stulman Jewish Studies Program at Johns Hopkins University. I would like to thank the Syndics of Cambridge University Library for providing me with the images of the documents displayed in this chapter. I am also grateful to Tamer el-Leithy, Eve Krakowski, Marina Rustow, Moshe Yagur, and Oded Zinger for their feedback and insights regarding this document and edition. All errors are my own. As this is a Geniza study within a papyrology volume, each Geniza shelfmark is preceded by "Gen." to mark its Geniza origin. Almost all Geniza shelfmarks cited here come from the Taylor-Schechter (T-S) Geniza Collection of Cambridge University Library (P.Cam.inv.). Geniza documents that are published in Khan 1993 are cited as P.GenizahCambr. along with their shelfmark.

2 Cambridge: Cambridge University Library, Taylor-Schechter Geniza Collection (hereafter Gen. T-S): 18 J 1.17v. On verso, Naʿim is not identified as a Nubian. She is identified as a Nubian on recto, where the scribe wrote a fatḥa above her name to indicate its pronunciation; Ṣabīḥ ʿAodeh read the name as the diminutive Nuʿaym, but this is incorrect (ʿAodeh 1992: no. 68; ʿAodeh 2008). The document on recto was first edited in Assaf 1940: 272, 276–277 no. 3, and later by Gil 1997, vol. 2: 918–920 no. 303. Gil identifies the scribe of the recto as Avraham b. Natan. For a revised edition of the recto, see Perry 2019.

3 On acknowledgments (*iqrār*s) from the medieval Middle East, see Little 1981; Lutfi 1983; Lutfi/Little, 1985; Khan 1993; Khan, 1994.

4 For further background on the Arabic contents of the Taylor-Schechter Geniza Collection, see

 | DOI:10.1163/9789004443877_007

Ṣabīḥ ʿAodeh first identified and published an edition and Hebrew translation of the document on verso in his PhD thesis (ʿAodeh 1992); he subsequently republished the document with additional commentary (ʿAodeh 2008). ʿAodeh's edition contains a few inaccuracies that this re-edition corrects. Further, since ʿAodeh first published this document, Geoffrey Khan (Khan 1993) has brought to light additional Arabic script documents from the Cairo Geniza that allow us to contextualize the form and formulae used within a wider field of Arabic scribal practices in Fāṭimid Egypt. Yūsuf Rāġib's editions of bills of sale for slaves and animals (Rāġib 2002–2006) also provide opportunities for comparative analysis that support a corrected reading of specific Arabic formulae in the document.[5]

1 Supplementary Deed of Sale for the Enslaved Woman Naʿīm

Gen. T-S 18 J 1.17v
Figure 6.1
33 high × 24 cm wide
1–10 Dhū l-Qaʿda 508/[March 29–April 7, 1115]
Cairo/al-Fusṭāṭ

ظ

١ انتقلت الجارية المسماة بباطنها وهي نعيم
٢ من ملك ست المنا ابنة هبة الله الإسرائيلية
٣ إلى ملك عبد المسيح بن مقارة بن هرون النصراني الكاتب
٤ وتسلمت ثمنها وقبـ[ـضـ]ـت من العين الوازن عشرين دينا[را]
٥ النصف من ذلك عشرة دنانير وضمنت الدرك في من
٦ يَدَّعِي ملكها وذلك في العشر الاول من ذي القعدة

Khan 1993; for a broader view of the collection's overall contents, see Reif 2000, Ben-Shammai 2002, and Reif 2002; for background on the Cairo Geniza's "discovery," wider global dissemination, and an introduction to historical studies based on these collections, see Goitein 1967–1993, Hoffman/Cole 2011, and Outhwaite/Bhayro 2011; for the study of domestic slavery based on Geniza documents, see Goitein 1967–1993, vol. 1: 130–147, Friedman 1972, and Perry 2014 and the literature cited there.

5 For bills of sale from Mamlūk Jerusalem, see Little 1981.

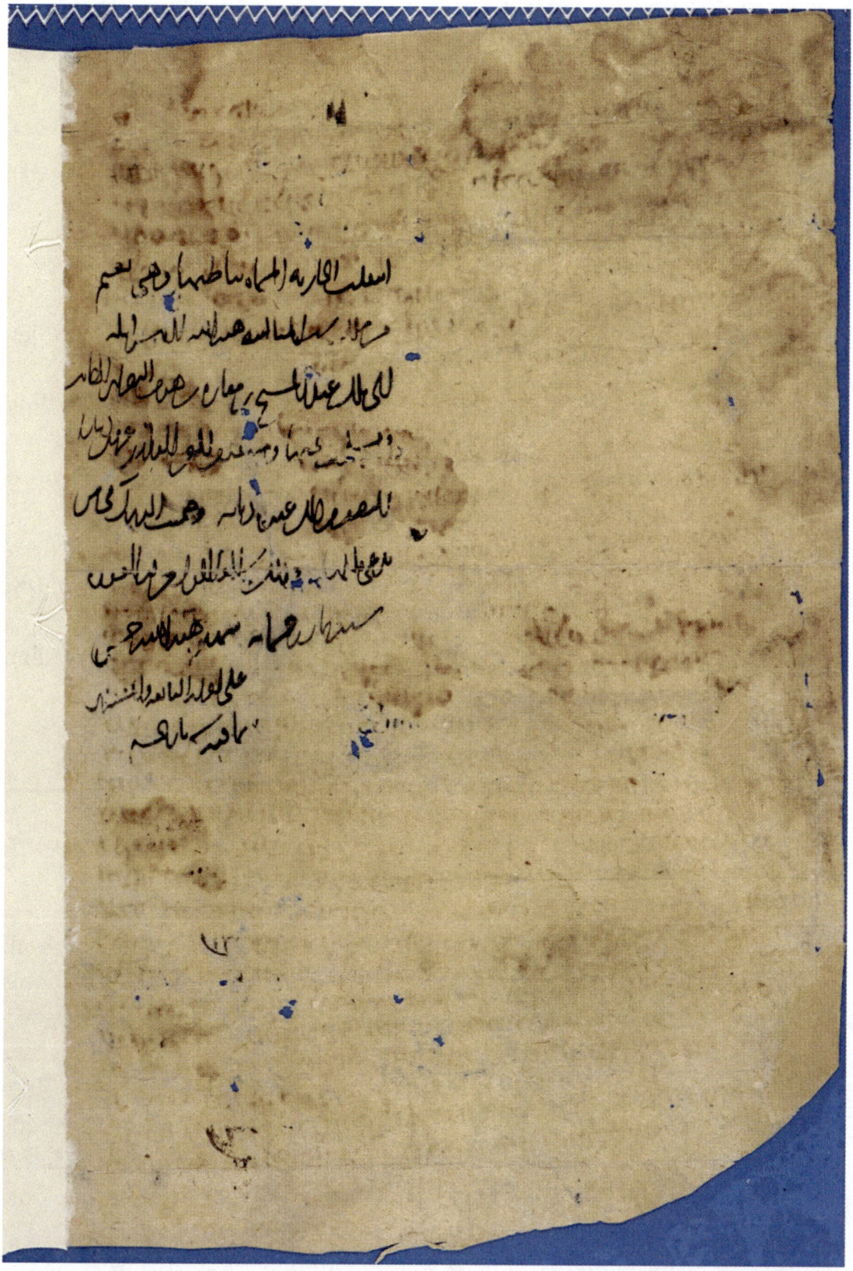

FIGURE 6.1 Gen. T-S 18 J 1.17 verso

٧ سنة ثمان وخمساية شهد هبة الله بن حسن

٨ على اقرار البايعة والمشتري

٩ بما فيه في تاريخه

Translation

1 The slave woman Naʿīm, named on the reverse document, was transferred
2 from the ownership of Sitt al-Munā daughter of Hibat Allāh, the Jew (fem.),
3 to the ownership of ʿAbd al-Masīḥ, son of Maqāra son of Ḥarūn, the Christian, the scribe.
4 She (Sitt al-Munā) received her (the slave woman's) price and took possession in coin of twenty weighed dinars—
5 half of which is ten dinars—and granted a warranty should anyone (else)
6 claim ownership of the slave woman. This was in the first ten days of Dhū al-Qaʿda
7 in the year five hundred and eight [March 29–April 7, 1115]. Hibat Allāh, son of Ḥasan, witnessed
8 the acknowledgment of the seller (fem.) and the buyer (masc.)
9 to what is herein according to this date.

Commentary

1–3 One unusual element of this supplementary deed is its opening formula *intaqalat al-djāriya fulāna min milk fulān¹ ilā milk fulān²*. As Khan notes, the use of *intaqala*, "it was conveyed," instead of *aqarra*, "he acknowledged," is characteristic of Mamlūk-era *iqrārs*.[6] Yet this *iqrār* predates the Mamlūk era by 135 years and begins *intaqalat al-djāriya*, "The slave girl is transferred." It is in lines 7–8 that the acknowledgment of the seller and buyer is mentioned in the context of the witness clause: *shahida fulān ʿalā iqrār al-bāʾiʿa wa-l-mushtarī*. In supplementary deeds for real estate from the Fāṭimid period discussed below, the verb *aqarra* is used.

The phrasing *al-djāriya al-musammā bi-bāṭinihā*, "the slave girl named on the recto side of it (the document)," refers to the Aramaic and Judaeo-Arabic bill of sale on recto.

6 Khan 1993: 9.

2 The Arabic name Hibat Allāh corresponds to the Hebrew name for men, Natan (or Natanel, "Gift of God)." On the recto, Sitt al-Munā is referred to as "the daughter (*bat*) of Natan."

3 ʿAodeh renders the end of line 3 as *al-ṭabīb* instead of *al-kātib*.[7] He also notes that the Christian buyer named was a known associate of the seller Sitt al-Munā's deceased husband Nahray b. Nissim. Nahray was a prominent merchant in 11th-century Fusṭāṭ.[8] In Nahray's account records, we find an ʿAbd al-Masīḥ mentioned as a recipient of payments and credits: Gen. T-S G J198v, col. I, ll. 14, 19, trans. Goitein 1966: 43–51; Gen. T-S. Ar. 54.15b, col. I, l. 19; col. II, l. 2, trans. Goitein 1966: 38–42. Business and family letters found in the Cairo Geniza indicate that it was common for relatives and business associates to sell slaves to each other and to help each other purchase slaves, see Perry 2014: 52–53.

5 *al-niṣf min dhālika ʿasharat danānīr*: The statement of the price twice, first as 20 dinars and then in this manner, is meant to prevent any later falsification of the document aimed at changing the price. This practice is found commonly in medieval Arabic documents.[9] Grohmann notes that this practice was used in Demotic and Greek documents, and concludes that the practice is "a borrowing or a continuation of a usage common to Egyptian clerkship."[10]

5–6 ʿAodeh reads *wa-ḍaminat bi-dhalika an lā taddaʿī milkahā*.[11]
Ṭaḥāwī observes that the authors of *shurūṭ* (contract stipulations) do not commonly include *darak* (warranty) formulae in contracts for movable property unless it is of considerable value. In such cases, as with slaves, for instance, the *darak* clause is included. Wakin adds that for valuable movable property, such as slaves, the *darak* clause is carefully included in the contract.[12] Scribes in the Fāṭimid period do not, however, invariably include the *ḍamān al-darak* clause in bills of sale for slaves: P.GenizahCambr. 56 = Gen. T-S. Ar. 42.174 (483/1090). Only one (P.Little PurchaseDeeds 4; 784/1382) of the six Mamlūk-era bills of sale edited in Little 1981 contains a *ḍamān al-darak* clause.[13]

---

7 ʿAodeh 1992: no. 68 and 2008: 196.
8 ʿAoddeh 2008: 200. For further information about the merchant Nahray b. Nissim and his activities, see Ackerman-Lieberman 2010: 548 and the references listed in Goitein 1967–1993: vol. 6: 80–81 and Goldberg 2012: 422 s.v. Abū Yaḥyā.
9 Wakin 1972: 53–54; Khan 1994: 34 n. 106.
10 Grohmann 1934–1962, vol. 1, 152–153.
11 ʿAodeh 1992: no. 68; ʿAodeh 2008: 196–197.
12 Wakin 1972: 62.
13 P.LittlePurchaseDeeds 4. See the discussion in Little 1981: 323–324.

The exact formula used here, *ḍaminat al-darak fī man yaddaʿī milkahā*, is not to my knowledge found in other edited Arabic documents. In Arabic documents from the Cairo Geniza, warranty clauses are most commonly nominal ones that begin with the conjunctive *fa-* (e.g., *fa-mā adraka hādhā al-mushtarī…*), which "indicates that the obligation of the seller is being construed as a consequent of the conclusion of the sale."[14]
Less commonly in the Geniza, as in our document, warranty formulae are verbal clauses that begin with the third-person verb *wa-ḍamina*(*t*). This is more common in leases in the Geniza,[15] e.g., *wa-ḍaminat al-ādjira li-l-mustaʾdjir al-darak fī dhālika* (P.GenizahCambr. 24.31 = Gen. T-S. Ar. 51.110; 520/1126). The use of the verbal clause is found, e.g., in *wa-ḍamina Idrīs b. Muḥammad b. Ṭāhir radd al-darak* (P.Berl.Arab I 10.16–17; 406/1015); *wa-ḍaminat al-bāʾiʿa al-darak* (P.Vente 13.9–11; 1284); *wa-taḍammana al-bāʾiʿ li-l-mushtarī minhu djamīʿ al-darak fī dhimmatihi* (P.Cair.Arab I 65.20–21; 441/1050).
It is not unusual for warranty clauses to include guarantees against a future hypothetical (or even an anticipated and named) claimant to the property being sold. Such clauses are also constructed using nominal or verbal forms of *dʿw*:[16] *wa-ḍamina Idrīs ibn Muḥammad ibn Ṭāhir radd al-darak fa-matā mā djāʾa muddaʿī aw wārith aw ghayruhu kāna ʿalā Idrīs ibn Muḥammad al-nafādh bi-dhālika ʿalā aṣḥābihi* (P.Berl.Arab I 1.16–18; 406/1015); *wa-ḍamina Dhī l-Nūn ibn ʿAbdallāh li-Yuhannis ibn Abrāhām al-darak fī hādhā al-ḥimār ḥimār dhakar matā iddaʿā waladuhu ʿalayhi bi-daʿwā kāna ʿalā Dhī l-nūn khalāṣ Yuḥannis hadhā minhu* (P.Vente appendix 2.10–11; 5th/11th century, a bill of sale for a donkey). P.Vente 3 (late 3rd/9th century) lacks the *ḍaman al-darak* clause of later bills of sale, but specifies that the Berber slave woman being sold lacks specific defects in her physical person as well as *wa-lā daʿwā fīhi wa-lā ḥurra wa-lā masrūqa*. These parallels suggest that the scribes who wrote *ḍamān al-darak* clauses had a certain amount of flexibility in how they could precisely formulate the language in a given document.

7–8 According to Khan, this witness clause is representative of the declaration generally used in Arabic contracts found in the Geniza. See Khan 1993: 29.

14 Khan 1993 27, 36. On *ḍamān al-darak* clauses in documents of sale, see Wakin 1972: 33; 60–63; 81 n. I.2.38; 89–91; 95–96 n. I.6.0; Rāġib 2002–2006, vol. 2: 93–97; 109.

15 Khan 1993 28.

16 Wakin 1972: 63–64; Little 1982: 22.

2 Gen. T-S 18 J 1.17v and 12th-Century Scribal Practices in Fusṭāṭ/Cairo

As the commentary above demonstrates, Gen. T-S 18 J 1.17v contains specific formulae that highlight elements of an Egyptian scribe's repertoire in early 6th/12th century Fāṭimid Egypt. The scribe's choice of *intaqalat* instead of *aqarrat* indicates that this practice was in use well before the Mamlūk period in deeds of acknowledgment that supplemented original bills of sale written on the reverse side of the document.[17] The particular formulation of the *ḍamān al-darak* warranty clause is also unusual among the published Arabic script documents. Though the substantive meaning of the phrase has parallels in other 5th/11th century Egyptian documents, the use of *fī man yaddaʿī milkahā* reflects the choices of this particular scribe and not adherence to a set formula.

When we set aside other supplementary deeds from the Cairo Geniza, Gen. T-S 18 J 1.17v also underscores the manner in which scribes reused the versos of bills of sale to record a subsequent transaction for the same property. Khan analyzes supplementary deeds for real estate and notes that they fit into the genre of the *faṣl* (supplementary deeds).[18] In *Nihāyat al-arab*, al-Nuwayrī provides instructions for writing a *faṣl* from the *shurūṭ* manual *Mukhtaṣar al-mukātabāt al-badīʿa fī-mā yuktabu min umūr al-sharīʿa* attributed to Abū ʿAbdallāh Muḥammad ibn ʿAbd al-Raḥmān al-Makhzūmī known as Ibn al-Ṣayrafī (d. 653/1255):[19]

وإنْ أَحضَر البائعُ من يدِه كتابا يَشهَد له بصحّة مِلكه للمَبيع كَتَب: وأحضَر هذا البائع من يده كتابا يتضمّن ابتياعَه الدّارَ المذكورة، وأصولا له، وسَطَّر عليها فصولا بهذه المبايَعة، وتَسلَّم المشترِى ذلك توثقةً له، وحُجةً لليوم ولِما بعده.

If the seller presents a document that attests to his valid ownership (of the property for sale), he (the scribe) writes: "This seller presented a document and a deed that certifies his ownership of the aforementioned house." Add to it supplements (*fuṣūlan*) about this purchase and the buyer receives this as his proof and it serves as a guarantee from now and henceforth.[20]

---

17 Cf. Khan 1993: 9.

18 Khan 1993: 9 n. 10.

19 See Khan 1993: 49–50, where Khan notes that the editor of *Nihāyat al-arab* confuses Ibn al-Ṣayrafī (d. 653/1255) with ʿAbū Bakr Muḥammad ibn ʿAbdallāh al-Ṣayrafī (d. 330/941). See also Daftary 1997: 114.

20 Nuwayrī 1923–1997, vol. 9: 26.

In several of the bills of sale (*fuṣūl*) for real estate that Khan edited, scribes reuse the verso of the original document for a supplementary deed that they explicitly call a *faṣl* and in which they reference the contents of the deed on recto.[21] Commonly, the *faṣl* identifies the seller as one of the parties named on the reverse page using the phrase *al-musammā bi-bāṭinihi*. The original document on recto is also referenced by the scribe in the formulae that identify the property. For example, in the supplementary deed in which an apothecary gifts a portion of his house (the purchase of which is documented on recto) to his son-in-law, the scribe describes the shares of the house being gifted as *min djamīʿ al-dār al-mawṣūfa al-maḥdūd[a] al-muḥallayya bāṭini hadhā al-kitāb al-madhkūr alladhī dhakara hadhā al-mutaṣaddiq annahā lahu wa-fī milkihi milkan ṣaḥīḥan* (P.GenizahCambr. 13v.5–7 = Gen. T-S. Ar. 53.61). Thus the scribe obviates the need to reiterate the restricting and accessory formulae for the identification of the property by referring to "all of the house described (regarding) its boundaries and features (written) on the reverse of this aforementioned document."[22]

Another important and understudied feature of these *fuṣūl* in particular, and supplementary deeds in general, is their physical arrangement on the verso (see Figs. 6.5–8 below). As the images of the *fuṣūl* for real estate illustrate, such supplementary deeds have extremely wide margins in comparison to the recto, though the text is aligned on the page in a variety of ways. In one case, the scribe writes the text on the verso so that the lines terminate at the same edge of the page as do the lines on the recto.[23] In another example, the scribe terminates the lines on the verso into the edge that begins the right margin on the recto.[24] In two examples, the scribe appears to have roughly centered the supplementary text on the verso.[25] Despite the variation in how scribes placed the text of these supplementary deeds on the verso, each technique prevents

21 P.GenizahCambr. 5 = Gen. T-S. Ar. 53.70; 9 = Gen. T-S. Ar. 53.60; 13 = Gen. T-S. Ar. 53.61; 23 = Gen. T-S. Misc. 29.24. *aqarra Yūsuf ibn Yaʿqūb al-Isrāʾīlī al-ṣaydalānī al-maʿrūf yawma-ʾidhin bi-l-fudjli ʿinda shuhūd hādhā al-faṣl* (P.GenizahCambr. 13v.2); *aqarra Abū l-Ḥasan ʿAlī ibn Muḥammad ibn Aḥmad al-maʿrūf bi-ibn al-Ṣīnī al-mutaṣarrif bi-l-Dji[fār] bi-Miṣr wa-huwa al-mushtarī al-musammā bi-bāṭinihi ʿinda shuhūd hādha al-fa[ṣl* (P.GenizahCambr. 5v.2–3 = Gen. T-S. Ar. 53.70).

22 Khan translates this as "all the house described and defined with regard to its boundaries and its features on the recto of this document." See Khan 1993: 121. For the structures of Arabic bills of sale, see Wakin 1972:37–72; Little 1981: 333–336; Khan 1993: 20–22; Rāġib 2002–2006, vol. 2: 13–120.

23 P.GenizahCambr. 5 = Gen. T-S. Ar. 53.70.

24 P.GenizahCambr. 13 = Gen. T-S. Ar. 53.61.

25 P.GenizahCambr. 9 = Gen. T-S. Ar. 53.60; 23 = Gen. T-S. Misc. 29.24.

FIGURE 6.2 Gen. T-S 18 J 1.17 recto
© CAMBRIDGE UNIVERSITY LIBRARY

the document's owner from cutting away the text of the verso so that the recto text remains completely intact. In this manner, a scribe could arrange the text on the verso to effectively cancel the deed on the recto without obscuring or damaging the original text.[26]

While the scribe of the supplementary deed for the sale of Naʿīm does not use the term *faṣl*, his choice of wording and reuse of verso share much in common with the *fuṣūl* edited by Khan. The text on the verso both acknowledges the bill of sale on the recto (*al-djāriya al-musammāh bi-bāṭinihā*) and omits essential information—in this case the Nubian origin (*djins*) of the slave—that is provided on the recto.[27] The scribe also uses very wide margins. The verso text is justified to the left side of the page (33 × 24 cm) with margins of 12 cm (right), 5.5 cm (top), and 13 cm (bottom). As in *fuṣūl* for real estate, the scribe's decision to organize the verso text in this manner effectively cancels the deed on the recto and prevents the document's owner from cutting away the supplementary text and using the original bill of sale to make a future, spurious claim to ownership of the slave woman.

In his instructions for writing a *faṣl* for a real estate transaction, al-Ṣayrafī tells the scribe to give the supplementary document to the new buyer—which would entail that the new buyer also receive the original bill of sale. In the *fuṣūl* for property that Khan edited, it appears that this is likely what happened: where the relevant text is legible, the buyers in the *fuṣūl* are all Jewish parties even though the original owners named on the rectos were not Jews.[28] It is

---

26 I wish to thank Tamer el-Leithy, Eve Krakowski, and Marina Rustow for suggesting this connection during a 2015 workshop supported by a Collaborative Research Grant from the National Endowment for the Humanities for the project "The Cairo Geniza as a Source for the History of Institutions and Scribal Practices in the Medieval Near East."

27 The *djins* (ethnonym) of the slave is a descriptor that is almost invariably included in Arabic, Judaeo-Arabic, and Aramaic bills of sale in medieval Egypt; see Rāğib 2002–2006, vol. 2: 30–33 s.v. *ğins*. The Iraqi-Jewish legal scholar Hai Gaon (d. 1038) instructs scribes in his Book of Formularies to record the geographic origin of the slave in bills of sale whether it is "Indian, Canaanite, Greek, Libyan, (or) Zanji (east African)"; see Assaf 1930: 28. For Mamlūk Jerusalem, see the discussion of *djins* and their treatment in *shurūṭ* manuals in Little 1981: 304–306.

28 P.GenizahCambr. 5v = Gen. T-S. Ar. 53.70v, 9v = Gen. T-S. Ar. 53.60v, 23v = Gen. T-S. Misc. 29.24v. P.GenizahCambr. 13v = Gen. T-S. Ar. 53.61v is a deed of gift in which the recipient is also Jewish. See also P.GenizahCambr. 56 = Gen. T-S. Ar. 42.174, an Arabic bill of sale for a slave sold by a Christian scribe to a Jewish man. Cf. ʿAodeh 1992: no. 5. Khan and ʿAodeh read the end of l. 4 differently. Thanks to Oded Zinger for pointing out this discrepancy to me. Jews in Fāṭimid Egypt might seek out a Muslim court for a variety of reasons even if their issue could legally be handled by a Jewish court; see Zinger 2018. Krakowski also analyzes instances in which Jewish parties in medieval Egypt patronized Muslim courts; see Krakowski 2018: 77–78. For example, a Jewish woman sued her brother in a Muslim court

most likely that the Jewish owners of these documents (and their heirs) then retained these documents and deposited them into the Geniza when they no longer had use for them.

In the case of the supplementary deed for the slave woman Naʿīm, however, it seems more likely that the document remained the property of the Jewish seller Sitt al-Munā and that this fact explains why the document was found in the Geniza. Within the Cairo Geniza, there is a large sub-corpus of documents that relate to the activities of Sitt al-Munā's widower, the merchant and communal leader Nahray b. Nissim.[29] Since Sitt al-Munā does not appear as a principal party or litigant in other Geniza records, one possible reason that the document is in the Geniza is because it was part and parcel of the larger Nahray b. Nissim family and mercantile archive.

If Sitt al-Munā or a Jewish scribe retained the document, then what record would the buyer ʿAbd al-Masīḥ have of his purchase? The same scribe who wrote the supplement on the verso may well have written a second document that served as a bill of sale for ʿAbd al-Masīḥ. As Phillip Ackerman-Lieberman has demonstrated, scribes composed multiple versions of documents for the same transaction. Ackerman-Lieberman studied two 13th-century Geniza bills of sale for the same slave that are not copies of each other, but are both customized to the requirements of the documents' owners.[30] Naʿīm's sale to ʿAbd al-Masīḥ was another transaction in which the contracting parties would have benefitted from having a scribe draw up multiple deeds, each tailored separately to the needs of the buyer and seller. For ʿAbd al-Masīḥ's own interests, it would have behooved him to possess a complete bill of sale drawn up in a Muslim court (as opposed to just a supplementary deed) in order to minimize any future complications should he wish to sell the slave to a Christian, Muslim, or Jewish buyer. Since the recto of the document was written in a somewhat archaically stylized Aramaic, a new Arabic script bill of sale written according to Muslim scribal conventions would have been all the more appealing to ʿAbd al-Masīḥ.

Another reason the document would have been retained and later deposited into the Geniza has to do with Jewish scribal practices. Jewish scribes retained

over a slave sale: Gen. T-S. Misc.23.8, ll. 7–8. I have prepared an edition of this document that will soon be available through the Princeton Geniza Project database.

29 For further information about this merchant Nahray b. Nissim and his activities, see Ackerman-Lieberman 2010: 548 and the references listed in Goitein 1967–1993: vol. 6: 80–81 and Goldberg 2012: 422 s.v. Abū Yaḥyā.

30 Gen. T-S 6 J 1.7+Gen. T-S 13 J 4.2 and Cambridge University Library, Oriental Collection (Or.): Gen. Or. 1080 J 273; both edited in Ackerman-Lieberman 2011: 14–23.

and consulted Arabic script documents drawn up in Muslim courts for their own information. Marina Rustow has demonstrated how Jewish communal figures adopted elements of the Fāṭīmid chancery style in the latter half of the 11th century and employed these features in their own petitions and letters to express their own authority and legitimacy.[31] Recent work by Eve Krakowski and Marina Rustow on the formulae used in Jewish marriage contracts further illustrates how not only Jewish scribes, but also litigants themselves, were familiar with Arabic scribal practices and the content of Muslim family law.[32]

In addition, 11th- and 12th-century bills of sale for slaves indicate that Jewish scribes engaged with the larger Fāṭimid Egyptian scribal and legal culture. For example, a late 11th-century bill of sale in Arabic script records the sale of the "carob-colored" (*kharrūbīyat al-lawn*) slave woman Qiwām to a Jewish man by another Christian scribe. The document appears to be a copy or a draft because it lacks the witness clauses necessary to validate the contract.[33] One of this document's interesting features is a short anonymous note written across the top of the manuscript's verso in Judaeo-Arabic: *ruqʿat Qiwā[m] al-djāriya*, "the record for Qiwām the slave woman." And on the other side of a crease indicating that the document was folded in half, we find: *min Ibn Zurʿa*.[34] This note suggests that this Ibn Zurʿa sent the bill of sale to a Jewish party—perhaps to a Jewish scribe for his own dossier or archive. As this suggests, Jewish scribes were familiar with the formulae and physical layout of Muslim bills of sale and supplementary deeds for slaves. For example, Ackerman-Lieberman also notes the scribe's use of the Arabic *ḍamān al-darak* warranty clause in the two aforementioned versions of a Judaeo-Arabic and Aramaic bill of sale for the same slave from 1226.[35] Jewish scribes had examples of Aramaic formularies for warranties at their disposal in manuals for the composition of legal documents, and early 12th-century bills of sale use these formulae.[36] Yet, over the course of the 12th

31 Rustow 2014. On the question of why so many Arabic script documents (petitions in particular) are preserved in the Geniza, see Rustow 2010; Rustow 2019a; Rustow 2019b; Rustow 2020.

32 Krakowski/Rustow 2014. See also Ackerman-Lieberman 2015 and Zinger 2018.

33 Gen. T-S. Ar. 42.174. On the witness clause in Muslim bills of sale, see Wakin 1972: 66–67; Khan 1993: 29.

34 Khan identifies this short text in Gen. T-S. Ar. 42.174. The scribe's writing of *ruqʿat Qiwām* with *tāʾ ṭawīla* in *status constructus* reflects a current practice in medieval Judaeo-Arabic, see Blau 1980: 40–41; Wagner 2010: 39–40.

35 On *ḍamān al-darak*, see the commentary to Gen. T-S 18 J 1.17v, ll. 5–6 above and the sources cited there, as well as Friedman and Goitein 2008: 385 n. 43. Ackerman-Lieberman 2011: 13.

36 The Aramaic bill of sale for Naʿīm on recto of our document contains elaborate guaran-

and 13th centuries, these scribes continued to employ Judaeo-Arabic formulae and Islamic forms in their composition of slave bills of sale, thus demonstrating what Krakowski and Rustow call knowledge of "the ambient legal traditions" at play in the medieval Middle East.[37]

One Geniza scribe's composition of a supplementary deed of sale for the slave woman Musk provides striking textual and visual evidence of how the ambient legal culture inflected how Jewish notaries recorded legal documents for their clients. In 560/1165, Mevorakh b. Natan, a scribe well known to Geniza scholars, drew up a Judaeo-Arabic and Aramaic bill of sale that records Musk's sale by Abū ʿAlī the perfumer to Abū al-ʿAlā al-Levi for 18 dinars.[38] In comparison to Geniza bills of sale from the first decades of the 12th century, Mevorakh b. Natan employed a host of Judaeo-Arabic formulae in contrast to the Aramaic phrases used by his predecessors.[39] In lieu of the Aramaic guarantees and warranties used on the recto of our document, for example, Mevorakh uses Judaeo-Arabic formulary to express that the seller has informed the buyer about defects in the slave woman, including *wa-amrāḍhā al-bāṭina fīhā wa-l-ẓāhira*, "her hidden and apparent diseases."[40]

For the purposes of the present study, however, Mevorakh's reuse of the verso to write a supplementary deed for the subsequent sale of Musk is even more compelling (see Figure 6.4 below).[41] Mevorakh composed this supplementary deed using extremely wide margins, just as we see in our document for the sale for Naʿīm. Mevorakh's document is badly damaged and the top left corner of the deed is missing, but the right margin is preserved and comprises 13 cm of a 24-cm-wide piece of paper. Similarly to the bill of sale on the recto, Mevorakh composed the supplement by drawing on both Judeao-Arabic and Aramaic formulae.

---

tees and warranty clauses that draw (often verbatim) on formulae both from Hai Gaon's formulary (Assaf 1930: 27–29) for a bill of sale for a slave and from formulae in the Babylonian Talmud (Giṭṭin 86a); see Perry 2019.

37 Krakowski/Rustow 2014: 135. Ackerman-Lieberman 2015 argues that there was a resurgence of Hebrew documentary production in the 13th century.

38 Gen. T-S 13 J 37.12r (dated Tammuz 1476 Seleucid era/1165), see Goitein 1967–1993, vol. 1: 139–140; 435 n. 69; Friedman 1986: 352; 379. On Mevorakh b. Natan, see the references in Goitein 1967–1993, vol. 6: 71–72.

39 See Gen. T-S 16.188 (1105); Gen. T-S 18 J 1.17r (1108); Gen. T-S 18 J 1.16 (1108).

40 Gen. T-S 13 J 37.12r, ll. 16–17. Cf. Rāgib 2002: II. 69–70.

41 Gen. T-S 13 J 37.12v. This document also appears to be in the hand of Mevorakh b. Natan.

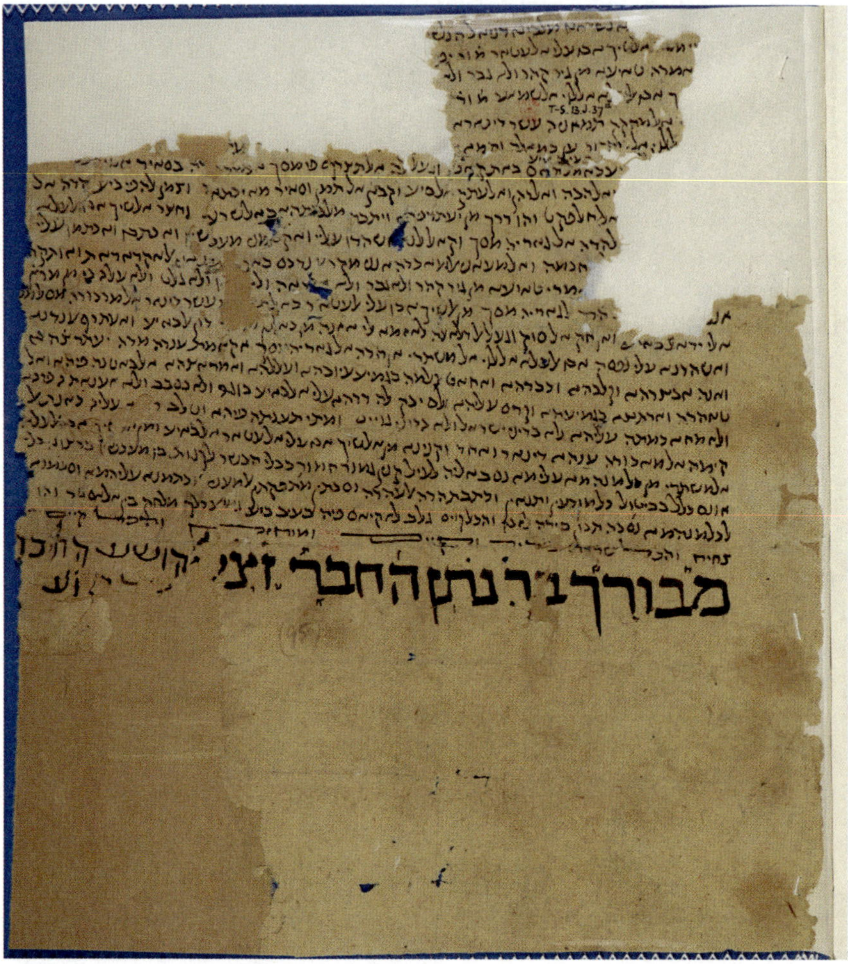

FIGURE 6.3 Gen. T-S 13 J 37.12 recto
© CAMBRIDGE UNIVERSITY LIBRARY

The first surviving line begins with a reference to the buyer named on the recto, *al-shaykh Abū al-ʿAlā* [*al-Levi* …].[42] The partial text on the next line marks the end of one phrase and the beginning of another: *bi-bāṭinihā wa-iʿtaraf ʿi*[*ndanā*…].[43] By comparing Mevorakh's use of *bi-bāṭinihā* here with its use in our document, we can infer that this phrase identifies the slave woman Musk,

42 Gen. T-S 13 J 37.12v, l. 1. Abū al-ʿAlā al-Levi's full name is legible at the end of l. 11.

43 Gen. T-S 13 J 37.12v, l. 2.

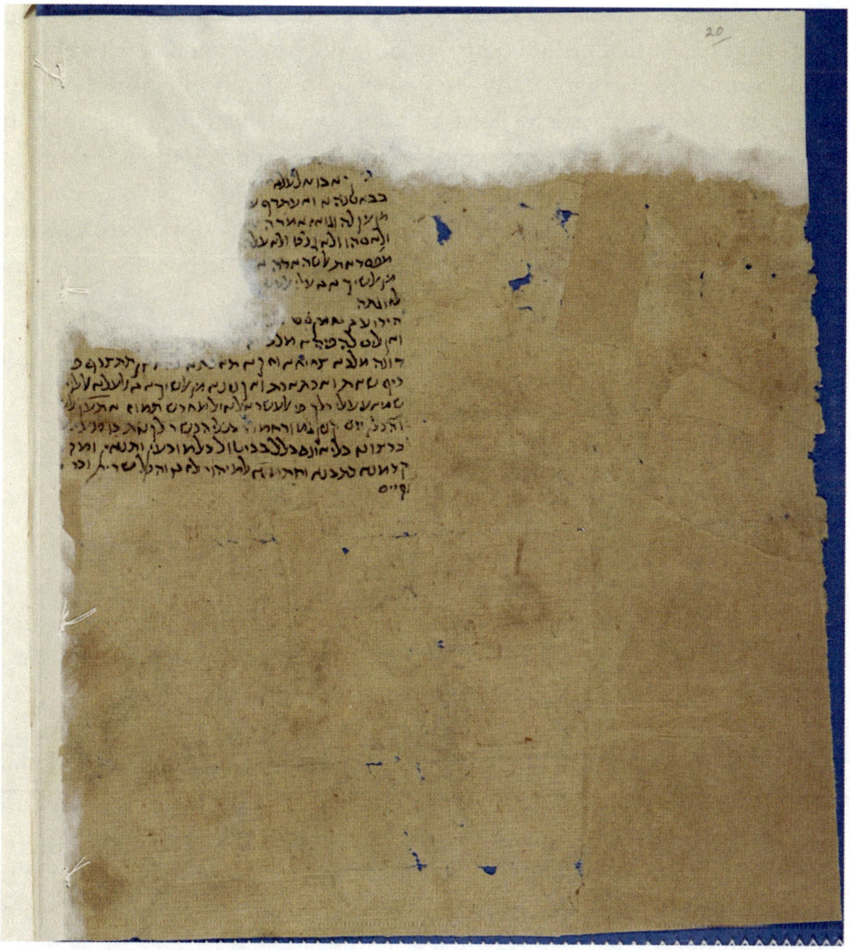

FIGURE 6.4 Gen. T-S 13 J 37.12 verso
© CAMBRIDGE UNIVERSITY LIBRARY

"(named) on the reverse document."[44] The next phrase, "(Abū al-ʿAlā al-Levī) acknowledged be[fore us...]," signals the beginning of the seller's testimony before witnesses that, in this case, he is placing the slave woman under the control of his wife, "to do with (or dispose of) as she wishes."[45]

44 Gen. T-S 13 J 37.12v, l. 2; cf. Gen. T-S 18 J 1.17v, l. 1.

45 Gen. T-S 13 J 37.12v. The obliteration of a large section of the text makes it difficult to ascertain the exact terms of this agreement. It seems almost certain that Abū al-Alā al-Levi is transferring his ownership of Musk to his wife completely. See lines 6–7: *min al-shaykh*

Both Mevorakh's choice of Judaeo-Arabic formulae and his physical reuse of the verso suggest that he and other Jewish scribes were familiar with Muslim legal documents and that they adapted specific elements from the wider Egyptian legal culture to serve the needs of their Jewish clients and litigants.[46] In this case, we are able to observe how Jewish scribes adopted forms for supplementary bills of sale during the mid- to late 12th century in Egypt, a practice that other Arabic Geniza documents from Muslim courts show in use a bit earlier in the second half of the 5th/11th century and more frequently in the first decades of the 6th/12th century.[47]

3 Prospects for the Use of Supplementary Deeds in Historical Research

Bills of sale and supplementary deeds such as our document (Gen. T-S 18 J 1.17) and Gen. T-S 13 J 37.12 present an unusual opportunity for the investigation of the social history of the medieval Middle East because they allow researchers to study multiple, related transactions that involve some of the same parties and a single unit of property—whether that property is a human being or a portion of a house located in a specific district of Fāṭimid Fusṭāṭ.

For the study of medieval slavery in the Islamic world, it is an uncommon opportunity to be able to follow an individual slave (or slave family) across time and through the hands of multiple owners.[48] In the case of the Nubian slave woman Naʿīm, our document traces part of her life's trajectory from service in the household of the widow Sitt al-Munā between 1108–1115 to ownership by a Christian scribe, ʿAbd al-Masīḥ. Among the corpus of slave names I have compiled from Geniza documents dating from the late 10th to the 13th centuries, Naʿīm is only found as an enslaved person's name between the year 1098 and

Abū [al-]ʿAl[ā] al-Le[vi... (7) li-zawdjatihi [...]. Line 9 indicates that he relinquishes complete ownership of the slave woman: *wa-an laysa lahu fīhā milk[an....* Finally, in lines 10–11, *dūnahu milkan ṣaḥīḥan wa-ḥaqqan thābitan lahā an tataṣarrafa f[īhā ...] (11) kayfa shāʾat* illustrates that the wife has the right to dispose of Musk "as she wishes."

46 Ackerman-Lieberman 2011; Krakowski/Rustow 2014.

47 Based on Khan's datings of the *fuṣūl* edited in Khan 2013 = P.GenizahCambr. The supplementary deed edited above, Gen. T-S 18 J 1.17v, dates to 508/1115.

48 In addition to Gen. T-S 18 J 1.17 and Gen. T-S 13 J 37.12 discussed here, P.Vente 3; 4; 10; 11 and appendix nos. 3; 4; 5 pertain to multiple transactions (or legal acts) documenting some of the same slaves. See also Little 1982 and my reconstruction of the life course of the slave Wafāʾ based on Geniza documents in Perry 2017: 136. The lives of enslaved and freed women are also the subject of Perry 2016.

the 1130s. The earliest instance is a bill of sale for "the Nubian woman called Naʿīm" (*al-nūbiyya al-madʿūʾa Naʿīm*) from the year 1098. An enslaved woman with the name Naʿīm is identified as property contested between a man and wife between 1127 and 1138. In 1177 a freed woman named Naʿīm is listed on an alms list as the recipient of three dirhams.[49] Might these three women be the same person? Enslaved women were commonly sold multiple times over the course of their lives, frequently among owners' and sellers' personal and business networks.

Additional pieces of evidence that may relate to this woman's life are a series of alms lists recorded in the autumn of 1107. In these lists, edited by Mark R. Cohen, Jewish communal officials record the presence of a person identified only by her *ism* Naʿīm as the recipient of bread loaves in October and November 1107.[50] Enslaved women, as well as freed women, appear occasionally in these lists as recipients of bread flour or clothing. The Naʿīm of 1107 is not designated as either, however.

It is not possible to confirm with certainty that the Naʿīm on the alms lists of 1107 is indeed the same woman who was sold as a slave in 1098 and then again in 1108 and 1115. Yet such a life trajectory is plausible based on what we know about both the nature of the documentary corpus and the practice of slavery in medieval Egypt. The documentary Geniza corpus related to slaves is particularly dense for the period from the late 11th through the first half of the 13th century. As such, historians are able to study the connections between individuals, families, and their descendants over the course of generations. Slaves were both members of these households and commodities that circulated among them.

There are a host of possibilities that could explain Naʿīm's trajectory—if she is indeed the same woman. Perhaps, by 1107, her owner had died without freeing or bequeathing her to an heir, thus making Naʿim indigent. Her reappearance as an enslaved woman in 1108 belonging to Sitt al-Munā could be explained by a range of circumstances, from kidnapping and coerced enslavement to an act of self-dedition on Naʿīm's part.[51] Documentary sources rarely provide us a glimpse into the actual mechanisms of enslavement, though they are more forthcoming on the logistics involved in transporting slaves to their

49 Naʿīm is in contrast to more common female slave names such as Tawfiq and Saʿādah; see Perry 2014: 75–82. There is a bill of sale for the Nubian slave woman Naʿīm (1098) (Gen. T-S 12.93, ll. 10–11). An enslaved woman Naʿīm is contested property in Gen. Halper 342. The alms list from 1177 is Gen. T-S NS 324.132. See Yagur 2017: 287. We do find the name of the free woman Sitt al-Naʿīm mentioned in Gen. T-S 12.531r as the widow of Abū ʿAlī the singer.

50 Gen. T-S. Misc. 8.9, col. IV, l. 7; Gen. T-S 10K15.15, Gen. T-S K 15.50; and Gen. T-S K 15.113; all these documents are translated in Cohen 2005: 107–163.

51 Franz 2014: 95.

FIGURE 6.5 Gen. T-S. Ar. 53.61 verso
© CAMBRIDGE UNIVERSITY LIBRARY

FIGURE 6.6 Gen. T-S. Ar. 53.61 recto
© CAMBRIDGE UNIVERSITY LIBRARY

FIGURE 6.7 Gen. T-S. Ar. 53.70 recto
© CAMBRIDGE UNIVERSITY LIBRARY

بسم الله الرحمن الرحيم

FIGURE 6.8 Gen. T-S. Ar. 53.70 verso

end users.[52] Yet as the supplementary deeds presented here suggest, opportunities may abound in the thousands of unedited Arabic papyri and Geniza documents that will allow us to reconstruct the social history of domestic slaves and members of other marginal groups who were so integral to life in the medieval Middle East. It is my hope that by highlighting the visual features of supplementary deeds and their relationship to their parent texts, scholars will be able to more readily identify and make use of such documentary records for the social history of these subjects.

Bibliography

Sources

Cambridge University Library, Taylor-Schechter Genizah Collection (Gen. T-S)[53]
T-S 8 J 11.13*
T-S 12.531r (unpublished)
T-S 12.93 (unpublished)
T-S 13 J 37.12r+v (unpublished)
T-S 16.188*
T-S 16.208*
T-S 18 J 1.16*
T-S 18 J 1.17r*
T-S 18 J 1.17v

al-Nuwayrī, Shihāb al-Dīn Aḥmad b. ʿAbd al-Wahhāb. (d. 733/1332). 1923–1997. *Nihāyat al-arab fī funūn al-adab*. 33 vols. Cairo: al-Muʾassasa al-Miṣriyya al-ʿĀmma li-l-Taʾlīf wa-l-Tardjama wa-l-Ṭibāʿa wa-l-Nashr.

P.Berl.Arab I, see below Abel 1896.
P.Cair.Arab I–VI, see below Grohmann 1934–1962.
P.GenizahCambr., see below Khan 1993.
P.LittlePurchaseDeeds, see below Little 1981.
P.Vente I–II, see below Rāġib 2002–2006.

52 Perry 2014: 47–54; Perry 2017: 135.

53 High-resolution images of these documents are available in the Friedberg Genizah Project database http://www.jewishmanuscripts.org, Geniza document images in the Cambridge Digital Library http://cudl.lib.cam.ac.uk/collections/genizah. * = Document transcription available in the Princeton Geniza Browser.

Research

[Abel, Ludwig.] 1896. *Ägyptische Urkunden aus den königlichen Museen zu Berlin, Arabische Urkunden, Part 1*. Berlin: Weidmann, 1896. [P.Berl.Arab I]

Ackerman-Lieberman, Phillip I. 2010. "Nahray ben Nissim." In *Encyclopedia of Jews in the Islamic World*, ed. Norman A. Stillman. Leiden: Brill, vol. 3: 548.

Ackerman-Lieberman, Phillip I. 2011. "Legal Writing in Medieval Cairo: 'Copy' or 'Likeness' in Jewish Documentary Formulae." In *From a Sacred Source: Genizah Studies in Honor of Professor Stefan C. Reif*, ed. Ben Outhwaite and Siam Bhayro. Études sur le judaïsme médiéval, vol. 42. Cambridge Genizah Studies Series, vol. 1. Leiden: Brill, 1–24.

Ackerman-Lieberman, Phillip I. 2015. "Legal Pluralism among the Court Records of Medieval Egypt." In *Bulletin d'études orientales* 63: 79–112.

ʿAodeh [ʿAwda], Ṣabiḥ 1992. *Ha-mikhtavim ha-ʿaraviyim shel ha-soḥarim ha-yehudim bi-Genizat Qahir be-meʾah ha-aḥat esreh* [Eleventh-Century Letters of Jewish Merchants from the Cairo Geniza]. Unpublished PhD thesis, Tel Aviv University.

ʿAodeh, Ṣabīḥ. 2008. "Sitt al-Munā, ha-isha ha-retzuya: sheṭar mekhirat shifḥa mi-shenat 1115 La-SeFira Ha-Notzrit she-nimtza ba-Geniza" [Sitt al-Munā, the Desired Woman: A Bill of Sale for a Slave Woman from the Year 1115 CE Found in the Geniza]. In *ʿAle ʿAsor: Divre ha-veʿida ha-ʿasirit shel ha-ḥevra le-ḥeker ha-tarbut ha-ʿaravit ha-yehudit shel yeme ha-benayim* [ʿAle ʿAsor: Proceedings of the Tenth Conference of the Society for Judaeo-Arabic Studies], ed. Daniel Lasker and Haggai Ben-Shammai. Jerusalem: Ben-Zvi Institute, 195–202.

Assaf, Simḥa. 1930. "Sefer ha-Sheṭarot" [Book of Formularies]. In *Tarbiz* 1 (3, Supplement): 5–72.

Assaf, Simḥa. 1940. "ʿAvadim ve-soḥer ʿavadim be-yeme ha-benayim" [Slaves and the Slave Trade in the Middle Ages]. In *Zion* 5: 271–280.

Ben-Shammai, Haggai. 2002. "Medieval History and Religious Thought." In *The Cambridge Genizah Collections: Their Contents and Significance*, ed. Stefan Reif and Shulamit Reif. Cambridge University Library Genizah Series, vol. 1. Cambridge: Cambridge University Press, 136–149.

Blau, Joshua. 1980. *Diqduq ha-ʿaravit ha-yehudit shel yeme ha-benayim* [A Grammar of Medieval Judaeo-Arabic]. 2nd ed. Jerusalem: Magnes.

Cohen, Mark R. 2005. *The Voice of the Poor in the Middle Ages: An Anthology of Documents from the Cairo Geniza*. Princeton: Princeton University Press.

Daftary, Farhad. 1997. "al-Ṣayrafī." In *The Encyclopaedia of Islam: New Edition*, ed. C. Edmund Bosworth et al. Leiden: Brill, vol. 9: 114.

Franz, Kurt. 2014. "Slavery in Islam: Legal Norms and Social Practice." In *Mediterranean Slavery Revisited (500–1800). Neue Perspektiven auf mediterrane Sklaverei (500–1800)*, ed. Stefan Hanss and Juliane Schiel. Zürich: Chronos, 51–141.

Friedman, Mordechai A. 1972. "Master and Slave Girl: Two Geniza Documents." In *Gratz College Annual of Jewish Studies* 1: 56–63.

Friedman, Mordechai A. 1986. *Ribbui nashim be-yisra'el: meqorot ḥadashim mi-Genizat Qahir* [Jewish Polygyny in the Middle Ages: New Documents from the Cairo Geniza]. Jerusalem: Bialik Institute.

Gil, Moshe. 1997. *Be-malkhut Yishma'el be-tequfat ha-geonim* [In the Kingdom of Ishmael]. 4 vols. Publications of the Diaspora Research Institute, vols. 117–120. Tel Aviv: Tel-Aviv University.

Goitein, S[helomo] D. 1966. "Bankers Accounts from the Eleventh Century A.D." In *Journal of the Economic and Social History of the Orient* 9: 28–66.

Goitein, S[helomo] D. 1967–1993. *A Mediterranean Society: The Jewish Communities of the Arab World as Portrayed in the Documents of the Cairo Geniza.* 6 vols. Berkeley: University of California Press.

Goitein, S[helomo] D., and Mordechai A. Friedman. 2008. *India Traders of the Middle Ages: Documents from the Cairo Geniza.* Études sur le judaïsme médiéval, vol. 31. Leiden: Brill.

Goldberg, Jessica L. 2012. *Trade and Institutions in the Medieval Mediterranean: The Geniza Merchants and Their Business World.* Cambridge Studies in Economic History. Cambridge: Cambridge University Press.

Grohmann, Adolf. 1934–1962. *Arabic Papyri in the Egyptian Library.* 6 vols. Cairo: Egyptian Library Press. [P.Cair.Arab. I–VI]

Hoffman, Adina, and Peter Cole. 2010. *Sacred Trash: The Lost and Found World of the Cairo Geniza.* Jewish Encounters. New York: Nextbook.

Khan, Geoffrey. 1993. *Arabic Legal and Administrative Documents in the Cambridge Genizah Collections.* Cambridge Library Genizah Series, vol. 10. Cambridge: Cambridge University Press. [P.GenizahCambr.]

Khan, Geoffrey. 1994. "An Arabic Document of Acknowledgement from the Cairo Genizah." In *Journal of Near Eastern Studies* 53: 117–124.

Krakowski, Eve. 2018. *Coming of Age in Medieval Egypt: Female Adolescence, Jewish Law, and Ordinary Culture.* Princeton: Princeton University Press.

Krakowski, Eve, and Marina Rustow. 2014. "Formula as Content: Medieval Jewish Institutions, the Cairo Geniza, and the New Diplomatics." In *Jewish Social Studies: History, Culture, Society* n.s. 20: 111–146.

Little, Donald P. 1981. "Six Fourteenth Century Purchase Deeds for Slaves from Al-Ḥaram Al-Sharīf." In *Zeitschrift der Deutschen Morgenländischen Gesellschaft* 131: 297–337. [P.LittlePurchaseDeeds]

Little, Donald P. 1982. "Two Fourteenth-Century Court Records from Jerusalem Concerning the Disposition of Slaves by Minors." In *Arabica* 29: 16–49.

Lutfi, Huda. 1983. "A Study of Six Fourteenth Century Iqrārs from Al-Quds Relating to Muslim Women." In *Journal of the Economic and Social History of the Orient* 26: 246–294.

Lutfi, Huda, and Donald P. Little. 1985. "'Iqrārs from Al-Quds: Emendations." In *Journal of the Economic and Social History of the Orient* 28: 326–330.

Perry, Craig. 2014. “The Daily Life of Slaves and the Global Reach of Slavery.” Unpublished PhD thesis, Emory University.

Perry, Craig. 2016. “Conversion as an Aspect of Master-Slave Relationships in the Medieval Jewish Community.” In *Contesting Inter-Religious Conversion in the Medieval World*, ed. Yaniv Fox and Yosi Yisraeli. London: Routledge, 135–159.

Perry, Craig. 2017. “Historicizing Slavery in the Medieval Islamic World.” In *International Journal of Middle East Studies* 49: 133–138.

Perry, Craig. 2019. “An Aramaic Bill of Sale for the Enslaved Nubian Woman Naʿīm.” In *Jewish History* 32: 441–449.

Rāġib, Yūsuf. 2002–2006. *Actes de vente d'esclaves et d'animaux d'Egypte médiévale*. 2 vols. Cahiers des Annales Islamologiques, vols. 23; 28. Publications de l'Institut Français d'Archéologie Orientale 893; 955. Cairo: Institut Français d'Archéologie Orientale.

Reif, Stefan C. 2000. *A Jewish Archive from Old Cairo: The History of Cambridge University's Genizah Collection*. Culture and Civilization in the Middle East. Richmond: Curzon.

Reif, Stefan C. 2002. “A Centennial Assessment of Genizah Studies.” In *The Cambridge Genizah Collections: Their Contents and Significance*, ed. Stefan C. Reif and Shulamit Reif. Genizah Series, vol. 1. Cambridge: Cambridge University Press, 1–35.

Rustow, Marina. 2010. “A Petition to a Woman at the Fatimid Court (413–414 A.H./1022–23 C.E.).” In *Bulletin of the School of Oriental and African Studies* 73: 1–27.

Rustow, Marina. 2014. “The Diplomatics of Leadership: Administrative Documents in Hebrew Script from the Geniza.” In *Jews, Christians, and Muslims in Medieval and Early Modern Times: A Festschrift in Honor of Mark R. Cohen*, ed. Arnold Franklin et al. Christians and Jews in Muslim Societies, vol. 2. Leiden: Brill, 306–351.

Rustow, Marina. 2019. “Fatimid State Documents.” In *Jewish History* 32: 221–277.

Rustow, Marina. 2019b. “The Fatimid Petition.” In *Jewish History* 32: 351–372.

Rustow, Marina. 2020. *The Lost Archive: Traces of a Caliphate in a Cairo Synagogue*. Jews, Christians, and Muslims from the Ancient to the Modern World. Princeton: Princeton University Press, 2020.

Wagner, Esther-Miriam. 2010. *Linguistic Variety of Judaeo-Arabic in Letters from the Cairo Genizah*. Études sur le judaïsme médiéval, vol. 41. Leiden: Brill.

Wakin, Jeanette. 1972. *The Function of Documents in Islamic Law: The Chapters on Sales from Ṭaḥāwī's Kitāb Al-Shurūṭ Al-Kabīr*. Albany: State University of New York Press.

Yagur, Moshe. 2017. *Zehut datit u-gevolot kehilatiyim be-ḥevrat ha-Geniza (me'ot 10–13): gerim, ʿavadim, mumarim* [*Religious Identities and Communal Boundaries in Geniza Society (10th–13th Centuries): Proselytes, Slaves, Apostates*]. Unpublished PhD thesis, Hebrew University.

Zinger, Oded. 2014. “Women, Gender and Law: Marital Disputes According to Documents from the Cairo Geniza.” Unpublished PhD thesis, Princeton University.

Zinger, Oded. 2018. "'She Aims to Harass Him': Jewish Women in Muslim Legal Venues in Medieval Egypt." In *AJS Review* 42: 159–192.

CHAPTER 7

Social Embeddedness in the Legal Arena according to Geniza Letters

Oded Zinger

1 A Marriage Scandal in Ashkelon

Sometime before 1085, the Jewish community of Ashkelon was in an uproar over a marriage scandal.[1] A certain Joseph b. Menasse was supposed to marry a girl named Djawzīya. Joseph, who seems to have been a merchant plying the Egypt-Palestine route, arrived in Ashkelon only to discover that a certain Ṣedaqa had betrothed his son to Djawzīya less than eight days before. Joseph was outraged and sought justice. The local Jewish court ruled that Djawzīya must be divorced, but Ṣedaqa's son would not hear of it. The case was brought before the local court two or three more times, with no result. Ṣedaqa (or his son) conditioned granting the divorce on Joseph's taking an oath that he would not marry Djawzīya, which Joseph refused to do. Ṣedaqa brought the case before two prominent Fatimid commanders in Palestine who ordered that that an unprejudiced Jewish court (*madjlis bi-lā taḥāmul*) be convened to rule on the matter. Djawzīya reportedly announced that if she were to be taken by means of the government or by force (*bi-sulṭān aw bi-shidda*), she would throw herself into a well and kill herself.[2]

1 This study is revision of a subsection from Chapter Four of my doctoral dissertation, Zinger 2014. I am grateful to Miriam Frenkel for her helpful comments on the revised study. Thanks also to the editors of this volume, Andreas Kaplony and Daniel Potthast, for their corrections and suggestions. Support for the revision was provided by the Center for Jewish Studies at Duke University. I would similarly like to thank the Syndics of Cambridge University Library for providing me with the images of the documents published in the Appendix and for the permission to display them. I further develop my thoughts on the social embeddedness of the legal arena in medieval Egypt in the first chapter of the book I am currently preparing for publication. *Italics* in a quoted passage indicate a Hebrew word in a Judeo-Arabic text. Since this is a Geniza study within a papyrology volume, each Geniza shelfmark is preceded by "Gen." to mark its Geniza origin. Abbreviations used for Geniza shelfmarks are found before the Bibliography below.

2 Gen. T-S 13J1.1, ed. Gil 1983: doc. 593; also ed. ʿAodeh 1992: doc. 61; see important discussion and partial translation in Goitein 1967–1993, vol. 3: 75–76. In recto line 15, I read *mā lā bi-tham(ā)niyat ayyām*. For my understanding of *sulṭān*, see Zinger 2018: 168–169.

 | DOI:10.1163/9789004443877_008

We know of this case because the Geniza preserved Joseph's Arabic script letter to Abraham b. Isaac the scholar (*ha-talmid*), a well-known banker and judge in Fusṭāṭ.[3] Joseph informed Abraham that a letter describing the case was on its way from Ashkelon with one of Joseph's Maghribī companions (*maghribī min aṣḥābī*). It appears that Joseph asked Abraham to be present when the letter arrived and be the first to obtain an answer from a certain higher authority in Fusṭāṭ.[4] It should be noted that these were years of upheaval for the Palestinian Yeshiva as it moved from Jerusalem to Tyre and, later, elsewhere. Therefore, when Joseph countered Ṣedaqa's appeals to Muslim authorities by appealing to a Jewish authority in Fusṭāṭ (stressing that he should rule according to "the laws of Israel"),[5] this should be seen as creative maneuvering on his part, rather than following a strict protocol based on clear-cut jurisdiction.[6]

Especially interesting is the way Joseph frames his request to Abraham. We can detect three different levels at which Joseph tries to convince Abraham to help him. First, there is the Maghribī connection—Joseph was probably a Maghribī (i.e., hailing from the Maghreb); Abraham b. Isaac was a Maghribī; the letter was carried to Fusṭāṭ by a Maghribī; and whoever was supposed to make the final ruling was either a Maghribī or closely allied to the Maghribīs.[7] Second, we notice the obligation based on kinship: "Our matter obligates you because your family and our family are one. The matter of this girl obligates

---

3 On Abraham b. Isaac, see Cohen 1980: 108; Friedman 1986: 255–261; ʿAodeh 1992: 6–7.

4 In his description of the letter, Goitein writes that Joseph asked Abraham to go see the Nagid, Mevorakh b. Saʿadya, and press him for a favorable ruling. However, the Nagid is not mentioned directly in the letter. As often happens with Geniza documents, the crucial passage happens to be written where the document is hardest to decipher. ʿAodeh read lines 3–4 in the recto's margins as *wa-qad irtaḍaynā bi-kutub kitāb ilā* [*l-rayyis li-sharḥ*] *al-ḥāl* and translated *al-rayyis* as "the Nagid." However, I read *wa-qad irtaḍaynā bi-kutub kitāb ilā sayyidinā* [*yashra*]*ḥ al-ḥāl*. Since throughout the letter Joseph addresses Abraham in the second person, *sayyidinā* appears to refer to a higher authority, rather than to Abraham himself. Since the letter cannot be dated precisely, it is impossible to determine to whom Joseph is referring. The most likely candidates are Mevorakh b. Saʿadya (whose first term as a Nagid lasted until 1082), David b. Daniel (head of the Jews from 1082 to 1094), Yehuda ha-Kohen b. Yosef (the famous "ha-Rav"), and Nahray b. Nissim. Joseph addresses Abraham as *al-dayyān*, "judge"; however, the use of this title for Abraham is inconsistent and does not help in dating the letter. For one example from 1092, see Gen. T-S 20.31.

5 Gen. T-S 13Ja1.1r margins.5.

6 These were the very years in which the head of the Jews was consolidating his control over legal institutions in Egypt; see Cohen 1980, 174. For the contemporary dispute as to whether Ashkelon was part of Palestine, see Yagur 2012: 71–73 ("our" document is mentioned on p. 73).

7 See the candidates in note 4 above. For interesting maneuvering in obtaining a ruling on a query, this time keeping the matter secret from any Sicilian in Fusṭāṭ, see Gen. T-S 12.371, ed. Gil 1997: doc. 775.

Umm Abū Naṣr, may God protect him."[8] It is not certain whether Joseph and Abraham were related by blood, by marriage, or whether Joseph is merely using the rhetoric of kinship (what anthropologists used to call fictive kinship).[9] The reference to the mother of Abū Nasr (whose identity is not known) as someone apparently connected to both Abraham and Djawzīya seems also to be another kinship card brought into play. Finally, Joseph reminds Abraham that Djawzīya's father supplicated before him, "so act in this matter as your wisdom sees fit."[10] We do not know the context of this supplication; Abraham b. Isaac, after all, had his own connections to Ashkelon and may have been related to the bride's father, but it is clear that the mention of the father's supplication is used to obligate Abraham to lend a hand in resolving Djawzīya's marriage scandal in Joseph's favor.[11]

This letter gives us a precious "backstage" view into the dynamics of a legal dispute. Usually we only know about premodern legal systems, whether Jewish or Muslim, either from prescriptive literary sources that tell us how the legal system should work or, if they survive, from the products of the legal system: deeds, court notebooks, and responsa. As important as such sources are, they tend to present us with a picture of the judicial system as separate from and often blind to social considerations such as class, patronage, and kinship ties.[12] Non-legal sources such as letters or memoirs, if they are available, may offer a different vantage point on the operations of justice.[13] The Cairo Geniza contains many personal and communal letters, written by litigants, communal

8 Gen. T-S 13J a1.1v.2–3.

9 Goitein thought that Joseph and Abraham were not actually related because *ahluka wa-ahlunā wāḥid* (which he translated as "my family is your family") is "an expression used in urgent requests directed to a person with whom the writer is not related"; Goitein 1976: 75. A study of how people expressed the obligation of kinship in Geniza documents would be most welcome. For a few similar examples, see Gen. T-S 10J6.10r.22–23 (*wa-ahluka anā wa-huwa*, "for I and he are your family"); Gen. CUL. Or. 1080 J35r.19, ed. Gil 1997: doc. 156 (*wa-anā wāḥid minkum*, "I am one of you"). In these examples there is no indication of actual family relationship. In Gen. Bodl. MS Heb. d66.57v13, ed. Goitein 1980: 327–332, a Jewish judge instructs his son to request a favor from the Muslim governor of Jerusalem and to tell the governor that they are "from his family" (*wa-taqūl lahu inna naḥnu min ʿāʾilatihi*).

10 Joseph wrote "your wisdom" in Hebrew, but in Arabic script *b-ḥ-kh-m-ʾ-t-ʾ-kh*. Upon reading the letter, Abraham wrote down to himself the meaning in Hebrew *b-ḥ-k-m-t-k*. The expression harks back to Kings I 2:6 and appears in a similar context also in Gen. T-S 12.371r.11, ed. Gil 1997: doc. 775.

11 For Abraham's own marriage scandal in Ashkelon, see Friedman 1986: 255–261.

12 There have been many studies on legal documents from the Cairo Geniza. For the most recent one, see Ackerman-Lieberman 2014.

13 See, for example, Ergene 2003: 111–113; 119–122; 131.

leaders, judges, and other interested parties, that reveal the complex interplay of law, local politics, and social embeddedness in legal disputes among medieval Jewish communities of the Eastern Mediterranean.

Such material allows us to complement the view "from above" offered by prescriptive works with a view "from below" that examines how the complex legal system was experienced by ordinary people. Exploring legal practice permits us to bridge the often dichotomous view of "law" versus "practice."[14] By viewing individuals as consumers of legal services, we can explore how they navigated the legal arena through their personal networks, as shaped by class, patronage, and kinship.[15] Exploring how legal processes were embedded in society, we may be able to write social histories of law in the medieval Islamic world. While such an undertaking is clearly beyond the confines of the present contribution, in what follows I present a taste of what Geniza letters can offer to such an undertaking through the examination of several letters about marital disputes.

2 Marriage Reconciliation in a Delta Town

Sometime before 1091, Naḥūm b. Manṣūr, a resident of the delta town of Malīdj, wrote a letter to Abū Kathīr, the *parnas* (communal official) in Fusṭāṭ, thanking him for securing a document (*kitāb*) that helped save the marriage of Naḥum's daughter. The cause of the marital discord is unclear, but it seems that local authorities failed to resolve it.[16] Therefore, a woman, probably Naḥum's wife, traveled from Malīdj to Fusṭāṭ and through Abū Kathīr's involvement brought back the document that stated that the husband must pay the delayed marriage payment in full.[17] Naḥum's letter, edited in full in the Appendix, attests to how the legal process was interwoven with communal drama and personal relationships both as the events played out locally in Malīdj and in the relationship between the delta town and the Jewish center in the capital.

14 On the Jewish side, see Zinger 2014: 7. On the Islamic side, see Stilt 2011: 1–2. For Late Antiquity, see Humfress 2009: 381–383.

15 For studying the legal arena from the point of view of its consumers, see Smail 2003.

16 See note to line 12 in the edition below for a possible cause of the conflict.

17 Naḥūm writes about "the woman" (*al-mara*). Goitein is probably correct in suggesting that he is referring to his wife; see Goitein 1967–1993, vol. 3: 213. The exact nature of the *kitāb* is not stated. It could have been a letter, a rescript to a petition, or a legal responsum. It seems to me that because it contained a clear legal ruling and was read out publicly in the synagogue it was probably a responsum, or at least functioned as such. Both Geonic and contemporary responsa were often read out publicly in the synagogue.

Naḥum describes to Abū Kathīr, who was almost certainly Ephraim ha-kohen b. ʿEli, a communal official well known from other Geniza documents, what took place when the document was brought to Malīdj:[18]

> The woman came from you and I found with her a letter. The *cantor, judge* Menasse …, my lord Ibn Maḥbūb the elder Abū al-Faradj, and the *cantor* from Ashkelon took it. They were a group of people assembled in the synagogue. (They) read the letter, examined what was in it, and did exactly what it said. They instructed the young man, who is the husband of my daughter, that there shall be no exception, except that he pay her the delayed marriage settlement. The young man yielded and kissed my head and the head of her mother. They made amends between us and we all yielded.[19]

Naḥum's letter offers us a glimpse of the emotional and communal drama involved in resolving a marital dispute. The local synagogue was the heart of communal life. There the community came together for worship, the authority of the communal leadership was announced and recognized, the charitable activities of the community took place, and the court was usually held. The document from the capital apparently contained a simple legal instruction: the husband must pay the delayed marriage settlement (*mu'akhkhar*).[20] However, declaring the legal ruling publicly in the synagogue by the leaders of the community added dramatic and political elements beyond the strict legal ruling. The result of reading the ruling also went beyond the dry letter of the law. Instead of the husband paying the delayed marriage settlement, reading the legal ruling and instructing the errant husband led to a dramatic climax that resolved with the husband yielding and submitting. The husband submitted to the authority of Jewish law, the authority of the center, the local leadership who proclaimed the ruling, and, last but not least, to his in-laws, as symbolized in the dramatic gesture of kissing them.[21] When Naḥum writes that the communal leaders "made amends between us and we all yielded," we can see the community coming together after conflict and reaffirming its *communitas*.[22]

18 On Ephraim ha-kohen b. ʿEli, see note 50 below.

19 Gen. T-S 10J10.13r.8–13. See a full edition in the Appendix. (As mentioned in note 1 above, *italics* signify words in Hebrew.)

20 It is quite likely that the ruling was framed as "unless the husband desist from such and such, he ought to pay the delayed marriage settlement."

21 Interestingly, he does not kiss his wife, and for all we know she may not have even been present in the synagogue.

22 *Communitas* is a term used by Victor Turner to refer to the spirit of togetherness felt by a

The resolution of this marital dispute demonstrates the intertwining of communal drama and politics with the legal process.

Beyond the drama that took place at the local Malīdj synagogue, the letter also attests to how obtaining the decisive ruling from the center in Fusṭāṭ depended on social relationships with the center in Fusṭāṭ. We can see how these relationships functioned by looking at how Naḥum addresses his benefactor at the beginning and end of the letter:

> The *Creator of All* knows how much longing I have for my lord and master, the venerable *parnas*, my elder, my honor and my dignity, the one who is there for me at times of calamities. I ask the *Creator of All* to keep you alive, protect you, and make your end good ... May (God) protect your son, Ibn Kathīr, and gladden you with him. I pray for you night and day. You are there for me in every calamity. I boast of (knowing) no one but you. To everyone who talks to me, I say: "My lord the *parnas*, he shall obtain a ruling for me." (Here appears the description of the events in the synagogue) ... I send you the most favorable and most perfect greetings, and greetings to your son, and greetings to ʿAyyāsh. Thank him in my place, may I not be deprived of you and may I not be deprived of him, for what he did with the woman.
>
> The writer of these words (i.e., the scribe) ... who made the connection with you, kisses your hands and sends you the most favorable and most perfect greetings. He, I, and my uncle pray for you with the *Torah scroll* in the synagogue of Malīdj. I ask the *Creator of All* to keep you alive, my master the *parnas*. *May He fulfill for you the biblical quote: "The Lord is thy keeper; the Lord is thy shade upon thy right hand"* (Psalms 121: 5) ... I wrote (this letter) in a time of haste in the evening, otherwise I would have wished to pray a lot for my lord the *parnas*.[23]

Beyond the regular epistolary conventions, this letter is saturated with expressions of patron-client relationship.[24] The recipient's benefaction (obtaining the ruling in the daughter's favor) is reciprocated by public declarations of exclu-

---

community during or after a ritual; see Turner 1969: 94–165. Here the community comes together after the conflict has been resolved; however, the feeling of togetherness is not based on a sense of equality, but on a public display of submission to one's in-laws, local leadership, and the center in Fusṭāṭ.

23 Gen. T-S 10J10.13r2–8, 15–20 and right-hand margins.

24 On expressions of patron-client relationship, see Cohen 2005a: 187–188; Cohen 2005b: 10–12; Rustow 2008: 341–382; Rustow 2009: 365–390.

sive loyalty ("I boast of (knowing) no one but you"), by spreading the patron's fame ("To everyone who talks to me, I say: 'My lord the *parnas*, he shall obtain a ruling for me'"), and by the assurance that the client is praying on his behalf (as declared in the letter's opening, closing, and postscript).[25] It is important to stress that the patron's favor here is not merely charitable assistance or a letter of recommendation, but is obtaining a favorable legal ruling.[26] Furthermore, the decisive document was obtained in the absence, and apparently even without the knowledge, of the husband. We see how assistance in the legal arena is integrated into the broader social calculus of reciprocal benefactions characteristic of patron-client relations in the Geniza.

The letter is particularly illuminating insofar as it conveys to us not merely a dyadic relationship between a client and a patron but a whole network of ties connecting the periphery to the center. In Malīdj we have the writer, his uncle, and the *cantor*, Ibn Ghāzfīnī, who establishes the connection with the capital. In the capital, we have the *parnas* Abū Kathīr (probably Efraim b. ʿEli) and his son Ibn Kathīr. A certain Abū al-Faradj Ibn Maḥbūb is mentioned as present in the synagogue at the dramatic reconciliation and later as present in Fusṭāṭ, and apparently constitutes another link between Malīdj and Fusṭāṭ. Thus, obtaining the favorable ruling from Fusṭāṭ was a group effort arranged through a network of ties.[27]

3 Marriage Reconciliation in the Calculus of Reciprocity

We get an especially valuable vantage point on the social factors involved in settling a marriage dispute in two letters written probably around 1071 or slightly afterward by Shela b. Mevasser of the Naḥum family to Surūr b. Ḥayyim of the Ben Sabra family.[28] Shela was a communal leader and a judge in Alexan-

---

25 The obligation of the client to spread the fame of the patron is found in many letters, e.g., in Gen. T-S 10J19.7r.11. It is interesting to compare this to the duty of wives to declare publicly the merits of their husbands as found in Islamic literary sources; see el-Cheikh 2002: 187. The opposite practice, declaring someone's infamy publicly in the market, is also known from the Geniza, see Goitein 1961; 149 and Gen. T-S 13J13.27, ed. Gil, *Ishmael*, doc. 238. For the client praying for his patron, see the remarkable petition for assistance of a poor man to a lady in Gen. T-S NS 99.10.

26 Another interesting example is found in Gen. T-S 8J17.25. I plan to explore the question of how Jews in medieval Egypt obtained responsa in a future study.

27 On the functioning of social networks in the Jewish community, see Frenkel 2006: 207. On commercial networks, see Goldberg 2012: 123–143.

28 On the dating of the letter, see the edition. On the Ben Naḥum family, see Goitein 1967–

dria starting in the seventh decade of the 11th century until the beginning of the 12th century.[29] So in the time of our letter, he was at the beginning of his career. Surūr b. Ḥayyim was older than Shela and was already an established merchant in Fustat.[30] From Shela's first letter to Surūr we learn that Surūr's daughter was married in Alexandria to a certain Shabbat.[31] The marriage ran into trouble and Shabbat wanted to divorce his wife. Shela reconciled the couple and then informed the concerned father of the wife. In the same letter he also requested Surūr's help with a certain Andalusian refugee. Jewish communities would often provide wandering paupers with just enough means to reach their next destination, thus relieving the local community of the burden of providing for them.[32] The letter shows how spousal reconciliation figured in a reciprocal calculus of benefactions that also encompassed charity:

1993, vol. 5: 553 n. 229, and Frenkel 2006: 74–75. The Ben/Ibn Sabra family seems to have had the worst of luck when it came to marriage. Some of the most vivid Geniza letters that deal with marital strife are associated with this family. See Gen. T-S 10J9.13, translated in Goitein 1967–1993, vol. 3: 175–176 (recently I identified Gen. CUL Or. 1080 3.46 as a letter written by the same woman on the same topic to "my brother" Abū ʿUmar, who is probably Mevorakh b. Abraham Ben Sabra's son; see Gen. Heid. Hebr. 28 (= Arab 27), recto 18, ed. ʿAodeh 1992: doc. 19). For other examples, see Gen. T-S 10J12.1, ed. Zinger 2014: 367–380 and discussed pp. 277–305; Gen. DK 238.4 (old XIII), discussed in Zinger 2014: 304–305.

29 In Gen. T-S 12.8 + T-S 10J4.9, which seems to be dated to 1070, Shela already carries the title of judge (*dayyan*). The next dated document is Gen. T-S 28.6c, from 1074 (here Shela is not titled the judge). The last dated document for Shela is Gen. T-S 20.129, dated 1101 or 1104. See more information in note 57 below. For Shela's career in general, see Frenkel 2006: 74–86 (the dating of some of the documents there requires revision).

30 Surūr b. Ḥayyim Ben Sabra signed a Fustat deed of release in 1049 (Gen. T-S 20.23), a *ketubba* (marriage contract) in 1059 (Gen. Bodl. MS Heb. a 3.43), and a partnership agreement in 1061 (Gen. IOM D 55 8). Gen. T-S NS J360 is a letter from Alexandria to Fusṭāṭ describing Surūr as slandering key figures in Fusṭāṭ, among them Yehuda ha-kohen b. Joseph, "the Rav," and Yehuda b. Saʿadya; ed. Gil 1991: doc. 449a. Gen. CUL Or. 1080 J264 and Gen. T-S 8J22.6 are two letters written by Surūr's other son-in-law, Mevorakh b. Yizḥaq; ed. Frenkel 2006: doc. 46 and 100. While in these letters Mevorakh b. Yizḥaq does not identify himself as part of the Ben Sabra family, when writing to someone outside the family, he adds "Ben Sabra" to his name; see Gen. T-S 10J6.10. Finally, it is likely that Ḥayyim b. Sasson b. Ḥayyim Ben Sabra who signed Gen. ENA 4020.21 is Surūr's (= Sasson's) son.

31 Shabbat is mentioned in a letter written by Surūr's other son-in-law, Mevorakh b. Yizḥaq; see Gen. CUL Or. 1080 J264r.24, ed. Frenkel 2006: doc. 100. From this letter we learn that Shabbat's *kunya* (paedonymic) was Abū al-Faradj.

32 By carrying letters of recommendation, such as the one in our document, these wander-

> It has been some days now that Shabbat and the girl (*al-ṣabīya*) quarreled, and he was on the verge of divorce. I did not cease to coax him and his brothers gently, may God endow them with life. They spared no effort (in this matter). You must, may God protect you, write to them and thank them for what they have done.
>
> I settled the matter as is desired. They are in complete blessing; calm your heart in this matter. For I am here for you more than any brother and friend. For your favor is upon us and upon anyone who comes to Miṣr, may God make you stay this way forever.
>
> The bearer of this letter is a *cantor* from the people of al-Andalus, *poor* and exiled from his land. … He asked me to write on his behalf to a man with *fear of heaven and industry*. I could not think of anyone as fitting as my lord, the elder, may God protect you. I ask you to act with him as is characteristic of you, as your beautiful custom has been with any *passerby*. … Speak to my lord, *the excellent ḥaver*, on his behalf so he can strive for him for *heaven's sake*.[33]
>
> Whatever need my lord and elder has, it will honor me to fulfill it. May you never deprive me of your letters, for I rejoice in them.[34]

Previous scholars commented separately on the two sections of the letter (the spousal reconciliation and the assistance to the poor foreigner). Read together, however, it is clear that these two sections are interconnected. The favor the writer has done by solving the recipient's daughter's marital friction is presented as a demonstration of the fact that "I am here for you more than any brother and friend." The writer presents his intervention as merely befitting his own and his congregation's relationship with the recipient, given the latter's favor to them and to "anyone who arrives at Fusṭāṭ"—a statement that sets the stage for his request, in the subsequent section, for just such a favor for a foreigner headed to Fusṭāṭ. Recommending the foreigner for assistance in Fusṭāṭ is important to Shela and Surūr's ongoing relationship because partaking in

ing paupers served as a useful communication network between members of the Jewish elite; see Frenkel 2006: 224–226; Frenkel 2014: 59–66. See also Cohen 2005b: 72–87.

33 A *ḥaver* is a member of the Palestinian Yeshiva. "The excellent *ḥaver*" is ʿEli b. ʿAmram, who by this time was the leader of the Rabbanites in Fusṭāṭ; see Bareket 2014. Notice how the number of Hebrew expressions (in italics) increases when the writer switches to write about charity.

34 Gen. T-S NS J120 + T-S. Misc. 28.11 b1–18; see full edition in the Appendix. In both this letter and the letter discussed below, Shela tends to divide the text with blank spaces before new topics are introduced. I have reflected these spaces with paragraph breaks.

charitable activity was a central social glue for the Egyptian Jewish elite.[35] The letter's conclusion once again solidifies the ties of reciprocal obligation.

Fortunately, the Geniza preserved another letter of Shela to Surūr which mentions the same case.[36] It seems that Surūr responded to Shela's first letter and thanked him for saving his daughter's marriage.[37] Shela then responded to Surūr's response and explained the reasons he had brokered peace between the quarreling couple:

> Regarding your thanks to me and my uncle[38] regarding what I have done for the benefit of your daughter, may God aid her and preserve her with her husband, it is a duty and obligation upon us for many reasons. The first reason is her loneliness and isolation (*li-waḥdatihā wa-inqiṭāʿihā*). Also, the well-being of the people of our city is incumbent upon me.[39] Also, out of respect to a lord like my master, the elder, may God guard him, whose favor is bestowed over high and low, may God, the exalted, make you always an exemplar of goodness.
>
> Regarding your filling in for me at the court of my master, the head (*rayyis*) "the fourth," may God prolong his honor, it was a favor and you did as is characteristic of you, may I not be deprived of you.[40]

35 See Frenkel 2006: 222–226. This is also probably why, toward the end of the letter, Shela suggests that Surūr also enlist the help of the excellent *ḥaver*, ʿEli b. ʿAmram.

36 In my dissertation, I was not aware of the join between Gen. T-S NS J120 and Gen. T-S. Misc. 28.11. Without the identity of the personalities provided by Gen. T-S. Misc. 28.11, I treated Gen. T-S NS J120 and Gen. T-S 13J17.5 as two separate cases; see Zinger 2014: 239–243. Two other joins between Geniza fragments related to Shela ought to be mentioned here. Gen. ENA 2805.2a, ed. Gil 1997: doc. 790 + Gen. ENA 2740.3, ed. Frenkel 2006: doc. 9 is a letter from Shela to the important Fusṭāṭ merchant-scholar Nehoray (Nahray) b. Nissim. Gen. T-S NS J334, ed. Frenkel 2006: doc. 93 + Gen. TS 12.717 is on the one side a letter to Abraham b. Jacob the cantor, complaining about Shela, his sons, and his brothers. On the other side is (a draft of?) a legal document about an inheritance case involving Eli *ha-kohen ha-parnas*; on him, see note 50 below. The latter join was suggested by the Genazim program in the Friedberg Project.

37 Sent from Fusṭāṭ to Alexandria, it was probably never deposited in the Geniza of the Ben Ezra synagogue in Fusṭāṭ.

38 Shela's uncle is mentioned also in the margins of Gen. T-S NS J120. In all probability, this was Bashīr of the Ben Naḥum family; see Frenkel 2006: 75.

39 Frenkel discusses this statement in Frenkel 2006: 199.

40 Gen. T-S 13J17.5r.6–16, ed. Frenkel 2006: doc. 67. This passage is discussed in Zinger 2014: 242–243, and Krakowski 2017: 262. "The fourth" (*al-reviʿi*) means the person fourth in line in the hierarchy of the Palestinian Yeshiva. The passage about the court of the fourth is important for the dating of the letters; see the edition below.

Shela then turns to discussing his dispute with a certain *rayyis* whose identity is not entirely certain.[41] After sending greetings to different members of the Ben Sabra family, Shela concludes the letter with:

> I know that the members of the Ben Naḥum family have no brothers or friends other than the Ben Sabra family, may God not deprive me of their lives.[42]

Shela conveniently lays out for us various factors involved in brokering marital settlements, moving from the general to the particular. First we have the general obligation toward a person in a weak position. The wife was supposedly suffering from isolation (*inqiṭāʿ*) in Alexandria since her father resided in Fusṭāṭ. This seems to be a trope used by Shela, as we know that Mevorakh b. Yizḥaq, who was married to her sister and belonged to the Ben Sabra family, resided in Alexandria and presumably could support her.[43] Next we have Shela's obligation to the well-being of his local flock. As a communal leader, he was charged with restoring peace between the members of his congregation, and especially between husband and wife. Then we have the duty stemming from the prominent position of his benefactor, "whose favor is bestowed over high and low." Finally, Shela mentions a personal favor he received from Surūr and concludes the letter with an acknowledgment of the special bond between the two families.

It is rare to have such a straightforward account of a judge explaining in private why he acted as he did. This letter allows us to see how the legal and non-legal domains intertwined, as concern for the socially weak, the obligation to restore peace, and personal ties of obligation came together to bring about a favorable outcome to a marriage conflict. At the same time, we see that Shela not only averted an ugly divorce, he also did not fail to use his success to obtain credit in his ongoing personal relationship with Surūr. Thus we see not only how social embeddedness figures in the legal arena, but also how the resolution of a legal dispute is integrated with matters of charity and the calculus of reciprocal favors.

---

41 Frenkel suggests "the *rayyis*" was either Judah b. Saʿadya or his younger brother, Mevorakh b. Saʿadya; see Frenkel 2006: 75 and 514. Another possibility is that Shela is referring to the "the *rayyis* the fourth" mentioned two lines above.

42 Gen. T-S 13J17.5r margins. 19–27.

43 On Mevorakh b. Yizḥaq, see notes 30–31 above. I plan to explore the gendered aspects and cultural meanings of social isolation (*inqiṭāʿ*) for Jewish women in medieval Egypt in a future study. For the time being, see Cohen 2005: 192–195 and note 13 especially, and Krakowski 2017: 63 and 66.

4 Conclusion

These three cases (in four documents) offer a taste of the rich material available in the Cairo Geniza for the study of legal practice in medieval Egypt "from below." Complementing the hundreds of deeds, fragments of court notebooks, and extant responsa, private letters provide a behind-the-scenes view of the workings of judges and communal leaders in resolving disputes. This perspective is usually missing in responsa and court records because we do not expect that a responder or a judge would mention for posterity his ongoing reciprocal relationship with the parties involved. With this material we can begin to explore the nature of justice in the Jewish communities of medieval Egypt and Palestine. In the letters explored above, we see how social embeddedness was an integral factor in pursuing marital disputes through a legal process. The horizontal and vertical relationships that were so central to the workings of trade, charity, and communal politics extended also to the legal arena.[44]

Furthermore, these documents allow us to explore how social embeddedness was used, both by the parties involved as well as by the legal authorities. Medieval Jewish judges in Egypt preferred to arrive at a mediated compromise rather than issue a decisive ruling.[45] Striving for compromise and reconciliation, legal authorities used, and were themselves entangled in, networks of social relations. The few documents explored above highlight the crucial role of middlemen between the parties and the legal authorities for the operation of these social relations. From Ashkelon, Joseph b. Menasse made an appeal based on kinship, Maghribī, and patronage ties to Abraham b. Isaac, who, despite being a judge himself, was supposed to obtain the ruling of a higher authority. From Malīdj, Naḥum b. Manṣūr wrote to a communal official who obtained for him a favorable ruling from a higher authority. These two letters, written from

44 On horizontal and vertical reciprocal relationships in trade, see Goldberg 2014: 273–286; for those in charity and communal politics, see Frenkel 2006: 207–232. The fact that social embeddedness was integral to the workings of the legal arena does not imply that legal doctrine was disregarded. Abundant Geniza court records and responsa outside the Geniza reveal that legal practice generally adhered to Jewish law; for the most recent study, see Ackerman-Lieberman 2014: 156–193. The examples explored above all involve resolving marital disputes, the field in which we might expect the greatest degree of social embeddedness. The material from the Geniza suggests that we need to find new ways of thinking about social embeddedness and adherence to legal doctrine that do not pose them as opposite poles in a zero-sum game; see the debate between David S. Powers and Lawrence Rosen in Powers 1991: 790–791; Rosen 2006: 820–821.

45 See Goitein 1967–1993, vol. 3: 334–335; Zinger 2014: 31–36.

the periphery to the center, reflect the way litigants employed social relations cultivated with well-placed middlemen to bring about a favorable outcome in the legal arena.[46]

Beyond the middlemen used by litigants, legal authorities themselves used middlemen and other parties to ensure the complicity of concerned parties. In Naḥum's letter we see how the husband's compliance was achieved through the participation of the local judge, two cantors, and a fourth person. In Shela's first letter we hear how Shela coaxed not only Shabbat but also his brothers, who played a crucial role in persuading Shabbat not to divorce his wife. Thus the involvement of middlemen and other parties, working in both directions, was central to the way social embeddedness operated in the legal arena and to a party's chances of obtaining a favorable outcome, as well as to the judge reaching a compromise and securing the parties' compliance. Frenkel has argued that the Jewish communities in medieval Egypt were led by a well-defined elite, tightly interconnected by bonds of trade, kinship, education, involvement in communal charity, and a shared cultural ethos.[47] In this respect, the letters of Shela reflect horizontal relations within the elite, since he exchanges with Surūr legal, charitable, and social favors, while the letter of Nahum reflects how non-elite members could obtain favors (in these cases of a legal nature) from the elite through the intercession of mid-level communal officials.

Law holds a privileged position in our modern society in general, and in Jewish and Islamic studies in particular. This privileged position often translates to a top-down approach that focuses on the courts as a manifestation of power or that examines how reality compares with the law as found in the legal codes. But the legal arena can also be examined from the perspective of the consumers of law, rather than its dispensers. Focusing on the experiences of litigants and the choices available to them requires bringing the law down from its pedestal and integrating it into the web of social relations and negotiations of everyday life. The small contribution made here has begun to explore how parties used their social relations to obtain a favorable outcome from the legal arena, and how legal authorities used the same social relations to ensure participation in the process and compliance with its outcome. The few documents examined above are merely the tip of the iceberg of the rich material available for the study of "law in action" in the Geniza. Exploring how individuals maneuvered the legal arena promises to teach us how individuals experienced the law (whether Jewish or Muslim) and to transform our understanding of legal insti-

46 See also Ergene 2003: 111.

47 Frenkel 2006: 207–232.

tutions. As a result, though law loses some of its awe and luster, we gain an appreciation of how it was integrated into social and cultural life and of the practical creativity of ordinary people in their dealings with the law.[48]

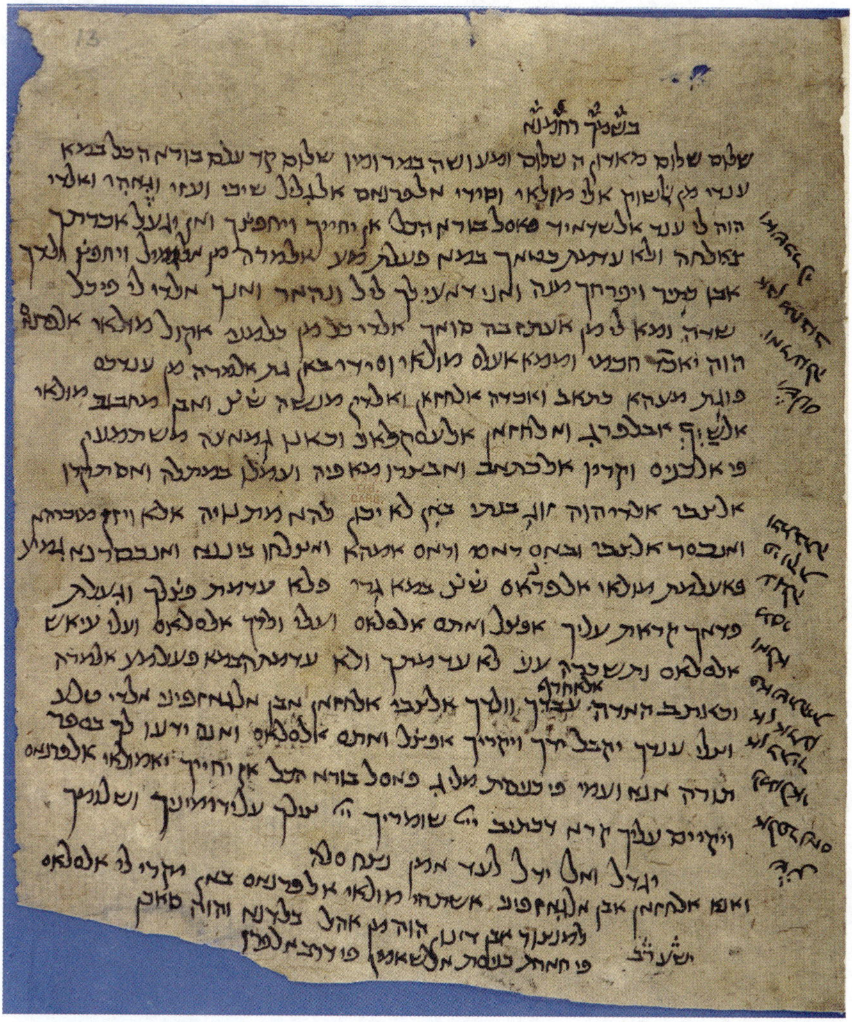

FIGURE 7.1 T-S 10J10.13 recto

48 This last paragraph draws on Zinger 2014: 271–272.

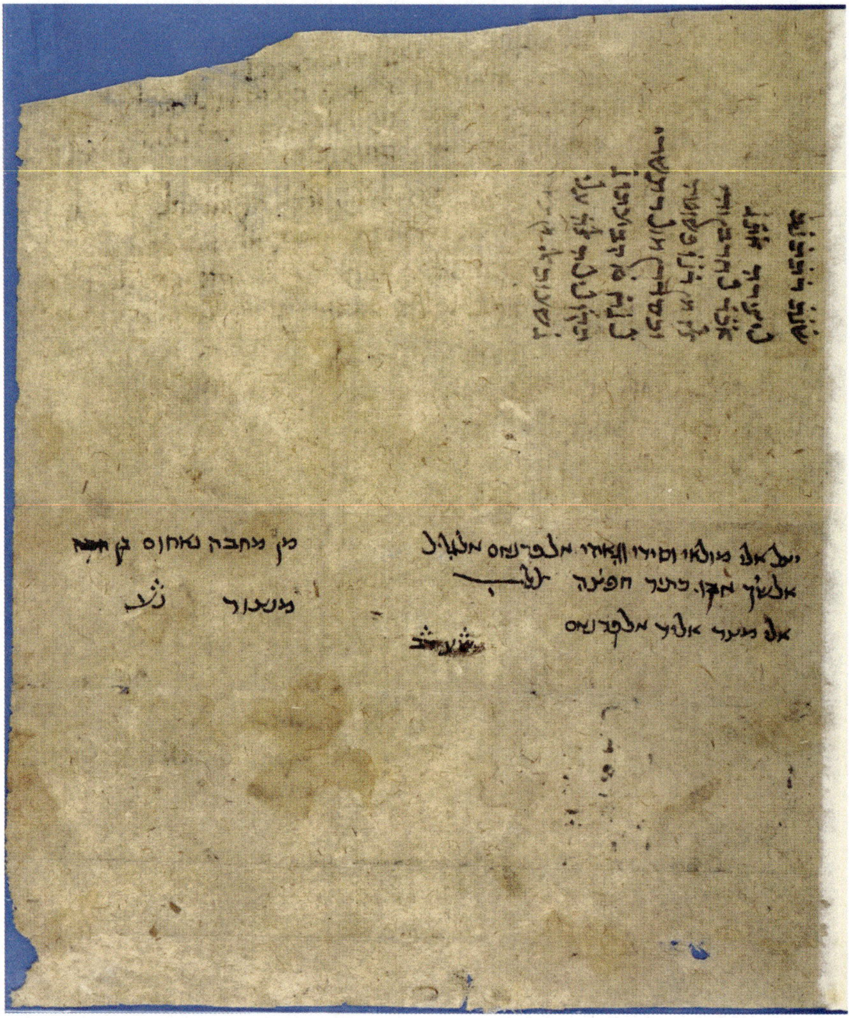

FIGURE 7.2 T-S 10J10.13 verso

5 No. 1: Marriage Reconciliation in a Delta Town[49]

T-S 10J10.13 rv
Figs. 7.1–2
16.5 high × 19.0 cm wide
Before September 1091
Sent from Malīdj to Fusṭāṭ

Brown paper. The writer inconsistently marks the Arabic *djīm* with a dot under the Hebrew *gimel*, a dot above the Hebrew *ṣade* for the Arabic *ḍād*, and on two occasions (lines 8 and 10) the Arabic *khā'* with a line over the Hebrew *kaf*. The verso contains a calendrical calculation in a different hand for 24 September 1091.

A letter from Naḥum b. Manṣūr to the *parnas* Abū Kathīr. Abū Kathīr is probably Ephraim ha-Kohen b. ʿEli, the *parnas* b. Yaʿīsh *ha-mumḥe*, "the expert."[50] Naḥum thanks Abū Kathīr for his help obtaining a *kitāb* from the capital that was read in public in the synagogue of Malīdj to great effect, thereby bringing about the reconciliation between Naḥum's daughter and her husband.

The letter is written in the good hand of the local cantor, Ibn al-Ghāzfīnī, who added a personal message at the bottom of the letter.[51]

בשמך רחמנא
שלום שלום מאדון השלום ומעושה במרומיו שלום קד עלם בורא הכל במא
ענדי מן אלשוק אלי מולאי וסידי אלפרנאס אלגִליל שיכי ועזי וגֶאהִי ואלדי
הוה לי ענד אלשדאיד פאסל בורא הכל אן יחייך ויחפצ̇ך ואן יגעל אכרתך
צ̇אלחה ולא עדמת כטאך במא פעלת מע אלמרה מן אלגמיל ויחפץ̇ ולדך
אבן כתיר ויפרחך מנה ואני דאעי לך ליל ונהאר ואנך אלדי לי פי כל
שדה ומא לי מן אעתז בה סואך אלדי כל מן כלמני אקול מולאי אלפרנאס
הוה יאכ̄ד חכמי וממא אעלם מולאי וסידי באן גת אלמרה מן ענדכם
פוגִת מעהא כתאב ואכדה אלחזאן ואלדין מנשה ש̇צ̇ ואבן מחבוב̇ מולאי

49 I first edited this document in my dissertation; see Zinger 2014: 359–366. Previously, it was mentioned in Goitein 1967–1993, vol. 3: 213; Golb 1974: 133. I have benefitted from Goitein's provisional transcription found in the Princeton Geniza Browser (PGB). In the transcriptions, I follow the Leiden Conventions for marking [lacuna], ⟦deletions⟧, and {scribal error}, deviating from the conventions only in marking ⸢uncertain readings.⸣

50 On Ephraim ha-Kohen b. ʿEli, see Zinger 2014: 359 n. 2. On his better-known father, see Cohen 1980: 110–113.

51 On Ibn al-Ghāzfīnī and his family, see Zinger 2014: 363–366, where I suggested understanding al-Ghāzfīnī as the *nisba* (attribution) of someone hailing from Qazvin, Iran. The fact that the cantor once placed a dot under the *gimel* in his name suggests he understood it as a *jīm* and obviously works against this suggestion.

10 אלשַׂיְךְּ אבלפרגׄ ואלחזאן אלעסקלאני וכאנו גׄמאעה משתמעין
11 פי אלכניס וקרין אלכתאב ואבצרו מא פיה ועמלו במתלה ואסתקרו
12 אלצבי אלדי הוה זוגׄ בנתי באן לא יכון להא מתנויה אלא ויזן מוכרהא
13 ואנכסר אלצבי ובאס ראסי וראס אמהא ואצלחו ביננא ואנכסרנא גׄמיע
14 פאעלמת מולאי אלפר/נ/אס שׂצׄ במא גׄרי פלא עדמת פצׄלך וגׄעלת
15 פדאך קראת עליך אפצל ואתם אלסלאם ועלי ולדך אלסלאם ועלי עיאש
16 אלסלאם ותשכרה עני לא עדמתך ולא עדמתה במא פעל מע אלמרה
17 וכאתב האדה // אלאחרף // עבדך וולדך אלצבי אלחזאן אבן אלגאזפיני אלדי טלע
18 וצלי ענדך יקבל ידך ויקריך אפצׄל ואתם אלסלאם ואנה ידעו לך בספר
19 תורה אנא ועמי פי כניסת מליגׄ פאסל בורא הכל אן יחייך יאמולאי אלפרנאס
20 ויקיים עליך קרא דכתיב יי׳ שומריך יי׳ צילך על יד ימיניך ושלומך
21 יגדל ואל ידל לעד אמן נצח סלה
22 ואנא אלחזאן אבן אלגׄאזפיני אשתהי מולאי אלפרנאס באן יקרי לי אלסלאם
23 ישׂע רׄב   למנצור אבן דינון הוה מן אהל בלדנא והוה סאכן
24 פי חארת כניסת אלשאמין פי דרב אלפרן

Right-hand margins

וכתבתה פי וקת עגלה מסי ואלא פאשתהית אן אדעו אן כתיר למולאי אלפרנאס שׂצׄ
ואשכר לי אבן מחבוב ואדעו לה ושלום

Verso

1 יצל אלי מולאי וסידי וגׄאהי אלפרנאס אלגׄליל   מן מחבה נאחום בן ⟦הבה⟧
2 אלש/י/ך אבו כתיר חפצׄה אללה
3 אלי מצר אליד אלפרנאס   מנצור נע
4 ישע רב

Translation

(1) *In Your name, Oh Merciful,*

(2) *Peace and peace again from the Lord of Peace and from Him who makes in heaven peace. The Creator of All* knows (3) how much longing I have for my lord and master the venerable *parnas*, my elder, my honor and my dignity, the one (4) who is there for me at times of calamities. I ask the *Creator of All* to keep you alive, protect you, and make your end (5) good. May I not be deprived of your letter concerning the good that you have done for the woman. May (God) protect your son, (6) Ibn Kathīr, and

gladden you with him. I pray for you night and day. You are there for me in every (7) calamity. I boast of (knowing) no one but you. To everyone who talks to me, I say: "My lord the *parnas*, (8) he shall obtain a ruling for me." I inform you, my lord and master, that the woman came from you (plur.) (9) and I found with her a letter. The *cantor*, *Judge* Menasse, (may the) R(ock) p(rotect him), my lord Ibn Maḥbūb (10) the elder Abū al-Faradj, and the *cantor* from Ashkelon took it. They were a group of people assembled (11) in the synagogue. (They) read the letter, examined what was in it, and did exactly what it said. They instructed (12) the young man, who is the husband of my daughter, that there shall be no exception, except that he pay her the delayed marriage settlement (13) The young man yielded and kissed my head and the head of her mother. They made amends between us and we all yielded. (14) I hereby inform my master the *parnas*, (may the) R(ock) p(rotect him), of what happened, may I not be deprived of your favor and may I be made (15) your ransom. I send you the most favorable and most perfect greetings, and greetings to your son, and greetings to ʿAyyāsh. (16) Thank him in my place, may I not be deprived of you and may I not be deprived of him, for what he did with the woman.

(17) The writer of these words (i.e., the scribe), your servant and child, the young man, the *cantor* Ibn al-Ghāzfīnī, who made (18) the connection with you, kisses your hands and sends you the most favorable and most perfect greetings. He, I, and my uncle pray for you with the *Torah scroll* (19) in the synagogue of Malīdj. I ask *the Creator of All* to keep you alive, my master the *parnas*. (20) *May He fulfill for you the biblical quote: "The Lord is thy keeper; the Lord is thy shade upon thy right hand" (Psalms 121:5). May your peace (21) ever increase and not decease. Amen neṣaḥ selah.*

(23) *Great Salvation!*

(22) (p.s.) I, Ibn al-Ghāzfīnī the *cantor*, ask my master the *parnas* to send my greetings (23) to Manṣūr Ibn Dinūn, who is from the people of our city and lives (24) in the neighborhood of the Palestinian synagogue, in the bakery alleyway (*darb al-furn*).

(Right-hand margins) (p.p.s.) I wrote (this letter) in a time of haste in the evening, otherwise I would have wished to pray a lot for my lord the *parnas*, (*may*) *G*(*od*) *p*(*rotect him*).

(p.p.p.s.) And thank for me Ibn Maḥbūb, I pray for him, *and peace*.

(Verso, address:) May it arrive to my lord, my master and my dignity, the venerable *parnas*, the elder Abū Kathīr, may God protect him. To Miṣr, to the hand of the *parnas*.

From him who loves him, Naḥum b. ⟦Hiba⟧ Manṣūr, (*may he*) *R*(*est in*) *E*(*den*)

Great Salvation!

Commentary

1 Above the Aramaic Basmala are four fleur-de-lis-like decorations.

2 *"Peace and peace again from the Lord of Peace and from him who makes in heaven peace"*: Echoing Job 25: 2, well known from the end of the Qaddish.

3 *wa-djāhī*: this word has both a dot under the *gimel* to signify a *djīm* and three dots for a *segol* (so apparently *wa-djēhī*).

4 *huwah* (see also lines 8, 12 and 23) appears in other Judeo-Arabic texts for *huwa*; see Gen. T-S NS 324.135 and see Blau 1989: 57.

5 *al-djamīl*: it seems as though the *gimel* was corrected, probably from a *kaf*.

9 *fa-wadjattu* < *fa-wadjadtu*. For *tt* < *dt*, see Blau 1989: 34. For the possible meanings of *kitāb* here, see note 17 above.

Four people took the letter: (1) the cantor, (2) Menasse the judge, (3) Ibn Maḥbūb Abū al-Faradj, and (4) the cantor from Ashkelon.

Menasse the judge is mentioned in the top part of Gen. T-S 20.93, a legal document from Fusṭāṭ describing another dispute in al-Malīdj. This legal record is glued to another legal document from Fusṭāṭ dated to 1094; see edition of the top part and discussion in Yagur 2017: 146–147 and 343–344. As Yagur notes, it is possible that this Menasse the judge is Menasse the judge b. Pinchas who is released from all claims in Gen. T-S 18J1.13, a 1085 deed from Alexandria.

10 It is possible that Ibn Maḥbūb Abū al-Faradj is identical with an Abū al-Faradj Ibn Maḥbūb who appears in a very interesting contemporary letter. Gen. T-S 12.288 is a letter from Shemarya b. Ephraim to Abū al-Faḍl Mevorakh b. Abraham of the Ben Sabra family (on him see the note to b recto 18 in the edition of the next document below) reporting how Shemarya negotiated the terms of the divorce on Mevorakh's behalf with Mevorakh's mother-in-law. In line 22, Shemarya sends greetings to Abū al-Faradj Ibn Maḥbūb, apparently an in-law of Mevorakh.

mushtamiʿīn < *mudjtamiʿīn*: see Blau 1989: 37 and 287.

11 *wa-ʿamilū bi-mithlihi*: see Blau 2006: 29 and 650

12 *wa-staqarrū al-ṣabī … bi-an* must mean something more active and authoritative than the usual *istaqarra al-amr bayn*, "the matter was agreed between."

wa-staqarrū al-ṣabī alladhī huwa zawdj bintī bi-an lā yakūn lahā mathnawiyya illā wa-yazin muʾakhkharahā: *Mathnawiyya* appears regularly in

Arabic legal documents as "reservation" or "exception." However, I wonder whether the meaning here should be understood as "double," meaning here a second wife, even though this meaning does not appear in Arabic dictionaries. According to this understanding, the translation would be: "they instructed the young man ... that she would not have a double without him paying her delayed marriage gift." After all, the basic meaning of the root is "double, second," and when Qurʾān 4:3 permits the taking of "two, three, four" wives, the "two" is expressed with *mathnā*. This would solve the awkwardness of *lā yakun lahā* in the sentence and would conform with what we know about polygyny in the Geniza, where usually a husband was not allowed to take a second wife without paying his wife her delayed marriage gift; see Friedman 1986: 7–23.

13 For *inkasara* as "cool off, yield, submit," see Goitein 1967–1993: vol. 3: 213; Blau 2006: 596; and Ullmann 1970: 182.

21 For *amen neṣaḥ selah*, see *Babylonian Talmud*, ʿEruvin, 54a: "Wherever (the Bible) states *netzaḥ*, *selah*, or *vaʿed*, the matter will never cease" (Koren translation). See also Malachi 1966 and Qoler 1969.

23 *yeshaʿ rav*: this is the writer's *ʿalāma* (a personal signature, cipher or, as in this case, motto), which also appears in the address. Above both the *shin* and the *resh*, a triangle of three dots is drawn. It seems *yeshaʿ rav* was written after the *amen neṣaḥ selah* of line 21. Then the scribe added his personal message in lines 22–24.

Right-hand margins

2 Above the *shin* in *shalom* there are three dots.

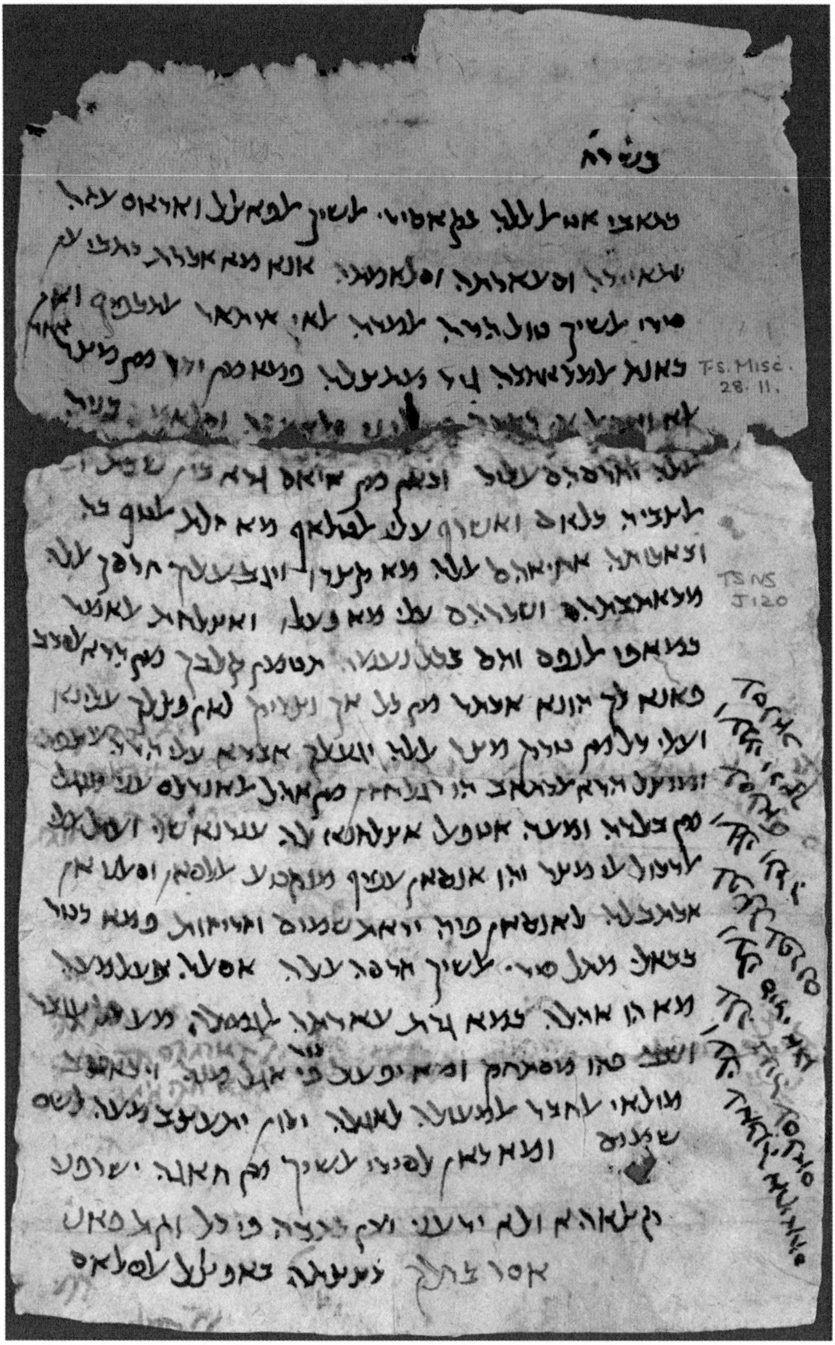

FIGURE 7.3 Gen. T-S NS J120 recto + Gen. T-S. Misc. 28.11 recto

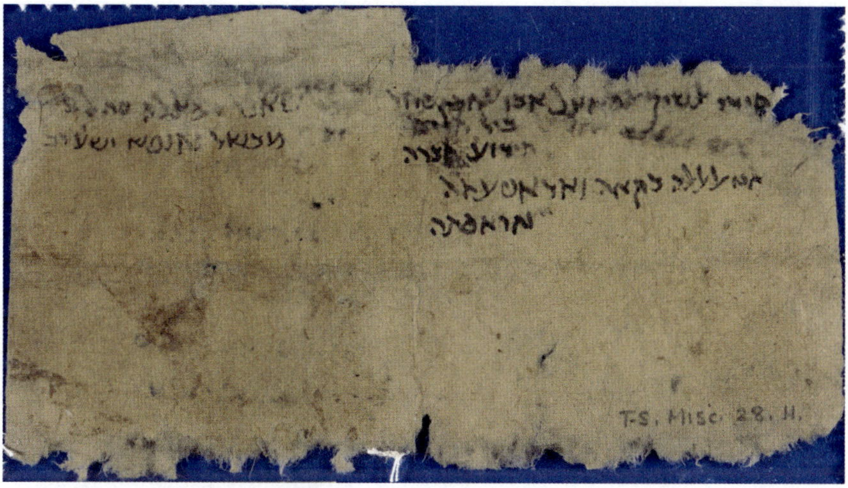

FIGURE 7.4 Gen. T-S NS J120 verso

6 No. 2: Marriage Reconciliation in the Calculus of Reciprocity[52]

Gen. T-S NS J120 rv + Gen. T-S. Misc. 28.11r
Figs. 7.3–4
(8.5 + 17.5) high × 16.5 cm wide
Probably 1071 or a little afterward
Sent from Alexandria to Fusṭāṭ

Paper, a rectangle piece. The text is almost completely extant, except the line in which the two fragments were torn. The text continues diagonally upside-down on the right-hand margins. In many places it is possible to read text from other parts of the letter due to ink transferring from the folding of the letter.

The join between the two fragments was proposed by the Genazim program in the Friedberg Project. Gen. T-S NS J120 was previously partially translated[53] and mentioned.[54] To the best of my knowledge, Gen. T-S. Misc. 28.11 has not been mentioned previously.

52 I have benefitted from Goitein's provisional transcription of Gen. T-S NS J120 found in the PGB.

53 Goitein 1967–1993: vol. 3: 213; Cohen 2005a: 45.

54 Goitein 1967–1993, vol. 2: 136 and 548 n. 58; vol. 5: 189 and 560 n. 21; 194 and 562 n. 54; 198–199 and 563 n. 74; 598 n. 17; Cohen 2000: 446; Cohen 2002: 322; Bareket 2017: 253 n. 110.

A letter from Sahl (Shela) b. Mevasser of the Ben Naḥum family to Abū al-Ḥasan Surūr b. Ḥayyim of the Ben Sabra family.[55] In the first part of the letter, Shela reports to Surūr how he saved the marriage of Surūr's daughter. In the second part, he asks Surūr to assist a poor Andalūsī foreigner. Gen. T-S 13J17.5, also written by Shela to Surūr, deals with the same marriage reconciliation and was written not long after the letter here published.[56]

The letter is not dated, and its date is not entirely certain. Shela begins to appear in dated Geniza documents in the seventh decade of the 11th century.[57] Since our letter mentions "the excellent *ḥaver*" (b recto 15), it could not have been written long after 1075, the latest year ʿEli b. ʿAmram, "the excellent *ḥaver*" and the head of the Palestinian congregation in Fusṭāṭ, appears in the Geniza.[58] A more precise dating between these years is offered by Shela's thanking Surūr for filling his place in "the court of my lord the head 'the fourth'" (*madjlis mawlāya al-rayyis al-reviʿi*) in Gen. T-S 13J17.5r14, written shortly after Gen. T-S NS J120 + Gen. T-S. Misc. 28.11. As Cohen already noted, "the fourth" can be a reference to Evyatar ha-Kohen b. Elijah, who was titled "the fourth" when he visited Fusṭāṭ in 1071.[59] So our letter can be dated generally to 1070–1075, with perhaps a more precise dating of 1071 or slightly afterward.

a (= T-S. Misc. 28.11) recto

בשׁ רחׄ
כתאבי אטאל אללה בקא סידי אלשיך אלפאצׄל ואדאם עזה
ותאיידה וסעאדתה וסלאמתה אנא מא אכרת כתבי ען
סידי אלשיך טול הדה אלמדה אלא{י} איתאר אלתכפיף ואן
כאנת אלמכאתבה גִיר מתצלה פמא {מן} ירד מן מצר אחד
אלא ואסאל ען ˹כברה˺ [פיב]˹לג˺ני סל˹א˺[מ]˹ת˺ה וסלאמ[ה] בניה

55 On Shela b. Mevasser, see Frenkel 2006: 74–86. On Surūr b. Ḥayyim, see note 30 above.

56 Gen. T-S 13J17.5 is edited in Frenkel 2006: doc. 67.

57 The Geniza preserved legal documents signed by Shela in Alexandria dated to 1070, 1074, 1077, 1088/9, and 1101/4; see Gen. T-S 12.8 + T-S 10J4.9, Gen. T-S 28.6c, ed. Frenkel 2006: doc. 41, Gen. T-S 16.138, Gen. ENA 4010.19 and Gen. T-S 20.129, respectively. Shela also appears in some legal fragments whose dates have not been preserved; see Gen. T-S 12.677 and T-S 20.121. The name Sahl b. Mevasser also appears in other deeds, but this is not "our" person; see Gen. T-S 16.132 (al-Banā, 999 C.E.), Gen. T-S 8.192 + T-S 16.153 (Fusṭāṭ, 1054) and Gen. T-S 12.79.

58 Gen. ENA 4010.IV.9, see Bareket 2017: 112.

59 Cohen 1980: 162; Gil 1983: 604–606.

b (= T-S NS J120) recto

אללה יחרסהם עליה (vacat) וכאן מן איאם גרא בין שבת ו'ב'[ין
אלצביה כלאם ואשרף עלי אלטלאק מא זלת אלטף בה
ובאכותה אחיאהם אללה מא קצרו ויגב עליך חרסך אללה
מכאתבתהם ושכרהם עלי מא פעלו (vacat) ואצלחת אלאמר
כמא פי אלנפס והם בכל נעמה תטמן קלבך מן הדא אלסבב
פאנא לך הונא אכתר מן כל אך וצדיק לאן פצ̇לך עלינא
ועלי כל מן טרק מצר אללה יגעלך אבדא עלי הדה אלצפה
ומוצל הדא אלכתאב הו רגל חזן מן אהל אלאנדלס עני מנגלי
מן בלדה ומעה אטפאל אצלחנא לה ענדנא שוי ועול עלי
אלדכול אלי מצר והו אנסאן עפיף מנקטע אללסאן וסאלני אן
אכתב לה לאנסאן פיה יראת שמים וזריזות פמא כטר
בבאלי מתל סידי אלשיך חרסה אללה אסאלה יפעל מעה
מא הו אהלה כמא גרת עאדתה אלגמילה מע כל עובר
ושב פהו מסתחק ומא יפעל // כיר // פי אגל מנה ויכאטב
מולאי אלחבר אלמעולה לאגלה יכון יתעצב מעה לשם
שמים (vacat) ומא כאן לסידי אלשיך מן חאגה ישרפני
קצ̇אהא ולא ידעני מן כתבה פי כל וקת פאני
אסר בדלך כ̇צצתה באפצ̇ל אלסלאם

b recto right-hand margins:

ועלי אלאכוה אחיאהם אללה בגיה אלסלאם ועלי סידי אבו אלפצ̇ל אלפרנס ועלי ולדה
אלסלאם ועמי יכצך אלסלאם

a verso

סידי אלשיך אלפאצל אבו אלחסן סרור   שאכר [ת]פצלה סהל [ביר]
ביר̇ חיים   מבשר נח נפש ישע רב
הידוע סברה
אטאל אללה בקאה ואדאם עזה
וחראסתה

Translation

a recto

(1) *In Y(our) N(ame), Oh M(erciful),*

(2) (This is) my letter (to you), may God prolong the life of my lord, the excellent elder, and make lasting his honor, (3) strength, happiness, and health. I have delayed my letters to (4) my lord the elder all this time only due to (my) preference to alleviate the burden (of your having to answer back). (5) Even though (our) correspondence was irregular, whenever someone comes down (the Nile) from Fusṭāṭ, (6) I ask about your news, and he informs me about your health and the health of your sons,

b recto

(1) may God protect them for you.

It has been some days now that Shabbat (2) and the girl (*al-ṣabīya*) quarreled, and he was on the verge of divorce. I did not cease to coax him (3) and his brothers gently, may God endow them with life. They spared no effort (in this matter). You must, may God protect you, (4) write to them and thank them for what they have done. I settled the matter (5) as is desired. They are in complete blessing; calm your heart in this matter. (6) For I am here for you more than any brother and friend. For your favor is upon us (7) and upon anyone who comes to *Miṣr*, may God make you stay this way forever. (8) The bearer of this letter is a *cantor* from the people of al-Andalus, *poor* and exiled (9) from his land. He has children with him. We have provided (*aṣlaḥnā*) something small for him and he intends (10) to go up to *Miṣr*. He is a modest and bashful (*munqaṭiʿ al-lisān*) person. He asked me (11) to write on his behalf to a man with *fear of heaven and industry*. I could not think (12) of anyone as fitting as my lord the elder, may God protect you. I ask you to act with him (13) as is characteristic of you, as your beautiful custom has been with any *passerby*. (14) For he is deserving. Whatever you do // will be good // in your most excellent benefits. Speak (15) to my lord, the *excellent ḥaver*, on his behalf so he can strive for him *for* (16) *heaven's sake*. Whatever need my lord and elder has, it will honor me (17) to fulfill it. May you never deprive me of your letters, for I (18) rejoice in them. I send you the best greetings of peace.

b recto right-hand margins

and to your brothers, may God endow them with life, (I send) the utmost greetings of peace, and to my lord, Abū al-Faḍl the *parnas*, and to his child, greetings. My (paternal) uncle sends you greetings.

b verso, address

(1 right) (To) my lord the excellent *elder*, Abū al-Ḥasan Surūr (2 right) b. Ḥayyim, (3 right) *known* as Sabra, (4 right) may God prolong his life and make lasting his honor (5 right) and protection. (1 left) (From) he who is grateful for his favor, Sahl [b.] (2 left) Mevasser, *may he rest in peace. Great Salvation!*

Commentary

ar4 *īthār al-takhfīf*: see Friedman 2016: 422.

ar5 *fa-mā* MN *yarid min miṣr aḥad*: the first MN seems to be a mistake in anticipation of *min* later in the line.

br3 *mā qaṣṣarū*: compare with *wa-mā qaṣṣarū awlād al-dayyān Sh(emaro) Ṣ(uro) fī ḥaqqinā*, Gen. T-S 13J21.24r.14–15, ed. Gil, Ishmael, doc. 99. See also Blau 2006: 548 and Friedman 2016: 821.

br4 *aṣlaḥtu al-amr kamā fī al-nafs*: in his partial translation, Goitein translated "I have settled the matter in a way you would have liked;" Goitein 1967–1993, vol. 3: 213. As far as I know, this expression appears in two other Geniza documents. In Gen. T-S 12.291v.8 we find *qāl lanā anā nukfīkum al-mūna wa-ʿalayya kamā fī l-nafs*. Goitein read the passage as *wa-ʿali[ma] bi-mā fī l-nafs* and is therefore of no help; Goitein 1968: 75–77 and English translation in Goitein 1973: 87–88. Gil corrected Goitein's transcription and translated "He told us: 'I shall spare you the expense, for I owe like (the man) himself (?)'" (my translation from Gil's Hebrew); Gil 1997: doc. 207. However, it seems as though the translation should be: "He told me: 'I will take care of the expense for you, it is upon me as is desired.'" The expression also appears in Gen. T-S 10J15.13, a difficult and remarkable letter previously unmentioned in the literature. In recto lines 5–6, I read: *wa-qad qaddamta anna l-kitāb yuḍīf ʿan istīfā(ʾ) mā fī l-nafs l(ā)kin laysa bi-yadika shayʾan wa-lā faʿalta anta shayʾan siw(ā) l-bakht wa-l-kans*, which I tentatively translate: "You previously wrote that the letter will add to the payment what is desired, but you have nothing in your hand and you have done nothing except divination and hiding." Outside the Geniza, the expression *ka-mā fī l-nafs* appears with some regularity in Arabic works. For one work in which it appears several times, see al-Dhahabī 1986, vol. 14: 199; vol. 15: 182; vol. 16: 463; 542; vol. 20: 368.

br10 *munqaṭiʿ al-lisān*: see Goitein 1967–1993, vol. 5: 563 n. 74; Cohen 2005a: 45.
For וסאלני compare with ישרפני in br16 and פאני in br17.

br11 *li-insān fīhi yirʾat shamayyim u-zrizut*: see Goitein 1967–1993, vol. 5: 194 and 598 n. 17.

br14 "Whatever you do // will be good // in your most excellent benefits:" Translation uncertain.

br15 *al-ḥavēr al-meʿule*: this is Eli ben ʿAmram; on him, see Bareket 2017.

br18 Abū al-Faḍl the *parnas* is Surūr's nephew, Mevorakh b. Abraham of the Ben Sabra family. In Shela's second letter (Gen. T-S 13J17.5), he refers to Abū al-Faḍl as *peʾer ha-parnasim*, "the glory of *parnasim*." In a 1090 deed, Mevorakh is called *ha-parnas rosh ha-parnasim*, "the *parnas*, head of the *parnasim*"; see Gen. T-S 12.583r9, ed. Weiss 1967: doc. 34.

br margins *wa-ʿammī yakhuṣṣaka al-salām*: see note 38 above.

Abbreviations Used for Geniza Shelfmarks

BL	London, British Library
Bodl.	Oxford, Bodleian Library
CUL Or.	Cambridge, Cambridge University Library, Oriental Collection
DK	Budapest, Hungarian Academy of Science, David Kaufman Collection
ENA	New York, Jewish Theological Seminary, Elkan Nathan Adler Collection
Heid	Heidelberg, Institute for Papyrology
IOM	Petersburg, Institute of Oriental Manuscripts of the Russian Academy of Sciences (previously "Institut Naradov Azii [INA]," Institute of the People of Asia)
T-S	Cambridge, Cambridge University Library, Taylor-Schechter Collection

Bibliography

Ackerman-Lieberman Phillip I. 2014. *The Business of Identity: Jews, Muslims, and Economic Life in Medieval Egypt*. Stanford Studies in Jewish History and Culture. Stanford: Stanford University Press.

ʿAodeh, Ṣabīḥ. 1992. *Ha-mikhtavim ha-ʿaraviyim shel ha-soḥarim ha-yehudim bi-Genizat Qahir ba-meʾah ha-aḥat esreh* [Eleventh-Century Arabic Letters of Jewish Merchants from the Cairo Geniza]. Unpublished PhD thesis, Tel Aviv University.

Bareket, Elinoar. 2017. *Eli Ben Amram and His Companions: Jewish Leadership in the Eleventh-Century Mediterranean Basin*. Eastbourne: Sussex Academic Press.

Blau, Joshua. 1989. *Diqduq ha-ʿAravit ha-Yehudit shel yeme ha-benayim* [A Grammar of Mediaeval Judeo-Arabic]. 2nd ed. Jerusalem: Magnes.

Blau, Joshua. 2006. *Milon le-ṭeqsṭim ʿaraviyim yehudiyim mi-yeme ha-benayim* [A Dictionary of Medieval Judeo-Arabic Texts]. Meqorot u-meḥqarim bi-teḥum leshonot ha-Yehudim. Jerusalem: Academy of the Hebrew Language.

el-Cheikh, Nadia Maria. 2002. "In Search for the Ideal Spouse." In *Journal of the Economic and Social History of the Orient* 45: 179–196.

Cohen, Mark R. 1980. *Jewish Self-Government in Medieval Egypt: The Origins of the Office of Head of the Jews, ca. 1065–1126*. Princeton Studies on the Near East. Princeton: Princeton University Press.

Cohen, Mark R. 2000. "Four Judaeo-Arabic Petitions of the Poor from the Cairo Geniza." In *Jerusalem Studies in Arabic and Islam* 24: 446–471.

Cohen, Mark R. 2002. "Halakha u-meṣiʾut be-ʿinyane ṣedaqa bi-tequfat ha-Genizah [Halacha and Reality in Matters of Charity during the Geniza Period]." In *Ha-Islam we-ʿolamot ha-shezurim bo: qoveṣ maʾamarim le-zikhrah shel Ḥava Laṣarus-Yafe* [The Intertwined Worlds of Islam: Essays in Memory of Hava Lazarus-Yafeh], ed. Naḥem Ilan. Jerusalem: Ben Zvi, 2002: 315–333.

Cohen, Mark R. 2005a. *Poverty and Charity in the Jewish Community of Medieval Egypt*. Jews, Christians and Muslims from the Ancient to the Modern World. Princeton: Princeton University Press.

Cohen, Mark R. 2005b. *The Voice of the Poor in the Middle Ages*. Princeton: Princeton University Press.

al-Dhahabī. 1986. *Siyar aʿlām al-nubalāʾ*, ed. Shuʿayb al-Arnaʾūṭ. 25 vols. Beirut: Muʾassasat al-risāla.

Ergene, Bogaç A. 2003. *Local Court, Provincial Society and Justice in the Ottoman Empire: Legal Practice and Dispute Resolution in Çankırı and Kastamonu (1652–1744)*. Studies in Islamic Law and Society, vol. 17. Leiden: Brill.

Franklin, Arnold E., et al., eds. 2014. *Jews, Christians and Muslims in Medieval and Early Modern Times: A Festschrift in Honor of Mark R. Cohen*. Christians and Jews in Muslim Societies, vol. 2. Leiden: Brill.

Frenkel, Miriam. 2006. *"Ha-ohavim ve-ha-nedivim:" ʿIlit manhiga be-qerev Yehude Aleksandriyah bi-yeme ha-benayim* ["The Compassionate and Benevolent": The Leading Elite in the Jewish Community of Alexandria in the Middle Ages]. Jerusalem: Ben Zvi Institute.

Frenkel, Miriam. 2014. "Pilgrimage and Charity in the Geniza Society." In *Jews, Chris-*

tians and Muslims in Medieval and Early Modern Times, ed. Arnold E. Franklin et al. Leiden: Brill, 59–66.

Friedman, Mordechai A. 1986. *Ribbuy nashim be-Yiśra'el: meqorot ḥadashim mi-Genizat Qahir* [Jewish Polygyny in the Middle Ages]. Tel Aviv: Bialik Institute.

Friedman, Mordechai A. 2016. *Milon ha-'Aravit ha-Yehudit mi-yeme ha-benayim: le-te'udot ha-Genizah shel Sefer Hodu u-le-ṭeqsṭim aḥerim* [A Dictionary of Medieval Judeo-Arabic in the India Book Letters from the Geniza and in Other Texts]. Jerusalem: Ben Zvi Institute.

Gil, Moshe. 1983. *Ereṣ-Yiśra'el ba-tequfah ha-muslemit ha-rishonah (634–1099)* [A History of Palestine 634–1099], vols. 2–3. Pirsume ha-Makhon le-ḥeqer ha-tefuṣot [Publications of the Diaspora Research Institute], vol. 41. Tel Aviv: Tel Aviv University.

Gil, Moshe. 1991. "Ereṣ-Yiśra'el ba-tequfah ha-muslimit ha-rishonah (634–1099): milu'im, he'arot, tiqqunim" [Palestine During the First Muslim Period (634–1099): Additions, Notes, and Corrections]. In *Teuda* 7 (= *Meḥqarim be-mada'e ha-yahadut* [Studies in Judaica]): 281–345.

Gil, Moshe. 1992. *A History of Palestine, 634–1099*. Cambridge: Cambridge University Press.

Gil, Moshe. 1997. *Be-malkhut Yishma'el bi-tequfat ha-ge'onim* [In The Kingdom of Ishmael], 4 vols. Tel Aviv: Tel Aviv University.

Goitein, S[helomo] D[ov]. 1961. "The Local Jewish Community in the Light of the Cairo Geniza." In *Journal of Jewish Studies* 12: 133–158.

Goitein, S[helomo] D[ov]. 1967–1993. *A Mediterranean Society: The Jewish Communities of the Arab World as Portrayed in the Documents of the Cairo Geniza*. 6 vols. Berkeley: University of California Press.

Goitein, S[helomo] D[ov]. 1968. "Misḥar ha-Yehudim ba-Yam ha-Tikhon bi-teḥilat ha-me'ah ha-aḥat eśre (II)" [Jewish Trade in the Mediterranean at the Beginning of the Eleventh Century (II)]. In *Tarbiz* 37: 48–77.

Goitein, S[helomo] D[ov]. 1973. *Letters of Medieval Jewish Traders Translated from the Arabic with Introductions and Notes*. Princeton: Princeton University Press.

Goitein, Shelomo Dov. 1980. *Ha-Yeshuv be-Ereṣ Yisra'el be-reshit ha-Islam u-vi-tequfat ha-Ṣalbanim le'or kitvei ha-Geniza* [Palestinian Jewry in the Early Islamic and Crusaders Times in the Light of the Geniza Documents], ed. Joseph Hacker. Jerusalem: Ben Zvi Institute.

Golb, Norman. 1974. "The Topography of the Jews of Medieval Egypt, Part II." In *Journal of Near Eastern Studies* 33: 116–149.

Goldberg, Jessica. 2012. *Trade and Institutions in the Medieval Mediterranean: The Geniza Merchants and Their Business World*. Cambridge Studies in Economic History. Cambridge: Cambridge University Press.

Goldberg, Jessica. 2014. "Friendship and Hierarchy: Rhetorical Stances in Genizah Mercantile Letters." In *Jews, Christians and Muslims in Medieval and Early Modern Times*, ed. Arnold E. Franklin et al. Leiden: Brill, 271–286.

Humfress, Caroline. 2009. "Law in Practice." In *A Companion to Late Antiquity*, ed. Philip Rousseau. Blackwell Companions to the Ancient World. Chichester: Blackwell, 377–391.

Krakowski, Eve. 2017. *Coming of Age in Medieval Egypt: Female Adolescence, Jewish Law, and Ordinary Culture*. Princeton: Princeton University Press.

Malachi, Zvi. 1966. "Le-ferush ha-milah 'ṣelah' ba-TaNaKH" [On the Meaning of the Word *Ṣelah* In the Bible]. In *Beit Mikra: Journal for the Study of the Bible and Its World* 11.3 (27): 104–110.

Powers, David S. 1991. "Review of *The Anthropology of Justice: Law as Culture in Islamic Society* by Lawrence Rosen." In *Journal of the American Oriental Society* 111: 790–791.

Qoler, Yiṣḥaq. 1969. "Le-hora'at ha-milah 'Selah'" [On the Meaning of the Word *Selah*]. In *Beit Mikra: Journal for the Study of the Bible and Its World* 14.4 (39): 58–76.

Rosen, Lawrence. 2006. "Review of *Dispensing Justice in Islam: Qadis and Their Judgments* by Muhammad Khalid Masud, Rudolph Peters and David Powers and *Intent in Islamic Law: Motive and Meaning in Medieval Sunni Fiqh* by Paul R. Powers." In *Middle East Journal* 60: 820–821.

Rustow, Marina. 2008. "Formal and Informal Patronage among Jews in the Islamic East: Evidence from the Cairo Geniza." In *al-Qanṭara* 29: 341–382.

Rustow, Marina. 2009. "Benefaction (*niʿma*), Gratitude (*shukr*), and the Politics of Giving and Receiving in Letters from the Cairo Geniza." In *Charity and Giving in Monotheistic Religions*, ed. Miriam Frenkel and Yaacov Lev. Studien zur Geschichte und Kultur des islamischen Orients: Beihefte zur Zeitschrift "Der Islam," vol. 22. Berlin: 365–390.

Smail, Daniel Lord. 2003. *The Consumption of Justice: Emotions, Publicity, and Legal Culture in Marseille, 1264–1423*. Conjunctions of Religion and Power in the Medieval Past. Ithaca: Cornell University Press.

Stilt, Kristen. 2011. *Islamic Law in Action: Authority, Discretion, and Everyday Experiences in Mamluk Egypt*. Oxford: Oxford University Press.

Turner, Victor. 1969. *The Ritual Process: Structure and Anti-Structure*. Ithaca: Cornell University Press.

Ullmann, Manfred. 1970. *Wörterbuch der Klassischen Arabischen Sprache, Band I*. Wiesbaden: Otto Harrassowitz.

Weiss, Gershon. 1967. "Documents Written by Hillel Ben Eli: A Study in the Diplomatics of the Cairo Geniza Documents." Unpublished MA thesis, University of Pennsylvania.

Yagur, Moshe. 2012. *Ben Miṣrayim li-Yerushalayim ha-ge'opoliṭiqah shel qehilat Yehude Ashqelon bi-tequfat ha-Genizah* [*The Geopolitics of the Jewish Community of Ascalon during the Classical Geniza Period*]. Unpublished MA thesis, Hebrew University Jerusalem.

Yagur, Moshe. 2017. "Zehut datit u-gevulot qehilatiyim be-ḥevrat ha-Genizah (me'ot 10–13): gerim, 'avadim, mumarim" [Religious Identity and Communal Boundaries in Geniza Society (10th–13th centuries): Proselytes, Slaves, Apostates]. Unpublished PhD thesis, Hebrew University Jerusalem.

Zinger, Oded. 2014. *Women, Gender and Law: Martial Disputes According to Documents from the Cairo Geniza.* Unpublished PhD thesis, Princeton University.

Zinger, Oded. 2018. "'She Aims to Harass Him': Jewish Women in Muslim Legal Venues in Medieval Egypt." In *AJS Review* 42: 159–192

PART 4

Mamlūk Documents

CHAPTER 8

How Documents Were Quoted in *Inshāʾ* Literature: A Comparison of P.Aragon 145 and Its Quotation by al-Qalqashandī

Daniel Potthast

1 The Historical Background of the 1293 Mamlūk-Aragonese Treaty

Not only the social and economic but also the political history of the medieval Arab world suffers from a lack of original documents. Though in Egypt thousands of documents have been found by excavation, and archives from the Fāṭimid period onward have been preserved in their historical context—such as the collections of St. Catherine's Monastery in the Sinai, several monasteries in Jerusalem, the Ḥaram al-Sharīf Collection, and the findings at the Umayyad Mosque in Damascus—vast periods of Arab history and many regions of the Arab world can only be analyzed by using literary sources. The *shurūṭ* (contract stipulation) and *inshāʾ* (composition manual) literature—works that defined the norms of writing legal and administrative documents and served as training books for prospective judges and secretaries—might serve as a replacement, since these manuals quote exemplary documents believed to be non-fictive. But we do not know in which ways the authors of these manuals altered the documents that they inserted into their works.[1] Though they claim to quote correctly—and though we can assume that the documents were not adapted to accord with the theory of Islamic Law or similar norms because they were specimens of documents for use in real life—we cannot not know for certain how precise the quotations are unless we can compare the original documents and their quotations.

Especially for the large numbers of legal documents about quotidian matters (sales, marriage and divorce contracts, receipts, written obligations, etc.), it is unlikely that we would find a pair of an original and its quotation. More promising are the administrative documents quoted in the *inshāʾ* literature. Docu-

1 Some literary quotations of documents were forged in an official chancery to show the skills of the chancery officials or the power of the issuer without being used as legal documents, while others were reworked originals from a totally different context; see Broadbridge, 2000: 86; Yüksel Muslu 2013: 253–254.

 | DOI:10.1163/9789004443877_009

ments from the circle of the ruler were rare, so a relatively high percentage of them were quoted. Strangely enough, a pair from among these documents has been known for more than 70 years without being analyzed properly: (1) a pact of mutual assistance between the Mamlūk sultan al-Ashraf Khalīl (1290–1293) and the Aragonese king Jaime II (1291–1327), concluded in 1293, is quoted by al-Qalqashandī in his *Ṣubḥ al-aʿshà* (Dawn of the Nightblind), and (2) the original is partly preserved in the Archivo de la Corona de Aragón in Barcelona. The edition of the document by Maximiliano Alarcón y Santón and Ramón García de Linares (1940, further quoted as P.Aragon 145) is based on al-Qalqashandī's quotation according to the modern print edition[2] and refers only in some cases to the major differences between the original and its quotation.[3]

What sources do we have? Al-Qalqashandī's text claims to be the indirect quotation of the complete treaty. His own *Vorlage* (template) was a quotation in the now lost *Tadhkīrat al-labīb wa-nuzhat al-adīb* by Muḥammad b. al-Mukarram,[4] secretary in the *dīwān al-inshāʾ* (chancery) during the reigns of sultans Qalāwūn (1279–1290) and al-Ashraf Khalil (1290–1293). From the original treaty in Barcelona, only the second half is preserved. In P.Aragon 145, two further fragments are described; they seem to have been lost in the eighty years since the 1940 edition of the document. According to the archive's statement, Maximiliano Alarcón y Santón wrote in unpublished notes that both these fragments had been glued to the back of the treaty. In addition to the original treaty and its quotation, we possess a quotation, in Ibn ʿAbd al-Ẓāhir's biography of the sultan Qalāwūn, of a 1290 treaty concluded between Aragon and the Mamlūks.[5] Since this treaty was concluded by al-Ashraf Khalīl's father Qalāwūn and Jaime's brother Alfonso III, it has, of course, a different narration of the negotiation and was mediated by other ambassadors. Also, the territories attributed to the Mamlūk Empire are less, since the last remains of the Latin Kingdom were conquered in the years between the 1290 and the 1293 treaty. The text of the clauses in the 1290 treaty accords with the text of the later treaty, however, so that it is a help for amendments of sections lost in that treaty.[6]

---

2 Al-Qalqashandī 1919: 63–70. The quotation of the treaty had already been edited by Amari 1883. Since both editions use the same manuscript, there are only minor differences.

3 The editions in Alarcón y Santón 1940/P.Aragon render the text of the documents carefully with only small slips of pen. However, the original vocalization has been left out and there are next to no metadata. Except for two fragments, in P.Aragon 145 only al-Qalqashandī's text or a mixed text was edited. Based on this, no diplomatic analysis is possible.

4 Al-Qalqashandī 1919: 70.

5 Ibn ʿAbd al-Ẓāhir 1961: 156–164.

6 Holt 1992 uses al-Qalqashandī's quotation in the opposite direction to gain a better understanding of the 1290 treaty.

The content of the 1293 treaty resembles that of late medieval commercial treaties between Islamic and Christian powers: its clauses codify the rights of Catalan merchants in Alexandria. This is exceptional because the Pope reacted to the 1291 Mamlūk conquest of Akko (Acre) with a trade embargo that most European powers did not override until the first decades of the 14th century. Ever since Aragon's 1282 conquest of Sicily against the Pope's will, however, it had been an enemy of the Papal States and the victim of a crusade (Aragonese Crusade 1284–1285), so that a trade agreement with the Mamlūks was an attempt to monopolize the Levantine trade. Because the possibility of a new crusade still existed, the treaty includes also several political and military clauses. The Aragonese king obligates himself to inform the sultan about any developments, to hinder them, and even to attack the organizers. Therefore, the agreement is an exchange of trade privileges in Egypt (and Syria) for military help—in case of a crusade—that divides the Latins and could even establish a second front in Europe.

Since Aragon and its enemies—France, the papacy, the Anjous—ended in 1295 their long lingering conflict (at the Treaty of Anagni), the 1293 Mamlūk-Aragonese treaty evidently had no great influence on their relations. Later Mamlūk-Aragonese relations focused only on intensifying their trade exchange.

The fact that the 1293 treaty was concluded without any temporal delimitation contradicts Islamic Law, which allows only a length of ten years (mostly interpreted as solar years).[7] We can appreciate this fact as a hint of correct quotation, since al-Qalqashandī does not alter the text. But since the Mamlūks had no opportunity after the conquest of Akko to expand into Christian territories, most of their treaties were concluded without delimitation[8]—other than those with the Andalusian and Maghrebian empires[9]—so that this contradiction to the theoretical ideals of Islamic Law was apparently not known by the secretaries of the *dīwān al-inshāʾ*.

7 Khadduri 1955: 220–222; Lohlker 2006: 23–38. The duration of a treaty is often explicitly stated in solar years (*aʿwām shamsīya*).

8 P.RuizOrsattiTratadoDePaz (= P.Aragon 154), P.WansbroughTreatyFlorence; P.WansbroughCommercialPrivileges.

9 *Three years*: P.Aragon 75; *four years*: P.Aragon 30; *five years*: P.Aragon 15; 27; 114; 161; P.AragonGranada pp. 325–329 (= P.MasalaMartino = P.Labartatratado); *ten years*: P.SilvestredeSacyGènes 1 (= P.AmariGenova 1 = P.BaudenDueTrattati 1); P.Aragon 116; P.Flor.Arab. 30; P.ChampollionDocuments XXXVII 5 (= P.SultanMérinide); P.AragonGranada pp. 298–300; P.Aragon. 140bis; *15 years*: P.SilvestredeSacyTraité; *20 years*: P.SilvestredeSacyGènes 2 (= P.AmariGenova 2 = P.BaudenDueTrattati 2); *30 years*: P.Flor.Arab. 38; P.RiberaTratado; *limited to the lifetimes of both signatories*: P.Aragon 1; *unlimited*: P.Aragon 3; P.Flor.Arab. 34; 35; 36.

The treaty's information about the Christian signatories is also problematic, since it refers not only to Jaime II but also to all the Christian empires on the Iberian Peninsula as partners. Next to Jaime II, his brothers Pedro, governor of Barcelona, and Alfonso, governor of Sicily, and his brothers-in-law Sancho, king of Castile, and Alfonso, pretender in Portugal, are included. Castile is understood as a most important kingdom with sovereignty (*kafāla*) over Aragon and Portugal. Several undisputed Portuguese or Aragonese territories, such as Valencia or the Algarve, were attributed to Castile. At the time the treaty was concluded, a civil war took place in Castile and Aragon in which the Castilian king Sancho was allied with the Portuguese king Dinis and not the pretender Alfonso mentioned in the treaty.[10] Since the treaty was negotiated with Aragonese ambassadors who probably spoke Arabic, it might be supposed that the literary transmission of the document bungled this part of the treaty, but the contemporaneous Catalan translation confirms these mistakes and obscurities.[11]

The 1293 treaty offers a very reduced formulary; it lacks any signs of corroboration—no *ʿalāma* or *mustanad* (a formula *ḥasaba l-marsūmi l-sharīfi*)—so that its legal validity is not assured. It probably was concluded by an oath as a performative speech act, as was the 1290 treaty, where the oath is quoted by Ibn ʿAbd al-Ẓāhir. The text of oaths was rarely quoted in treaties; instead it was written on a second document. The oath for the Christian could be performed by the ambassadors or handed in at a later time in written form. Since al-Qalqashandī explains that this treaty is the only one quoted by him that accords with the requirements of good chancery texts,[12] we can assume that the lack of any sign of corroboration was standard in peace treaties.

2 Parts of P.Corona de Aragón.inv. 145

The treaty consists of the following parts, in which the registry remark, invocation (complete in both versions), and (partial) protocol were preserved in the now lost fragment that Maximiliano Alarcón y Santón and Ramón García de Linares edited. The narration and clauses 1–4 are only preserved in

10 Holt 1990: 23–24 interprets the "Alfonso" not as a name but as a title used by the Mamlūk chancery for Iberian rulers, and refers to P.Aragon 146 as single clear documentary evidence for this use.

11 Masiá de Ros 1951: 166–270.

12 Al-Qalqashandī 1917: 70–71.

al-Qalqashandī's quotation. Clauses 5–16 and the eschatocol (closing protocol) are preserved in both versions.

Registry remark: An identification as an image of the original treaty (*ṣūrat hudna mubāraka*) naming the contractors. Probably only the treaty in the Mamlūk archive was understood as original, while the executed copies for the other signatories were designated as *ṣuwar*, or "copies."

Invocation: Basmala.

Protocol: The protocol identifies the kind of document and the signatories. The treaty names itself an *istiqrār al-mawadda wa-l-muṣādaqa*, "agreement of love and friendship." Interreligious treaties concluded by medieval Muslim rulers, especially when they included political and military parts, were legitimated by the friendship of the rulers. Since the 1293 treaty transgresses the boundaries of Islamic Law, this designation was preferred to the normal *ʿaqd al-ṣulḥ*, "an agreement on an armistice."[13]

Narration: A narration describes the circumstances of the negotiations, mentions the names of the Aragonese ambassadors, and lists the Christian signatories, while in parts 1 and 3 only Jaime is mentioned as partner of al-Ashraf Khalīl. The date of the treaty's conclusion is specified according to both the Christian (January 29, 1292)[14] and the Islamic calendar (Ṣafar 19, 692).

Clause 1: The most important clauses (for the Mamlūks) follow. At first, the territories of the Mamlūk Empire are defined,[15] and it is stated that within their borders the Aragonese will attack or harm no one.

Clause 2 defines the territories of Jaime II, in which any references to the other Iberian empires are missing. In a further inconsistency, however, the list includes the sovereign kingdom of Mallorca. It is stated that within their borders the Mamlūks will attack or harm no one.

13 Examples for the designation as *ʿaqd al-ṣulḥ* are P.Flor.Arab. 29, 30, 34, 38, as *kitāb al-ṣulḥ* P.Aragon 116, 140bis, as *kitāb muṣālaḥa wa-muʿāqada* P.Flor.Arab. 46, P.BaudenDueTrattati 1 and 2. All other peace treaties follow models not described in the *inshāʾ* literature.

14 Since in medieval Aragon the new year started with the feast of the annunciation (March 25th), this date correlates with January 29, 1293 in the modern calendar!

15 Ifrīqīya is mentioned as part of the empire. Since Aragon was interested in it to consolidate its rule of the Western Mediterranean, the Mamlūks included it to avoid conflicts in the case of a possible expansion to the west.

Clause 3 states that Aragon will fight the Pope, Genoa, Venice, the Knights Hospitaller, the Knights Templar, and the Frankish and Byzantine kings in the case of a war against the Mamlūks.

Clause 4 states that Aragon will not support its own allies if they participate in a war against the Mamlūks.

Clause 5 settles the problem of shipwrecks. The international treaties of the Late Middle Ages replaced regulations of customary law or Islamic Law[16] that allowed the rifling of the possessions of the shipwrecked yet also obligated their subjects to help protect and assist them.[17]

Clause 6 manages the handling of belongings of merchants who died on their travels. Their inheritance had to be restored to their ruler.[18]

Clause 7 prohibits piracy, a main problem of trans-Mediterranean trade,[19] and stipulates the rulers must restore goods stolen by pirates who are their subjects.

Clause 8 adds to the previous clause that the rulers will punish their subjects if they breach the treaty's clauses.[20]

Clause 9 forbids trade embargoes against the Mamlūks. Especially, the export of the strategic resources of iron, wood, and coal had to be allowed. Since these were necessary for warfare and the construction of ships, their export to Islamic empires had otherwise often been restricted.[21]

---

16 According to Islamic Law, foreigners had to enter the Islamic realm by an official way to be counted as *musta'min* and have the right of protection. Heffening 1925/1975: 37; Samarrai 1980: 13–14.

17 For further examples of similar regulations, see Holt 1995: 68; 83; 114.

18 For parallel clauses in treaties transmitted in literature: Holt 1995: 84; 101; in documents: P.ViladrichSultán 257–263.

19 Examples of letters that deal with the compensation for pirate attacks are P.Aragon 5; 42; 51; 52; 54; 57; 58; 59; 60; 61; 66; 103; 110; 111; 118; 120; 121; 129; 130 and 131.

20 This clause was for a long time a normal component of Arabic-Frankish treaties; Köhler 1991: 403.

21 Halm 1987: 212. In normal peace treaties and commercial agreements, forbidden goods (*mamnūʿāt*) were usually excluded. In P.Aragon 15 these are defined as horses (*khayl*) and weapons (*silāḥ*); there exists no treaty that forbids trading wood, iron, and coal. In military alliances, the exchange of mercenaries and war galleys was defined by their costs.

Clause 10 obligates the Christian signatories to free Muslim slaves. In the Late Middle Ages, Barcelona was a center of trade in Muslim prisoners, who were traded as slaves or held for ransom.

Clause 11 states that Islamic Law is the legal base of all business transactions in the Mamlūk Empire and that disputes must be settled according to it.

Clause 12 states that the belongings of Muslim merchants on Christian ships are to be protected. Possible losses must be restored by the Aragonese king. The treaty does not codify the legal basis of business transactions in Aragon. Like most medieval Arabic-Frankish trade agreements, the treaty seems to assume that overseas transport is operated mainly by European merchants.

Clause 13 forbids all subjects of the signatories to emigrate permanently to another empire, unless the emigrant converts to the other religion. Both empires had minorities of the other faith whose emigration was forbidden. Since the Aragonese Muslims provided an above-average part of the tax income, Jaime II had a major interest in avoiding their emigration. Their existence was well known in Egypt, and Mamlūk sultans advocated the rights of the Aragonese Mudéjares (Muslims permitted to live under Christian rule) in several letters. A major diplomatic goal of contemporaneous Maghrebian and Andalusian rulers was achieving permission for the Mudéjares to emigrate; accurate regulation of their taxes is inexplicit, since those contracts do not mention their amounts.[22]

Clause 14 settles Christian pilgrimage to the Holy Land. While in all other clauses the Christians signatories are mentioned as the "king Don Jaime and two brothers and his two brothers-in-law," the treaty grants only the three kings (Jaime and his brothers-in-law) the right to issue passports for the pilgrimage. The regulation of the pilgrimage often served as legitimation of treaties with non-Muslims, since the Christian signatory could justify himself by pointing to the fact that he had enabled the visits to Jerusalem.

---

22 P.Aragon 15.15: *an lā tamnaʿū man arāda l-khurūdj ilā arḍ al-muslimīn mina l-mudajjanīn al-sākinīn bi-arḍikum bi-ahlihim wa-awlādihim wa-an yubāḥa lahumu l-wuṣūl ilā arḍinā āminīn marfūʿan ʿanhum al-iʿtirāḍ min ghayr shayʾ yalzamuhum illā l-maghram al-muʿtād ʿalā mā djarat bihi l-ʿāda min ghayr ziyāda ʿalā dhālika*, "You do not hold off in your land Mudéjares living in your land who want to emigrate with their families and children to Muslim land. You allow them to arrive safely to our land without hindrance for them. The usual dues according to the old custom without any raise are necessary for them."

Clause 15 repeats the rules of clauses 1–4.

Clause 16 fixes the customs paid as the usual ones. Later commercial agreements often specify the amounts,[23] but here, most probably the normal tariffs established by customary Islamic Law were applied.[24] As trade places, Alexandria and Damiette are mentioned; Syria seems to be irrelevant for trade, probably because of the military conflicts with the Crusaders. Except for the pilgrimage to Jerusalem, no traveling inside the Mamlūk Empire seems to be permitted for Europeans.[25]

The eschatocol includes the information of the unlimited duration of the treaty, repeats the dating according to the Christian and Islamic calendars, and ends with the usual closing formulae (*istiṯnāʾ*, *taṣliya*, *ḥasbala*), yet has no authorization.

3 Edition of P.Corona de Aragón.inv. 145

P.Corona de Aragón.inv. 145
Figures 8.1–8
216 cm high × 13 cm wide
Ṣafar 19, 692 (= Jan. 29, 1293)/Janīr 29, 1292 (= Jan. 29, 1293!)
Cairo

The treaty is written on a paper scroll consisting of eight sheets. They are agglutinated after lines 10, 26, 42, 57, 74, 92 and 106. The height of a single sheet adds up to 32 cm, of which 2 cm are used as a glue flap. The width adds up to 13 cm, i.e., 1/4 ḏirāʿ. In most other preserved examples, the Mamlūks used larger formats (1/3 ḏirāʿ)[26] for international agreements, but even in letters the formats

23 E.g., P.Flor.Arab. 35; 36; P.RuizOrsattiTratadoDePaz (= P.Aragon 154).

24 According to Islamic Law, merchants from outside the Abode of Islam (*Dār al-islām*) had to pay an entry tax (*maks al-samāḥ*), a tax of 2 percent on money and the 20 percent *khums* tax on goods. If the merchant traveled to a city in the inland, especially Cairo, he had to pay the *wādjib al-dhimma*, an internal tariff of 10 percent. The "taxes according the custom" varied considerably and came along with other dues. Because of the importance of long-distance trade for the Mamlūk Empire, the tax rate dropped to ca. 10 percent at the end of the 15th century. See Labib 1965: 234–260.

25 Later treaties usually include clauses on traveling to Damascus for trade purposes and the permission to travel to Cairo for an audience at the Noble Portal.

26 P.ElezovicSpomenici 134; P.WansbroughTreatyFlorence.

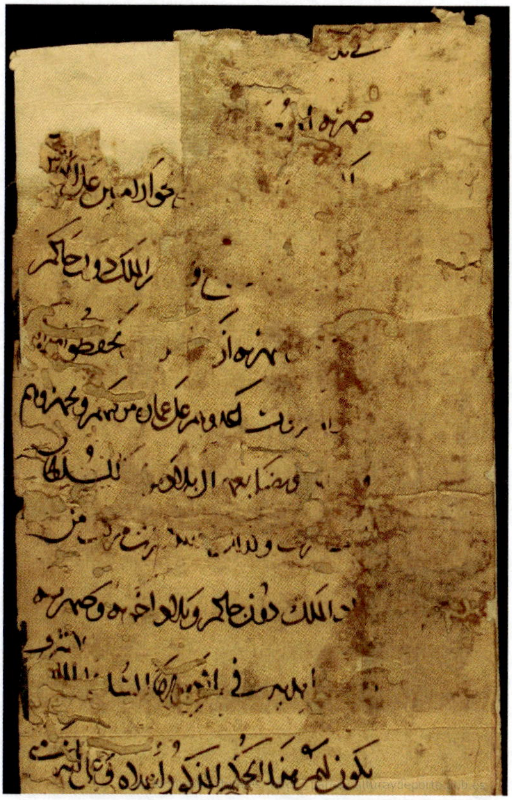

FIGURE 8.1
P.Corona de Aragón.inv. 145

vary considerably, so it can be assumed that there was no specified format for treaties with and letters for non-Muslims.

The treaty is glued on paper, so the verso is masked. For comparison with al-Qalqashandī's quotation of the treaty, this means that approximately half of the scroll is lost. In the preserved second half, the reading is complicated by holes at the left margin. The ink is partially abraded (especially in lines 1–5).

Like most Mamlūk documents of diplomatic exchange with Western Europe, the text is written with almost all diacritical dots and even some vocalization marks (*fatḥa* often, *ḍamma* and *shadda* sometimes, *kasra* rarely). If a word lacks dots in the original, I mention this in the text critical apparatus (in the next section below). All *hamza*s have been supplemented by me; exceptions are registered in the apparatus.

Specifics of the writing are: *alif*, *dāl*, *dhāl*, *rāʾ*, and *zāy* are often connected to the left. *Ḥāʾ*, *djīm*, and *ḥāʾ* resemble, especially in final form, the letter *ʿayn*. The upper stroke of medial *kāf* is written separately and resembles *fatḥa*. *Sīn* is occasionally marked by a little half-circle above.

[فـ]ـي بـ[ـلاد الملك دون جا كم وبلاد أخويه أو] صهْريه ا[.]...ُ َ[..يكون كل من فيها من] اَ[لتجار والبحارة والمال والمماليك والـ]ـجوَار آمنين عَلى الأ[نفـ]ـس [والأموال والبضائـ]ـع و[يلتز]م المَلك دون جَا كَم [أو أخويه أو صـ]ـهريه أَن [يخفروهم و]يَحفظُوا مرا[كـ]ـبـ[ـهم] [وأموالهم] ويساعدوهم عَلى عمارة مركبهم ويجهزوهم [أموالهم] وبضَائعهم إلى بلَاد مو[لانا] السُلطان [الملك الأشـ]ـرف وكذلك [إذا انـ]ـكسرت مركب من [بلـ]ـاد المَلك دُون جا كم وَبلاد أخويه وَصهريه [ومعـ]ـاهديه في بلاد مولاَنَا السُد[ـطان] الـ[ـمـ]ـلك [ا]لأشرف يكون لَهُم هَذَا الحُكم المذكُور أعلاه وَعلى أنه مَتى مَات أَحدٌ من تجَار المسْلمِين وَمن نصَارى

1 [فـ]ـى دـ[ـلاد 2 صهْريه 3 والـ]ـحوَار امبين 4 حَا كَم 5 [صـ]ـهريه ان يَحفظُوا 6 وساعدوهم عماره مركهم ويحهزوهم 7 بضَايعهم الى بلَاد 8 مركب 9 وَبلاد اخويه وَصهريه 10 فى بلَاد مولانا [ا]لاشرف 11 نكون انه مى 12 تجَار

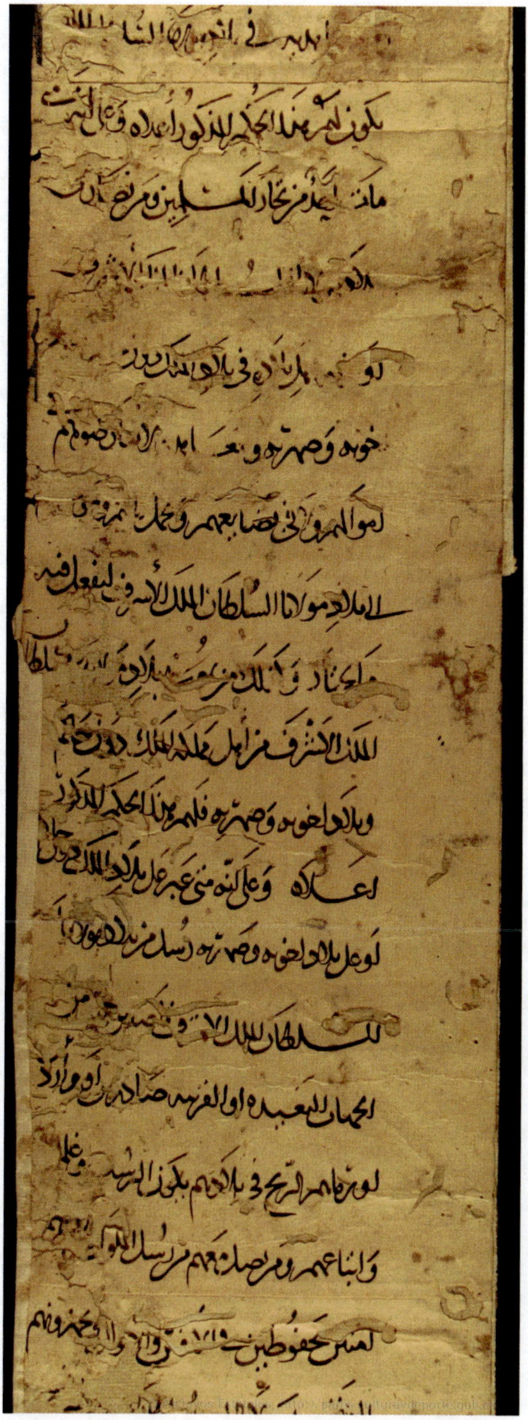

FIGURE 8.2
P.Corona de Aragón.inv. 145

13 [بـ]ـلَاد مولانا السُلطَان الـ[ـمـ]ـلك الأشرف

14 اَو [ذ]مة [أ]هلِ بلَاده في بلَاد الملك دون [جا كم وبلاد]

15 [أ]خويه وَصِهْريه ومعَاهد[يه] لا يـ[ـعَـ]ـارضوهم في

16 أموَالهم ولَا في بضَايعهم وَيحمل ما [لـ]ـهم ومَو[جودهم]

17 إلى بلادِ مَولانا السُلطَان المَلك الأشرف ليفعل فيه

18 مَا يختار وَكذلك من يمُوت ببلَاد مَو[لانا الـ]ـسُلطان

19 الملك الأَشْرَف من أهل مَملكة المَلك دُون جَاكم

20 وبلَاد أخويه وَصِهْريه فلهم هذَا الحكم المذكورْ

21 أعلَاه وَعَلى أنّه متى عَبر عَلى بلَادِ الملك دون جا[كم]

22 أَو على بلاد أخويه وَصِهْريه رُسل من بلاد مولانَا

23 السلطَان الملك الأ[شر]ف قاصدين جـ[ـهة] من

24 الجهات البَعيدة أو القريبَة صَادر[يـ]ـن أَو واردين

25 أو رماهم الرِّيح في بِلَادهم يكون الرسُل وغلما[نهم]

26 وَأتباعهم وَمن يصل مَعهم من رُسل الملوك [أو غير]هم

27 آمنين محَفُوظين في الأَ[نـ]ـفس والأ[مـ]ـوال ويجهزونهم

---

13 مولانا الاشرف 14 [ذ]مه بلَاده فى بلَاد 15 [أ]خوبه وصَهْربه فى د[ـعَـ]ـارضوهم 16 اموَالهم فى وَيحمل 17 الى بلادِ مَولانا الأسرف لىفعل فىه 18 ىحتار ىمُوت ببلَاد الـ[ـسلطان 19 الاَشْرَف مَملكه حَاكم 20 وبلَاد اخوبه وَصهْربه المدكورْ 21 اعَلَاه بلَاد دون حا[كم] 22 اَو بلاد اخوبه وَصهْربه بلاد مولانَا 23 الا[شر]ف 24 الحهاب البعيده او القرىبه اَو واردىن 25 او الرّىح فى بِلَادهم 26 ىصل 27 امنىن محَفوطين فى الاَ[نـ]ـفس والا[مـ]ـوال ىحزونهم

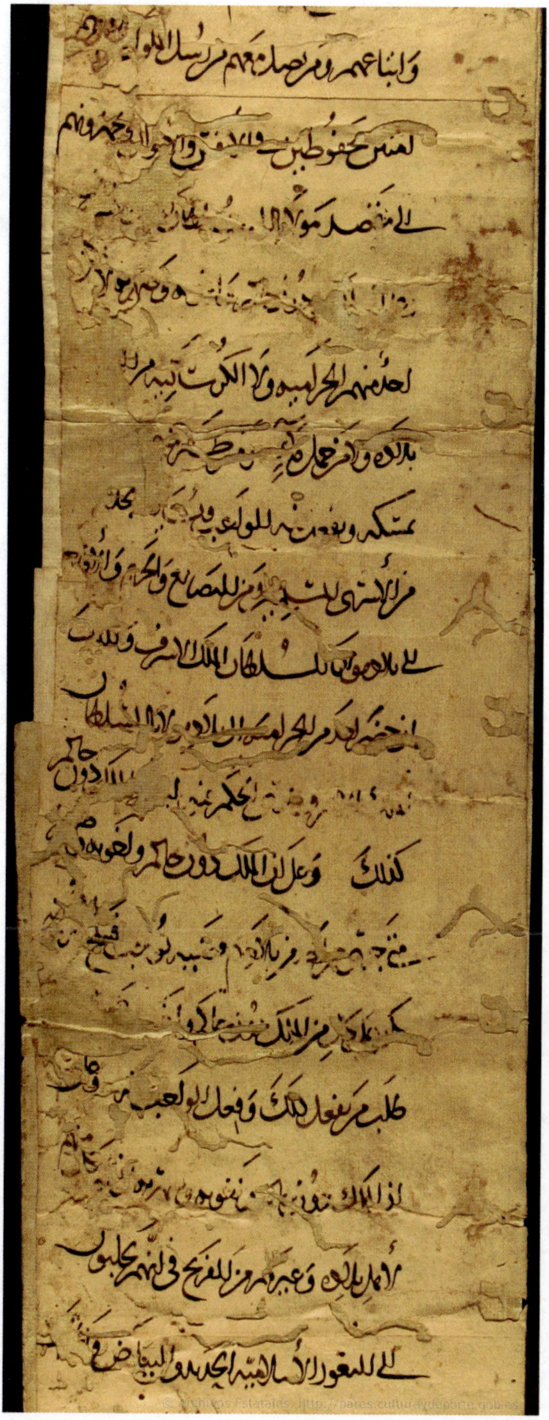

FIGURE 8.3
P.Corona de Aragón.inv. 145
© ARCHIVO DE LA CORONA DE ARAGÓN, BARCELONA

إلى مَقصد موَلَانا السُلطَان [الملك الأشرف] [وعلى أن] الـ[ـملك] دُون [جا كَم] وَأ[خويـ]ـه وَصهريه لا [يمكن] أحدٌ منهم الحرَامية ولَا الكُرسَالية من الـ[ـتزود من] بلَاده ولَا من حمل مآءٍ وَمـ[ـن] ظَـ[ـفـ]ـر به [من الحرامية] يمسكه ويفعل فـ[ـيـ]ـه الواجب ويـُ[ـسَير ما يـ]ـجد[ه معهم] من الأسْرى المسْلمين وَمن البَضائع وَالحرَ[يـ]ـم وَالأ[ولا د] إلى بلاد مولانا السُلطَان الملك الأشرف وَ[كذلـ]ـكَ إن حضَر أحَد من الحرامية إلى بلَاد مولانا السُلطان [الملك] الأشرف [يجري] الحكم [فيه] لبـ[ـلاد ا]لـ[ـمـ]ـلك دون جا كم كذلكَ وَعلَى أن الملك دُون جا كم وأخويه وصـ[ـهريـ]ـه متَى جرى من أَ[حد] مِن بلَادِهم قَضية تُوجب فَسخ ا[لمهاد]نة كـ[ـان] على كلٍ من الملك دُون جا كم وأَ[خويه وصهريه] طَلب مَن يفعل ذَلكَ وَفعل الوَاجب [فيـ]ـه وعلى أن المَلك دُون [جا كم] وأخويه وصهْريه [يفسح] كل منهم لأهلِ بلَادِه وَغَيرهم منَ الفَرنج في أَنَّهم يجلبون إلى الثغور الإسلاميّة الحَديد والبياض وَالخَ[ـشـ]ـب وغير ذلكَ وعلَى أنَّه متى أسر أحدٌ من المسلمين

28 الى مَولانا 29 وَا[خويـ]ـه وَصهريه 30 احدٌ الحرَاميه الكُرسَاليه 31 بلَاده طَـ[ـفـ]ـر 32 بمسكه وبفعل فـ[ـبـ]ـه الواحب 33 البَضاىع 34 الى بلاد مولانا الاسرف 35 ان احَد الحرامىَه الى بلَاد مولانا 36 الاسرف حاكم 37 ان حا كم اخوبه 38 اَ[حد] بلَادِهم قَضيه بُوجب فَسح ا[لمهاد]نه 39 حا كم واَ[خويه] 40 بفعل ذَلكَ الوَاحب 41 ان واخوبه وصهْربه 42 بلَادِه وَغَيرهم الفَرىح فى انَّهم يحلبون 43 الى البغور الأسلاميّه الحَدىد البياض وَالخَ[ـشـ]ـب 44 وعير انَّه اسر احدٌ المسلمن

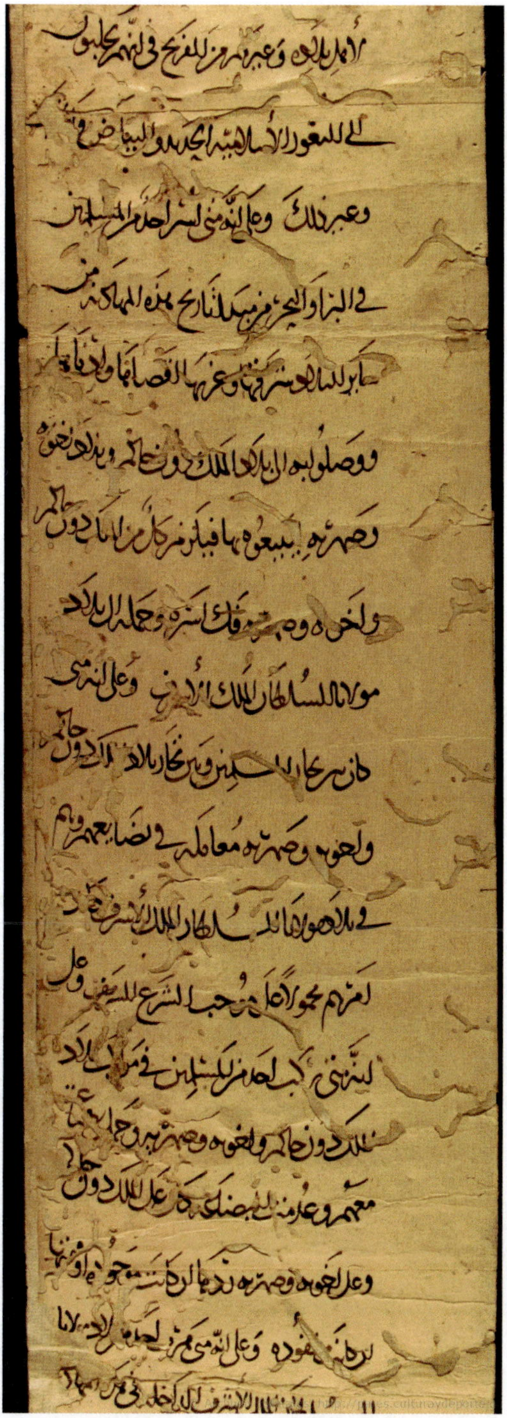

FIGURE 8.4
P.Corona de Aragón.inv. 145

في البر أو البحْر من مَبدأ تاريخ هذه المهادنة من سَاير البلَاد شَرقها وغربهَا أقصَاهَا وأدنَاهَا ووَصلُوا به إلى بلَاد المَلك دُون جاكم وبلاد أخويه وَصهْريه لِيَبيعُوه بها فيلَزم كلٌّ من الملك دون جاكم وأخو[يـ]ـه وصهر[يـ]ـه فَك أَسْره وحَمله إلى بلَاد مولانا السُلطَان المَلك الأشرف وعَلى أنه متى كان بين تجار المسلمين وَبين تجَار بلاد [المـ]ـلك دون جاكم وأخويه وَصهْريه مُعامَلة في بضَائهم وهم في بلَاد مولانَا السُلطَان الملك الأشرف كان أَمْرهم محمولًا علَى مُوجب الشَرع الشَريف وعلى أَنَّه متى ركب أحَد منَ المسْلمين في مَراكب بلَاد المَلك دُون جاكم وأخويه وصهْريه وَحمل بضاعتـ[ـه] معَهُم وعُدمت البضَاعة كـ[ـان] عَلى المَلك دون جاكم وعلى أَخويه وصهْريه ردَها إن كَانَت مَوجُودة أو [قيمـ]ـتها إن كَانَت مـ[ـفـ]ـقُودة وَعلى أنّه مَتى هرب أَحد من [بـ]ـلاد مولانا

45 فى او مَبدا تارىح المهادنه 46 سَاير البلاد وغرىهَا اقصَاهَا وادنَاهَا 47 الى حاكم وبلاد اخوىه 48 وَصهرىه لِيَبيعُوه ىها كلٌّ حاكم 49 وأخـ[ـيـ]ـه اَسْره الى ىلَاد 50 مولانا الأسرف انه مى 51 ىس ىحار المسلمىن وَىس ىحَار ىلاد دون حاكم 52 واخوىه وَصهْرىه مُعامَله فى ىضَايهم 53 فى ىلاد مولانا الأسرف 54 اَمْرهم مُوحب السَرىف 55 انَّه احَد المسْلمين فى ىلَاد 56 حاكم واخوىه ىضاعتـ[ـه] 57 البضَاعه حاكم 58 اَخوىه وصهْرىه كَانَت مَوحُوده او 59 ان كانَت مـ[ـفـ]ـقُوده انه مَى هرب اَحد مولانا

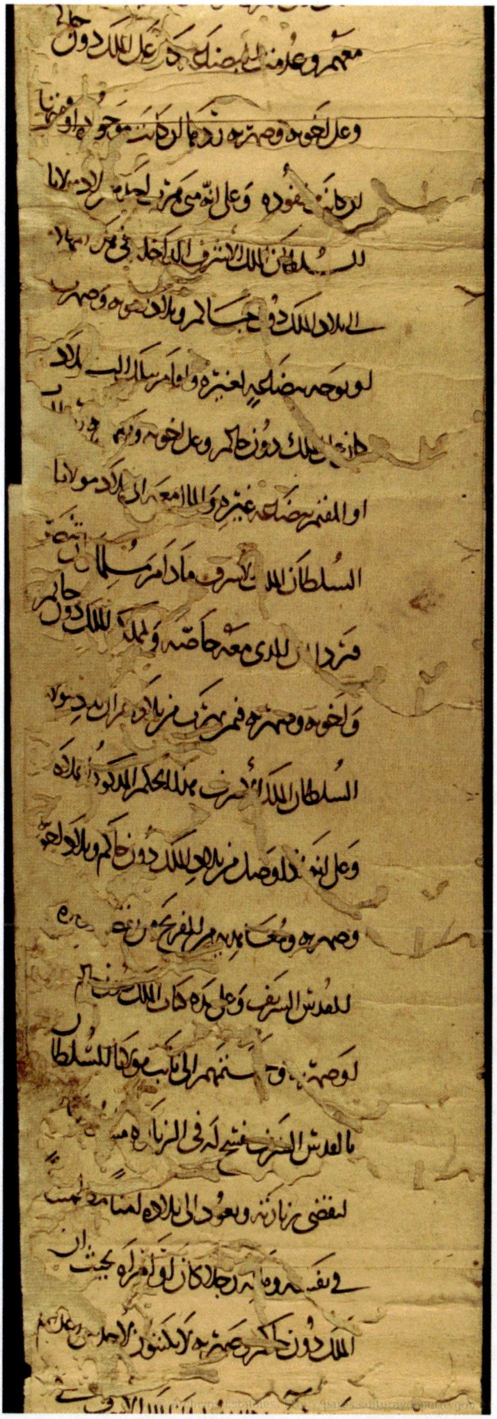

FIGURE 8.5
P.Corona de Aragón.inv. 145
© ARCHIVO DE LA CORONA DE ARAGÓN, BARCELONA

60 السُلطَان الملك الأشرف الداخلة في هَذ[ه الـ]ـمهاد[نة]
61 إلى بلاد المَلك دُون جَا كم وبلاد أ[خـ]ـويه وَصهريه
62 أو توَجه ببضَاعة لغيّره وأقَامَ بتلك البلَاد
63 كان على الملك دُون جا كم وعلى أخويه وَصهـ[ـريـ]ـه ر[د الهار]ب
64 أو المقيم ببضَاعة غيْره وَالمال معَه إلى بلَاد مولانا
65 السُلطَان الملك الأشرف مَا دَامَ مُسلِماً إن تنَصّر
66 فيَرد الـ[ـما]ل الذي مَعهُ خَاصّة وَلمملكـ[ـة] الملك دون جا كم
67 وَأخَويه وصهْريه فيمن يَهْرب من بلَادهم إلى بلادِ [مـ]ـولا[نا]
68 السُلطان المَلك الأشرف هذا الحكم المذكُور أعلَاه
69 وَعلى أنه إذا وَصل من بلادِ الملك دُون جا كم وبلَاد أخو[يه]
70 وصهريه ومُعَاهِديـ[ـن] من الفرنج من يقصـ[ـد ز]يارة
71 القُدسْ الشَريف وَعلى [يـَ]ـده كتَاب الملك دُون جا كم
72 أو صهْر[يه] و[خـ]ـتَمهم إلى نَائب مولَانا السُلطَان
73 بالقدس الشَريف [يـ]ـفسَح لَه في الزيارة مسـ[ـموحا]
74 ليقضي زيارَته ويعُود إلى بلاده آمناً مطمئناً
75 في نَفسه وَمالِه رجلا كانَ أَوْ امْرأَة بحيث ان
76 المَلك دُون جا كم وصَهْريه لَا يكتبون لأحد من أعد[ائـ]ـهم

---

60 الاشرف الداخله فى 61 الى بلاد وبلاد ا[خـ]ـوبه وَصهربه 62 او بوَحه بضَاعهٍ لغيّره واقَامَ سَلك البلاد 63 حا كم اخوبه [الهار]ب 64 او المقم بضَاعه الى بلَاد مولانا 65 الأسرف ان 66 فيَرد الدى خَاصّه حا كم 67 وَاخَوبه وصهْربه فمن يَهْرب بلَادهم الى بلادِ اعلَاه 68 الأسرف المدكور 69 أنه اذا بلادِ حا كم وبلَاد اخو[يه] 70 وصهربه الفرنج نقصـ[ـد] [ز]باره 71 القْدسْ السَريف كتاب حا كم 72 اَو الى نَاىب مولَانا 73 بالقدس السَريف فى الزبَاره 74 لىقضى زبارَته وبعُود الى بلاده امناً مطمساً 75 فى نَفسه اَوْ امْراَه بحيث 76 حا كم وصَهْربه يكتبون لا حد اعد[ائـ]ـهم

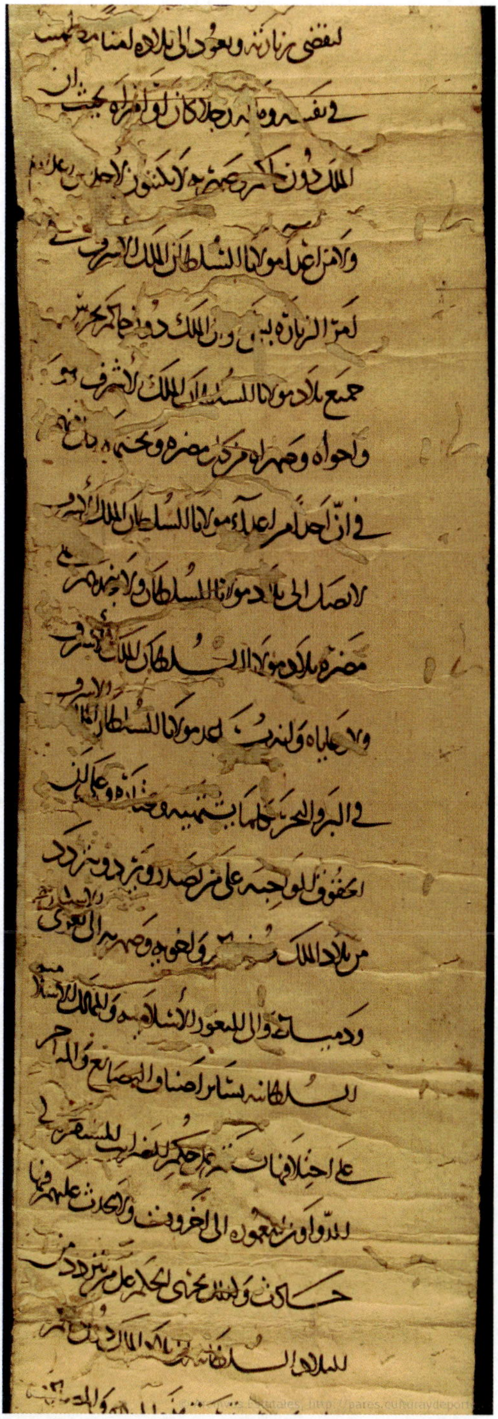

FIGURE 8.6
P.Corona de Aragón.inv. 145
© ARCHIVO DE LA CORONA DE ARAGÓN, BARCELONA

77 وَلَا من أَعْدَآء مولانا السُلطَان المَلك الأشرف في
78 أَمْر الزيارَة بـ[ـشـ]ـيء وأن المَلك دُون جاكَم يحرسْ
79 جَميع بلَاد مولانا السُلطَان المَلك الأشرف هوَ
80 وأخواه وَصهراه من كل مضرة وَيجتهـ[ـد] كل منهم
81 في أنّ أَحدًا من أعدآء مولانا السُلطَان الملك الأشرف
82 لا يَصل إلى بلَاد مولانا السُلطَان ولَا يجدهم على
83 مَضرّة بلَاد مولَانا السُلطَان المَلك الأشرف
84 ولَا رعاياه وَأنه يُسَاعد مولَانا السُلطَان المَلك الأشرف
85 في البَر والبَحْر بكلمَا يشتهيه ويختَاره وعَلى أَن
86 الحُقوق الوَاجِبَة عَلى من يَصدر ويَرد ويتردَد
87 من بلَاد المَلك دُ[ون جـ]ـاكم وَأخويه وَصهريه إلى ثغري الاسكندرية
88 وَدمياط وَإلى الثغور الأسْلَامية وَالممَالك الإسلامية
89 السُلطانية بسَائر أَصناف البضائع وَالمتاجر
90 عَلى اختِلَافها تَستمر على حُكم الضَرائب المستقرة في
91 الدّوَاوين المعمُورة إلى أَخر وقت ولَا يحدث عليهم فيها
92 حَادث وَكذلك يجْري الحكم عَلى من يتردد من
93 البلاد السُلطَانية إلى بلَاد المَلك دُون [جاكـ]ـم

---

77 اعْدآ مولانا الاسرف فى 78 اَمْر الزبارَه وان حا كَم بحرسْ 79 حَمع بلَاد مولانا 80 واحواه مضره بحتهـ[ـد] 81 فى انّ اَحدًا اعدآء مولانا الأسرف 82 بَصل الى بلَاد مولانا السُلطَان نجدهم 83 مَضرّه بلَاد مولَانا الأسرف 84 وَانه مولَانا الاسرف 85 فى البَحْر بكلمَا وبحتَاره اَن 86 الوَاجِبَه بصدر بتردَد 87 بلَاد وَاخويه وَصهربه الى بعرى الاسكندربه 88 وَالى النغور الاسْلَاميه الاسلامبه 89 السُلطانبه بسَار اَصناف البصابع وَالمباحر 90 احتِلَافها بَستمر الضَراىب المسقره فى 91 الدّوَاوبن المعمُوره الى اَخر وفت بحدث علبهم فبها 92 وَكدلك بتردد بحْرى مں 93 اللاد السُلطَانه الى بلَاد

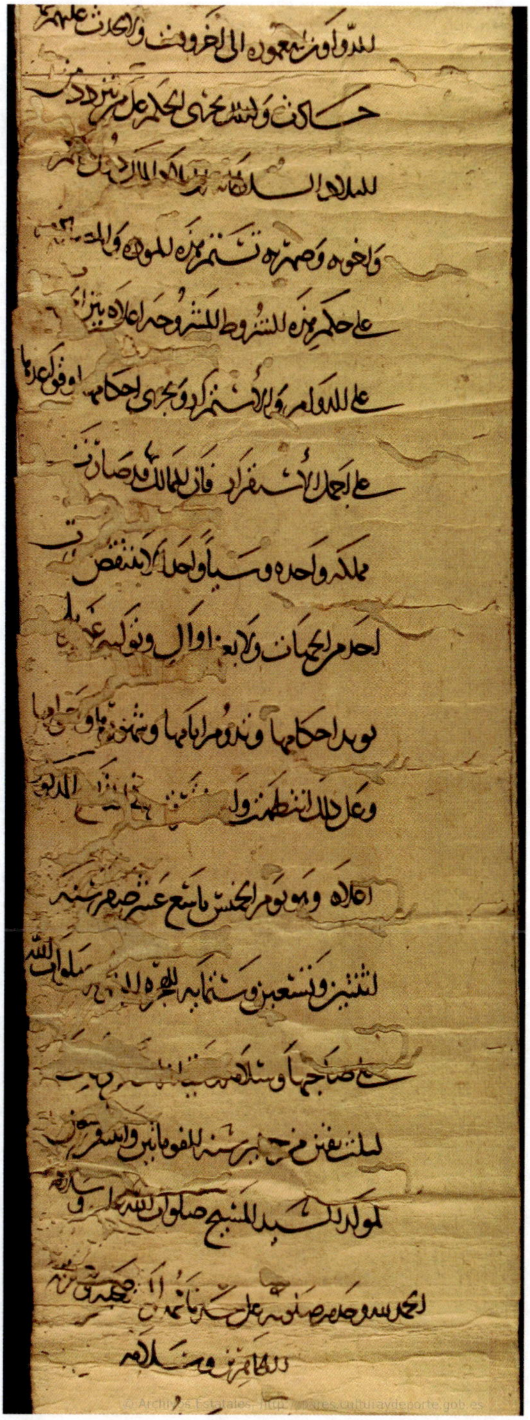

FIGURE 8.7
P.Corona de Aragón.inv. 145

94 وَأخويه وَصِهْريه تَسْتمر هَذه المودة وَالمصا[دقة]

95 على حكمِ هَذه الشُروط المَشرُوحَة أعلَاه بين الـ[ـجهات]

96 على الدوَام وَالأسْتمرَار وَتجري أحكَامِها وقوَاعدها

97 على أَجمل الأَسْقرَار فَإن المَمالك/ بها \قد صَارت

98 مملكَة وَاحدة وشَيًا وَاحدا لَا تنتقص [بمـ]ـوت

99 أحَد من الجهَات ولَا بعـ[ـز]ل وَالٍ وتَولية غَير[ه] بل

100 تؤيد أحكامها وتدُوم أيَامها وشهورْها و[أ]عوامها

101 وعَلى ذلك انتظمت وَا[ستقرت] في التَا[ريخ] المذكور

102 أعلَاه وَهو يوم الخميس تَاسع عَشر صفر سنَة

103 اثنين وَتسْعين وَستَماية للهجْرة النبو[يـ]ـة صَلوَات الله

104 على صَاحبهَا وسلَامـ[ـه ... الموافق]

105 لثلث بقين من [جنـ]ـير سنة الف وماتين وَاثنين و[تـ]ـسعين

106 لمَولد السيد المَسيح صلوات الله عـ[ـيه] وَسلامه

107 الحمد لله وَحده وَصلوَاتُه على سَيدنا مُحمد وآله وصَحبه وعترته

108 الطَاهرِين وسَلام

109 حسبنَا الله ونعم الوكيلُ

---

94 وَاخويه وَصهْريه المودة 95 المَشرُوحَه اعلاه بين 96 بجرى احكَامها 97 اَجمل بها قد 98 مملكَه وَاحده وسَيًا ننتقص 99 احَد من الحهَات بعـ[ـز]ل وتَوليه 100 يويد احكامها اىَامها 101 دلك انتطمت فى التَا[ر]ـح 102 اعلَاه يَوم الخمس تَاسع صعر سنَه 103 ستَمايه للهجْره صَلوَات 105 لبلث بقين سنه وَاسن [تـ]ـسعن 106 صلوات 107 وَصلوَاتُه سَدنا 108 للطَاهرِن 109حسنَا الوكلُ

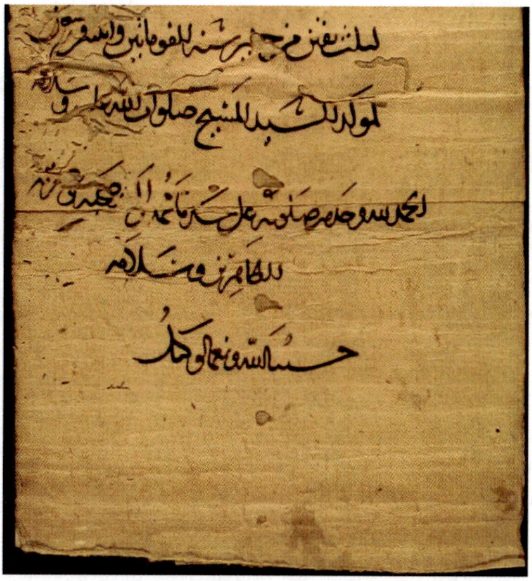

FIGURE 8.8
P.Corona de Aragón.inv. 145

4 Translation

[If one of the Muslim ships is shipwrecked]
1 [i]n the l[ands of King Don Djākim and the lands of his two brothers and]
2 his two brothers-in-law, [everybody who is in it,]
3 [merchants, sailors, (their) property, slaves, and] relatives are (to be) safe in [(their) lives,]
4 [property, and good]s. King Don Djākim, [his two brothers, and his two br]others-in-law
5 are [obligat]ed to [protect them, to] keep the[ir ships]
6 [and property,] to help them with the repair of their ships, and to provide them
7 [(passage) with their property] and goods to the lands of our [lord] al-Sulṭān
8 [al-Malik al-Ashraf]. In the same manner: [If ships] from the lands
9 of King Don Djākim or the lands of his two brothers, his two brothers-in-law, or his allies
10 are shipwrecked in the lands of our lord al-Sul[ṭān] al-[M]alik [a]l-Ashraf,
11 the above-mentioned rule will be applied. When
12 one of the Muslim or Christian merchants
13 [of the] lands of our lord al-Sulṭān al-[Ma]lik al-Ashraf,
14 or (one) of the *dhimmī* people of his lands (i.e., a Jew or Christian living under Muslim rule), dies in the lands of King Don [Djākim or the lands

15 of his] two brothers, his two brothers-in-law, or his allies, (no one is to) confront them in

16 their property and their goods, and he (is to) send what belongs to them and their possessions

17 to the lands of our lord al-Sulṭān al-Malik al-Ashraf, so that he (can) do with them

18 as he pleases. In the same manner: (For anyone) who dies in the lands of our l[ord al-S]ulṭān

19 al-Malik al-Ashraf (and who is) of the people of the kingdom of King Don Djākim,

20 or of the lands of his two brothers and two brothers-in-law, this above-mentioned rule will be applied

21 to them. When envoys from the lands of our lord al-Sulṭān al-Malik al-Ashraf

22 transit the lands of King Don Djākim or the lands of his

23 two brothers and two brothers-in-law and they strive (to reach) a

24 distant or nearby region, be it that they come or that they go,

25 or that the wind casts them into their lands, the envoys, their servants,

26 their entourage, and who(ever) comes with them of the envoys of kings and other rulers,

27 they are (to be) safe and protected in (their) lives and property and be sent (on)

28 to the destination of our lord al-Sulṭān [al-Malik al-Ashraf.]

29 K[ing] Don [Djākim], his two [brothers] and his two brothers-in-law,

30 none of them is to allow pirates and corsairs to [be victualed]

31 in his lands or to supply (themselves) with water. Who(ever) overwhelms some one of the pirates,

32 he [is to] seize him, do w[it]h him the necessary, and s[end what w]as foun[d with him]

33 of Muslim captives, goods, women, and chil[dren]

34 to the lands of our lord al-Sulṭān al-Malik al-Ashraf. In the same manner:

35 If one of the pirates comes to the lands of our lord al-Sulṭān

36 [al-Malik] al-Ashraf, the decision [will happe]n to him as in the [lands of] King Don Djākim,

37 in the same manner. King Don Djākim, his two brothers, and his two brothers-in-law,

38 if so[meone] from their lands conducts an affair by which this [tru]ce is canceled,

39 (then) King Don Djākim, his two [brothers, and his two brothers-in-law] are obligated

40 to search for whom[ever] does that, and to do the necessary with him.
41 King Don [Djākim,] his two brothers, and his two brothers-in-law (are to) allow everyone
42 from their land and other Franks to export
43 to the Islamic harbors iron, coal, wood,
44 and other (goods). When a Muslim is captured
45 on the land or on the sea, starting from the date of this truce,
46 from the remaining lands, from the east or from the west, from the most distant or the closest,
47 and they come with him into the lands of King Don Djākim and the lands of his two brothers
48 and two brothers-in-law to sell him there, King Don Djākim, his two brothers,
49 and his two brothers-in-law are obligated to dissolve his captivity and send him to the lands
50 of our lord al-Sulṭān al-Malik al-Ashraf. When
51 a business connection exists between Muslim merchants and merchants from the land
52 of [Ki]ng Don Djākim, his two brothers, and his two brothers-in-law concerning their goods,
53 while they are in the lands of our lord al-Sulṭān al-Malik al-Ashraf, their matters
54 are settled according to the imperative of the noble law.
55 When a Muslim travels on ships from the lands
56 of King Don Djākim, his two brothers, and his two brothers-in-law and has [his] wares
57 on them and the wares disappear, (then) King Don Djākim,
58 his two brothers, and his two brothers-in-law must return them, if they are found, or their value,
59 if they are lost. When somebody flees from the land of our lord
60 al-Sulṭān al-Malik al-Ashraf, during (the duration) of this truce,
61 to the lands of King Don Djākim or the lands of his two brothers and two brothers-in-law,
62 or turns (to them) with goods that do not belong to him and stays in those lands,
63 (then) King Don Djākim, his two brothers, and his two brothers-in-law must retu[rn the fugiti]ve,
64 or the person who stays with goods that do not belong to him, and his property to the lands of our lord

65 al-Sulṭān al-Malik al-Ashraf, as long as he is a Muslim. If he converts to Christianity,

66 he will send back his property that is peculiar with him, and (thereafter) he belongs to the kingdom of King Don Djākim,

67 his two brothers, and his two brothers-in-law. (For) who(ever) flees from their lands to the lands of [ou]r lo[rd]

68 al-Sulṭān al-Malik al-Ashraf, the above-mentioned rule (will also be applied).

69 If someone from the lands of King (Don) Djākim, the lands of his two brothers,

70 his two brothers-in-law, and his Frankish allies comes (in order) to achieve the pilgrimage

71 to the noble Jerusalem, and has with him a letter of King Don Djākim

72 or his two brothers-in-law and their seal for the governor of our lord the Sultan

73 in the noble Jerusalem, (then) the pilgrimage is for him possible and permitted,

74 so that he (can) perform his pilgrimage and return to his lands in safety and peace

75 for his life and property, be he a man or a woman, whereby

76 King Don Djākim and his two brothers-in-law do not write something for any one of their enemies

77 or the enemies of our lord al-Sulṭān al-Malik al-Ashraf in

78 the matter of the pilgrimage. King Don Djākim (therefore) protects

79 all lands of our lord al-Sulṭān al-Malik al-Ashraf—he,

80 his two brothers, and his two brothers-in-law—from every harm. Every one of them will struggle (to ensure)

81 that not one of the enemies of our lord al-Sulṭān al-Malik al-Ashraf

82 comes to the lands of our lord the Sultan. They will not help them

83 harm the lands of our lord al-Sulṭān al-Malik al-Ashraf

84 or his subjects. They support our lord al-Sulṭān al-Malik al-Ashraf

85 on land and on sea with everything he wishes for and selects.

86 The obligatory duties for (people) who enter, leave, and travel

87 from the lands of King D[on Dj]ākim, his two brothers, and his two brothers-in-law to the two harbors of Alexandria

88 and Damiette and the coasts and Islamic kingdoms

89 of the Sultan with all kind of goods and commodities,

90 corresponding to their difference, will persist according to the regulation of taxes that are fixed in

91 prospering *dīwān*s (i.e., chanceries) until the end of time. No innovation is therein established

92 against them. In the same manner: The rule will be applied for persons who travel from
93 the land of the Sultan to the lands of King Don [Djāki]m,
94 his two brothers, and his two brothers-in-law. This love and friendship will continue
95 according to the regulation of these above-explained clauses between the [contractors]
96 in continuity and persistence. Their rules and basics will be applied
97 with the most beautiful persistence, because the kingdoms have become by them
98 a single kingdom, a single thing that will not be dissolved [by the dea]th
99 of one of the contractors, nor by the deposition of a ruler nor the succession of another (ruler), but
100 his rule will be confirmed and his days, months, and years will persist.
101 (These clauses) were arranged and defined at the above-mentioned
102 date and it is Thursday, the nineteenth Ṣafar of the year
103 six hundred ninety and two of the emigration of the Prophet—may God honor
104 its tenant and grant him pea[ce. It corresponds]
105 to the antepenultimate (day) of [Jan]uary of the year one thousand two hundred [ni]nety-two
106 of the birth of the Lord, the Messiah—may God honor [hi]m and grant him peace!
107 Thanks to the single God! May God honor our Lord Muḥammad, his family, his companions, and his house!
108 And His peace for the pure ones!
109 Our sufficiency is God, and He is the best trustee.

5 Differences between the Original Treaty and al-Qalqashandī's Quotation

The most obvious differences between the two versions of the treaty are found in the formulaic parts: According to Alarcón y Santón's and García de Linares's edition of the lost beginning of the treaty, al-Qalqashandī omitted the Basmala when he quoted the treaty and abridged the titles of the Mamlūk sultan. He also ignored the eschatocol (lines 102–109) and abridged the *mawlānā s-sulṭān al-malik al-ashraf* of the original treaty to *al-malik al-ashraf*. In almost all documents, repeated formulae were of no interest for the dīwān's secretaries, since they had learned them early in their training. We can assume that the authors of the *inshāʾ* literature focused on the peculiarities of document writing, so that the nonformulaic parts of documents were rendered more closely in the manuals than were the formulaic ones.

In the preserved part of the main text, we find two main differences: The first lines (lines 1–4) of the original cannot be harmonized with al-Qalqashandī's quotation. Comparison with the 1290 treaty shows that several words defining the protected people in case of shipwreck are omitted. The Catalan translation confirms that the text of both treaties is here in agreement. Clause 7, concerning piracy (lines 29–37), is completely missing. So we can expect that in other *inshāʾ* works, too, some sentences and even complete clauses in documents were eliminated when the documents were quoted.

All other differences are minor. Since the text of the original often accords better with the rules of Classical Arabic grammar than does the text of al-Qalqashandī's *Ṣubḥ al-aʿshà*, we can assume that the errors in the quotation are probably result of the transmission of *the Ṣubḥ al-aʿshà* in manuscript form.

6: Al-Qalqashandī replaces the singular *markabihim* with the plural *marākibihim.*

8: Al-Qalqashandī replaces the singular *markabihim* with the plural *marākibihim.* Since it is the subject of the predicate *inkasarat,* only al-Qalqashandī's text fits the grammatical rules.

18: Al-Qalqashandī replaces *bi-bilād* with *fī bilād.*

20: Al-Qalqashandī adds *wa-muʿāhidīhim* after *bilād aḫawayhi wa-ṣihrayhi.*

22: Al-Qalqashandī omits *ʿalà*. In *akhawayhi wa-ṣihrayhi,* he replaces *aw* with *wa-*.

24: Al-Qalqashandī changes the order *al-baʿīda wa-l-qarība* to *al-qarība wa-l-baʿīda.*

25: Al-Qalqashandī replaces *yakūnu* with *takūnu,* so that his text does not accord with Classical Arabic grammar.

27: Al-Qalqashandī replaces the plural *yudjahhizūnahum* with the singular *yudjahhizuhum*. Since the text adresses all five Christian contractors, the text of the original fits better.

28: Al-Qalqashandī replaces *maqṣad* with *bilād*. The original fits better, since the clauses settle the transit of Mamlūk envoys to a third party and not only their return to Egypt.

48: Al-Qalqashandī omits *kull man.*

65: Al-Qalqashandī omits *amr.*

66: Al-Qalqashandī omits *fa-*.

72: Al-Qalqashandī omits *wa-ṣihrayhi.* The abridged mention of al-Ashraf Khalīl as *mawlānā s-sulṭān* (without the normal addition *al-malik al-*

Ashraf) in the original is reproduced by al-Qalqashandī as *al-malik al-Ashraf* (the form in which he always refers to the sultan).

76: Al-Qalqashandī omits *wa-ṣihrayhi* and adapts the predicate (*yaktubu* instead of *yaktubūna*). Together with the omission in l. 72, the meaning of clause 14 concerning the pilgrimage to Jerusalem is slightly changed; in the original not only the Aragonese king but also the Castilian and Portuguese kings are allowed to issue passports.

78: Al-Qalqashandī corrects a mistake in the original and replaces *wa-anna* with *wa-ʿalā anna.*

82: Al-Qalqashandī writes *bi-kulli-mā* not connected but as two words: *bi-kull mā.* As in l. 72, the abridged mention of the Mamlūk sultan as *mawlānā l-sulṭān* is rendered by al-Qalqashandī as *al-malik al-Ashraf.*

88: Al-Qalqashandī omits *al-islāmīya* after *al-mamālik.* Probably the doubling of a single adjective (*al-thughūr al-islāmīya wa-l-mamālik al-islāmīya al-sulṭānīya*) was perceived as a violation of stylistic ideals.

91: Al-Qalqashandī replaces the plural *al-dawāwīn al-maʿmūra* with the singular *al-dīwān al-maʿmūr.*

99: Al-Qalqashandī replaces *al-djihāt* with *al-djānibayn.* His dual form refers to a Christian and a Muslim side, while the plural of the original reflects that the treaty was concluded by six signatories.

Al-Qalqashandī concludes his chapter on Muslim-Frankish treaties—in which he quotes four further treaties in addition to the 1293 Mamlūk-Aragonese treaty—with some remarks on the style of these treaties.[27] In his view, only the Mamlūk-Aragonese treaty satisfies the stylistic ideals of Classical Arabic. He explains that the other treaties were probably negotiated word by word, so that that they were, rather, minutes of the agreements with no proper revision.[28] In their case, it has to be asked whether the modern edition of the *Ṣubḥ al-aʿshà* reproduces all their peculiarities, since their transmission offered opportunities for scribes to correct them. Especially the layout of these treaties remains unknown, for al-Qalqashandī does not describe it because he has a longer section devoted to layout. We can assume that Muslim-Christian treaties often did not conform to the layout of the Muslim chanceries. P.Aragon 153, a commer-

27 Al-Qalqashandī 1919: 70–71.

28 An example, from another region, is P.Aragon 2, a draft of the negotiations on a Naṣrid-Aragonese military alliance (1301), written partly in Spanish, partly in dialectal Andalusī Arabic. The actual treaty (P.Aragon 3) was, however, revised and written in proper Classical Arabic. The commercial treaty of 1430 between the Mamlūks and Aragon (P.Aragon 153) was also written in Middle Arabic and probably not revised.

cial treaty between Aragon and the Mamlūks (1430), is written carelessly on eight paper sheets, since it was concluded on Rhodes and not in Cairo. These differences in layout cannot be extracted from the *inshāʾ* literature; but they concern only documents written under special circumstances. The descriptions of (Mamlūk) layout by al-Qalqashandī and the actual Mamlūk documents accord.

Thus al-Qalqashandī's description is relatively exact. Only 19 of the 109 lines were omitted; more than 80 percent of the text shows only minor differences. The abbreviation of formulae common in documents can be observed as systematic alteration. As the *ka-dhā wa-ka-dhā* at the end of al-Qalqashandī's quotation indicates, he was mostly interested in the peculiarities of a document. Since we can assume that the formulae were replaced by placeholders in almost all the documents quoted in *inshāʾ* works, this literature can only serve in a very limited way as a source for the formularies of official letters and administrative and legal documents. The historical value of these quoted documents is in fact larger: some parts were omitted, probably unintentionally, but texts were not distorted. Even the problematic information on the contractors in al-Qalqashandī's quotation seems to be correct and reflects the uncertain knowledge of Europe in the Mamlūk chancery.

6 Conclusion

The textual closeness between original and quotation can be assumed for Mamlūk documents in the *inshāʾ* literature. The quality of the quotations of older documents remains in doubt. Further investigation is necessary: while we can at least hope to find more examples of parallel document transmission for Mamlūk times, for earlier times it is very unlikely that we will find documents that will allow us to determine how reliable the *inshāʾ* literature is. As a historical source, the document quotations from the times of their authors (and, as our example al-Qalqashandī's quotation shows, from a century ago) are relatively trustworthy. In regard to quotations of older documents, we can only speculate on their trustworthiness. The analysis of documents' formularies and special formulae cannot be undertaken only by studying the *inshāʾ* literature, however; its statements must be verified by other documents, since in the manuals only the extraordinary was reproduced carefully, while the usual was abbreviated. Besides this abbreviation, based on the reader's advanced knowledge as a scribe (*kātib*), possible further sources could be (1) references to outdated formulae that lived on in literature—such as al-Qalqashandī's mention of the formula *aḥmadu ilayka llāha alladhī lā ilāha illā huwa* as an introduction for letters, which is attested only in original letters from the 7th and 8th centuries, or (2) quotations of documents that were never sent or used in any way, but written for exercise or demonstration of scribal skills. In every case, transmitted literary documents must be used carefully—even if we know the technique of quoting better now, thanks to comparing al-Qalqashandī's quotation to the original 1293 Mamlūk-Aragonese treaty.

Bibliography

Alarcón y Santón, Maximiliano and Ramón García de Linares. 1940. *Los documentos árabes diplomáticos del Archivo de la Corona de Aragón*. Publicaciones de las Escuelas de Estudios Árabes de Madrid y Granada, vol. C 1. Madrid: Imprenta de Estanislao Maestre. [P.Aragon]

Amari, Michele. 1883. "Trattato stipolato da Giacomo II di Aragona col sultano d'Egitto il 29 gennaio 1293." In *Atti della R. Accademia dei Lincei* 11: 423–444.

Broadbridge, Ann. 2008. *Kingship and Ideology in the Islamic and Mongol Worlds*. Cambridge Studies in Islamic Civilization. Cambridge: Cambridge University Press.

Halm, Heinz. 1987. "Die Ayyubiden." In *Geschichte der arabischen Welt*, ed. Ulrich Haarmann. Munich: Beck.

Heffening, Willi. 1925/1975. *Das islamische Fremdenrecht bis zu den islamisch-fränkischen Staatsverträgen*. Beiträge zum Rechts- und Wirtschaftsleben des islamischen Orients, vol. 1. Hannover: Lafaire/Reprint: *Das islamische Fremdenrecht bis zu den islamisch-fränkischen Staatsverträgen: eine rechtshistorische Studie zum Fiqh*. Osnabrück: Biblio.

Holt, Peter M. 1990. "Al-Nāṣir Muḥammad's Letter to a Spanish Ruler in 699/1300." In *al-Masāq* 3: 23–29.

Holt, Peter M. 1992. "The Mamluk Sultanate and Aragon: The Treaties of 689/1290 and 692/1293." In *Tārīḫ: Papers in Near Eastern Studies* 2: 105–118.

Holt, Peter M. 1995. *Early Mamluk Diplomacy (1260–1290): Treaties of Baybars and Qalāwūn with Christian Rulers*. Islamic History and Civilization, vol. 12. Leiden: Brill.

Ibn ʿAbd al-Ẓāhir, Muḥyī d-Dīn. 1961. *Tashrīf al-ayyām wa-l-ʿuṣūr fī sīrat al-Malik al-Manṣūr*, ed. Murād Kāmil. Cairo: Wizārat ath-thaqāfa wa-l-irshād al-qawmī.

Khadduri, Majid. 1955. *War and Peace in the Law of Islam*. Baltimore: Johns Hopkins University Press.

Köhler, Michael A. 1991. *Allianzen und Verträge zwischen fränkischen und islamischen Herrschern im Vorderen Orient: eine Studie über das zwischenstaatliche Zusammenleben vom 12. bis ins 13. Jahrhundert*. Studien zur Sprache, Geschichte und Kultur des Islamischen Orients, N.F., vol. 12. Berlin: de Gruyter.

Labarta, Ana. 2018. "Edición del tratado de paz bilingüe de 1405 entre el reino de Granada y la Corona de Aragón." In *Saitabi: Revista de la Facultat de Geografia i Història* 68: 139–159.

Labib, Subhi Y. 1965. *Handelsgeschichte Ägyptens im Spätmittelalter (1171–1517)*. Vierteljahresschrift für Sozial- und Wirtschaftsgeschichte, vol. 46. Wiesbaden: Steiner.

Lohlker, Rüdiger. 2006. *Islamisches Völkerrecht: Studien am Beispiel Granada*. Bremen: Kleio.

Masala, María. 1993. "Martino l'umano: trattato di pace con Granada (1405)." In *Sardegna, Mediterraneo ed atlantico tra medioevo ed età moderna: Studi storici in memoria di Alberto Boscolo. Volume secondo: Il Mediterraneo*, ed. Luisa D'Arienzo. Rome: Bulzoni, 315–343.

Masiá de Ros, Ángeles. 1951. *La Corona de Aragón y los estados del norte de Africa: política de Jaime II y Alfonso IV en Egipto, Ifriquía y Tremecén*. Barcelona: Instituto español de estudios mediterrán.

P.Aragon. *See* Alarcón y Santón 1940.

al-Qalqashandī, Abū l-Abbās Aḥmad. 1919. *Ṣubḥ al-aʿšà* [*Dawn of the Nightblind*], vol. 14, ed. Muḥammad ʿAbd al-Rasūl Ibrāhīm. Cairo: Dār al-Kutub al-Sulṭānīya.

Samarrai, Alauddin. 1980. "Medieval Commerce and Diplomacy: Islam and Europe A.D. 850–1300." In *Canadian Journal of History/Annales canadiennes d'histoire* 15: 1–22.

Viladrich, Mercé. 1999. "Jaque al Sultán en el 'Damero maldito': edición y traducción de un tratado diplomático entre los mercaderes catalanes y el sultanato mameluco (1429)." In *L'expansió catalana a la mediterrània a la baica edat mitjana*, ed. Maria Teresa Ferrer i Mallol and Damien Coulon. Anuario de estudios medievales: anejos, vol. 36. Barcelona: Consell superior d'investigacions scientífiques, 161–205.

Yüksel Muslu, Cihan. 2013. "Attempting to Understand the Language of Diplomacy between the Ottomans and the Mamluks." In *Archivum Ottomanicum* 30: 247–267.

Index of Documents Quoted by Edition

Michail Hradek

Chrest.Khoury I
- 61 — 121

CPR XXXI
- 13; 14 — 60

O.Frange
- 89 — 65

P.AmariGenova
- 1; 2 — 187n

P.Aragon
- 1 — 187n
- 2 — 213n
- 3 — 187n, 213n
- 5 — 190n
- 15 — 187n, 190n, 191n
- 27 — 187n
- 30 — 187n
- 42 — 190n
- 51 — 190n
- 52 — 190n
- 54 — 190n
- 57 — 190n
- 58 — 190n
- 59 — 190n
- 60 — 190n
- 61 — 190n
- 66 — 190n
- 75 — 187n
- 103 — 190n
- 110 — 190n
- 111 — 190n
- 114 — 187n
- 116 — 187n, 189n
- 118 — 190n
- 120 — 190n
- 121 — 190n
- 129 — 190n
- 130 — 190n
- 131 — 190n
- 140 bis — 187n, 189n
- 145 — 186
- 146 — 188n
- 153 — 213
- 154 — 187n, 192n
- 161 — 187n

P.AragonGranada
- pp. 2–300 — 187n
- pp. 325–329 — 187n

P.AbbottLiteraryPapyri I
- 2 — 104

P.AbbottLiteraryPapyri II
- 13 — 89

P.BaudenDueTrattati
- 1 — 187n, 189n
- 2 — 187n, 189n

P.Berl.Arab. II
- 11 — 102
- 35 — 102

P.Brux.Bawit
- 127 — 59
- 128 — 59
- 129 — 59

P.Cair Arab.
- 291 — 102
- 317 — 70
- 377 — 118, 119, 120
- 378 — 118, 120
- 384 — 121
- 386 — 121

P.ChampollionDocuments XXXVII
- 5 — 187n

P.David-WeillLouvre
- 26 — 70

P.DiemKhalili
5 102

P.DiemVulgarismus 102

P.Flor.Arab.
29 189n
30 187n, 189n
34 187n, 189n
35 187n
36 187n
38 187n, 189n
46 189

P.GenizahCambr.
5 134n21, 134n23, 136n
9 134n
12 71
13 134, 136
24 132
25 71
56 131, 136n

P.GrohmannUrkunden
4 102n

P.GrohmannWirtsch.
2 71

P.Heid.Arab. II
7 71
18 71
69 102

P.Heid.Arab. III
8 70

P.HermitageCopt.
51 67

P.Jahn
14 71

P.Kellis V
5 64

P.Khurasan
32 102n

P.LittlePurchaseDeeds
4 131n

P.Lond. IV
1494 58

P.Lond.Copt. I
1050 59
1118 65
1214 60

P.Loth
2 102

P.Marchands II
11 70
42 71
V/1 16 71

P.MariageSeparation
45 71

P.RiberaTratado 187n

P.RuizOrsattiTratadoDePaz 187n, 192n

P.Ryl.Arab. I VI
18 70

P.Ryl.Arab. II
10 70

P.Ryl.Copt.
243 64

P.SilvestredeSacyGenes
1; 2 187n

P.SilvestredeSacyTraite 187n

P.Stras.Copt.
67 64

P.SultanMerinide 187n

P.Rain.Unterricht.Kopt.
307 60
309 60

P.Vente
3 132, 142n
4 142n
10 142n
11 142n
13 132

P.ViladrichSultan
257–263 190n

SBKopt. III
1440 64, 67
1448 67

General Index

Michail Hradek

Abū Aḥmad 86
Abū Bakr 92, 93
Abū Bakr ʿUbayd Allāh b. Abī Djaʿfar al-Miṣrī 108
Abū Dhārr al-Ghaffārī 89
Abū Hurayra 108
Abū ʿĪsā 106
Abū Isḥāq ʿAmr b. ʿAbd Allāh al-Sabīʿī 87
Abū l-Dardā' 78, 79
Abū Masʿūd 86
Abū Yaʿlā 76, 78, 79
Abū Yūnus 101
Abū ʿAbd al-Karīm al-Ḥārith b. Yazīd al-Ḥaḍramī al-Miṣrī 88
Abū ʿUmar 87, 159
ʿAbd al-Djabbār b. al-ʿAbbās al-Hamdānī 78, 79
ʿAbd Allāh b. Lahīʿa al-Ḥaḍramī 106, 108, 110, 114
ʿAbd Allāh b. Masʿūd 81
ʿAbd Allāh b. Yasār al-Aʿradj 88
Acre, *see* Akko
Account
  Accounting documents 4, 5, 6, 34, 59
  Arabic 59
  Book 118
  Coptic 59, 60
  Journal 5
  Ledger 119
  Paper 64, 67
  Papyrus 59
  Record 131
Acknowledgment (*iqrār*) 127, 130, 133, 162
Administration 4, 6, 59, 117
Administrative
  Center 8
  Document 59, 185, 214
  Record 3
Afghanistan 3, 6, 7
Agricultural
  Estate 118
  Produce 76
  Worker 119, 122
Aḥmad b. ʿAbd Allāh 92
Akhvamazda 7
Akkadian 3, 13, 39n
  Scribe 4
Akko 187
ʿalāma 171, 188
Alexander the Great 5, 11, 19
Alexandria 159, 161n, 162, 170, 173, 174n, 187, 192, 210
Alfonso
  Alfonso III, brother of Jaime 186
  Governor of Sicily 188
  Pretender in Portugal 188
ʿAlī 87
ʿAlī b. ʾAbī Ṭālib 92, 93, 94
ʿAlī b. Maʿbad 114
Ancient North Arabian dialects 49
Ancient South Arabian
  Alphabet 26
  Epigraphy 26, 27, 28, 35, 44
  Manuscript 38, 48
  Writing 27, 29, 33, 39
al-Andalus 160, 176
Aphrodito/Ishqaw 58
Arab
  Administration 59
  Conquest 3, 58, 64
Arabic
  Account 59, 64, 67
  Andalusi 213n
  Document 58, 60, 71, 131, 132
  Epigraphy viii
  Epistolography 60, 62n, 64
  Papyrology vii, 117, 118
  Poetry vii, 74n
  Scribal practice 128, 138
Aragon 186, 187, 188, 189n, 190, 191, 214
Aragonese
  Crusade 187
  King 186, 187, 191, 213
  Mudéjares 191
  Territory 188
Aramaeogram 13

Heterogram 13, 14, 15, 17, 18, 19
Logogram 13, 14, 16
Aramaic
Bactrian material 10
Bill of sale 136n, 138, 139
Formulae 138, 139
Imperial Aramaic 8, 17
Papyrus 4, 5, 12
Phrase 139
Scribe 4
Script 3, 19
Achaemenid
Bureaucracy 8
Empire 3, 4, 7, 13, 20
Archive 34, 112, 138, 185, 186, 189
Documentary 74
Literary 74
Mercantile 137
of Akhvamazda 7
Public 48
State 57
Arsames (Arsham) 10, 11n, 18
Artaxerxes 4
Ashkelon 152, 153, 154, 156, 163
al-Ashraf Khalīl 186, 189, 212
ʿasīb, *see* palm leaf-stalk
Asóka
Edicts of 12
Aswan 5
Elephantine 5, 10, 11, 19n
Syene 5
ʿAwn b. Abī Djuḥayfa 76, 78, 79, 80
Ayyūb al-Nuʿmānī 106

Bactra 7, 10, 11, 15, 18, 19
Bactrian 5, 12, 19
Aramaic material 6, 10, 11
Document 11, 20
Bagavant 7
bān (*Moringa*) 30n
Barley 120, 121
barsīm, *see* clover
Basmala 60, 61n, 62n, 89, 110n, 170, 189, 211
Behistun inscription 4, 5, 16n, 19n
Ben Ezra Synagogue, *see* Cairo Geniza
Bilingual(ism) 57, 60
Bill of sale 132, 136, 137, 138, 139, 143
Aramaic 130, 138, 139
Judaeo-Arabic 127, 130, 138, 139
Birchbark 12, 13, 20
Bone 32
Booklet 94, 95, 103, 114
Brahmi 12, 19
al-Bukhārī 76
Business 5, 41, 131, 143, 191, 209
Document 34, 41, 48
Letter 27, 62n, 76, 80
Butterfly bush (*Buddleja polystachya*) 30

Cairo (Miṣr) 128, 133, 160, 169, 176, 192, 214
See also Egypt (Miṣr); al-Fusṭāṭ
Cairo Geniza 117, 127, 128, 131, 132, 133, 137, 154, 163
Ben Ezra Synagogue 161n
Calque 16
Cambyses 4, 5
Cantor 156, 158, 160, 161n, 164, 167, 169, 170, 176
Castile 188
Chancellery 186, 210, 213
Fāṭimid chancellery style 138
Literature (*ʾinshāʾ*) 185, 186
Mamlūk style 188, 214
Manual 185, 212, 214
Official 185
Script 109
Text 188
Charity 159, 160n, 162, 163, 164
Civil war 93, 123, 188
Clause
Warranty 132, 133, 138, 139n
Witness 130, 132, 138
Clover (*barsīm*) 118, 120
Codex 103, 104
Coin 12, 14, 15, 16, 45, 130
Commercial
Agreement 190n, 192
Network 158n
Treaty 187, 213n
Communal
Charity 164
Figure 138
Leader 137, 155, 156, 158, 162, 163
Letter 154
Official (*parnas*) 143, 155, 156, 163, 164
Politics 157, 163
Contract
Divorce 185

Marriage (*ketubba*) 138, 159n
Contract stipulation (*shurūṭ*) 131, 135, 136, 212
Coptic
Account 60
Entagion 59
Letter 57, 59, 60, 61, 62, 64, 65, 66, 68
Papyrus 57, 59, 61
Scribe 65
Tax receipt 59
Corpus 5, 6, 10, 11n, 18, 19, 75, 89, 137, 142, 143
Court
Jewish 136n, 152
Muslim 136n, 137, 138
Notebook 154, 163
Record 163
Craftsmen 67, 117
Cuneiform 3, 11, 12, 13
Begat hieroglyph 3
Tablet 3, 12
Cursive 29, 60, 61, 68, 76, 104
Grafitti 28
Inscription 28
Script (*naskhī*) 28
Cyrus 4, 5

ḍaʿīf 73
Daizaka 9
Damascus 185, 192n
Damiette 192, 210
darak, *see* warranty
Darius 4, 16n
Dayr al-Naqlūn 64, 67
Deed
Legal 35n, 42, 43, 48n
of Sale 128, 139
Supplementary 130, 133, 134, 136, 137, 138, 139, 142, 147
Deir el-Naqlūn, *see* Dayr al-Naqlūn
Demotic 57, 131
Dinis, Portuguese king 188
Diplomatics (physical form of documents) 11, 13
diploun (measure) 59
Djarīr b. Ḥāzim b. Zayd Abū l-Naḍr al-Azdī al-ʿAtakī 106, 107, 108
Document
Bactrian 20
Business 34, 41, 48
Judaeo-Arabic viii
Mamlūk 193, 214
Script 128, 133, 138
Tax 75
Documentary 48, 139n, 143, 188
Papyrus 74, 75
Record 147
Text 26
Dossier 138
Draft 7, 112, 138, 161, 213
Transmission (*musawwad*) 113
Driver Letters 10, 11, 16, 18n, 19n
Ductus 13, 28
duʿāʾ 80, 114
Egypt (Miṣr) 3, 4, 5, 10, 12, 15, 57, 58n, 61n, 62, 65, 68, 74, 88, 93, 112, 136n27, 136n28, 142, 143, 152, 153n, 158n, 162n, 163, 164, 185, 187, 191, 212
Early Islamic 75, 117, 123
Fāṭimid 128, 133, 136n
See also Cairo (Miṣr); al-Fusṭāṭ

Elamite 4, 5, 19
Preponderance 5
Scribe 8
Elephantine, *see* Aswan
Empire 3, 4, 5, 191
Andalusian 187
Archaemenid 3, 7, 13, 20
Christian 188
Greco-Bactrian 12, 19
Iranian 20
Islamic 190
Maghrebian 187
Mamlūk 186, 189, 191, 192
Mesopotamian 20
Neo-Assyrian 26
Roman 20
Entagion 59
Epigraphy 26, 27, 28, 35, 44
Epistolography 60, 62n, 64
Estate 118, 119, 120, 121, 123, 130, 133, 134, 136
Agricultural 118
Manager 120
Ethiopic 40n, 46
Script 25n
Expositio 70

Farmer 59, 117, 119
faṣl, *see* supplementary deed
Fāṭimid
  Chancellery style 138
  Egypt 128, 133, 136n
  Fusṭāṭ 142
  Legal culture 138
  Period 130, 131, 185
  Scribal culture 138
al-Fayyūm 58, 60
  Fayoumic 61, 66
  See also Dayr al-Naqlūn
Formulae 60, 61, 74, 128, 133, 134, 188, 192, 211, 212, 214
  Arabic 64, 128
  Aramaic 138, 139
  Judaeo-Arabic 139, 142
  Warranty 131, 132
Furāt al-Kūfī 89, 93
al-Fusṭāṭ 112, 121, 128, 153, 155, 157, 158, 159, 160, 161n36, 161n37, 167, 170, 173, 174, 176
  Fāṭimid 131, 133, 142
  See also Cairo (Miṣr)

Gandhara 12
Geniza
  Jewish 48
  Letter 155, 159n
  See also Cairo Geniza
djins, *see* slave
Graffiti 28, 49n
Greek
  Documents 131
  Literary papyrus 74n, 109n
Guarantee 132, 133, 139
Guarantee-declaration (*enguetike homologia*) 58

Ḥadīth
  Papyrus 74, 75, 79, 109, 110, 112, 113, 114
  Scholar(ship) 75, 80
  Studies 75, 109
  Text 74, 75, 79, 111

Harvest 118, 119, 120, 121
Ḥasbala 69, 71, 192
Hashavakhshu 9
Hermoupolis, *see* al-Ushmūnayn
Heterogram, *see* aramaeogram
Hieroglyphic 57
Ḥudhayfa b. al-Yamān 87, 88

Ibn Abī l-Dunyā 104
Ibn Abī Shayba 76, 79, 87, 88
Ibn al-Mubārak 104, 108
Ibn al-Muqaffaʿ 14
Ibn Isḥāq 108
Ibn Masʿūd 106
Ideogram 16, 17, 18
idjāza (authorization) 80, 107, 111
ʿilb (*Zizyphus*) 30n
Imperial
  Aramaic 8, 17
  Policy 5
Imruʾ al-Qays 24, 25n, 26, 48, 49
India 3, 12, 13, 14, 136
Inscription
  Behistun 5, 16n, 19n
  Cursive 28
  Monumental 26, 28, 35n, 39n, 40n, 43, 47n
inshāʾ
  dīwān al-inshāʾ (chancellery) 186, 187
  Literature (composition manual) 185, 189n, 212, 214
International Society for Arabic Papyrology (ISAP) 7, 8
Invocation 20, 58, 61n, 66, 188, 189
ʾiqrār, *see* acknowledgment
Iranian Language 8, 13, 15, 18n
Islamicate world viii
Isnād 73, 75, 76, 79, 87, 88, 103, 113
Ishqaw, *see* Aphrodito
Istithnāʾ 192

Jaime II, brother of Alfonso III 188
Jedaniah 18
Jerusalem 153, 154n, 185, 191, 192, 210, 213
  Mamlūk 128, 136
Jewish
  Communal figure 138, 143
  Community 18, 152, 155, 158n, 159, 163, 164
  Court 136n, 152
  Egyptian Jewish elite 161
  Geniza 48
  Law 156, 163n

Marriage contract 138
Notary 139
Persian-Jewish heritage 6
Scribe 137, 138, 142
Journeymen (*adjīr, raqqāṣ*) 119, 120, 121, 122
Judaeo-Arabic 136, 138
Bill of sale 127, 130, 136n, 138, 139
Formulae 139, 142
Juniper (*Juniperus excelsa*) 30

Kalamos, *see* pen
Ketubba, see marriage contract
Kharoṣṭi 12, 13, 19, 20
Manuscript 12
Script 12
Khulmi 7

Law
Family 138
Jewish 156, 163n
Muslim 73, 108, 185, 187, 189, 190, 191, 192
Layout 138, 213, 214
Lease 118, 132
Annual 117
Leather 3, 4, 5, 6, 10, 11, 12, 17, 20, 27
Ledger, *see* account
Legal
Act 75, 142n
Deed 35n, 42, 43, 48n
Practice 155, 163
System 154, 155
Letter
Business 62n, 76, 80
Communal 154
Coptic 57, 59, 60, 61, 62n, 64, 65, 66, 68
Familiy 131
Genizah 155, 159n
Hieroglyph begat 3
Middle Sabaic 42
Monumental 28
Official 214
Paper 60, 61
Papyrus 60
Private 35n, 163
Ligature 61, 89
List 59, 64, 189
of alms 143
of goods 34
of ḥadīth 110
of names 34
of payments 120, 121
of supplies 7, 11
Literary
Archive 74n
Composition 26, 33
Papyrus 74, 75, 109, 110, 111, 112
Source 73, 117, 123, 154, 158n, 185
Text 19, 34n, 74, 80, 109
Litigant 137, 138, 142, 154, 164
Loanword 18, 61, 67
Logogram, *see* aramaeogram
al-Madjlisī 89

Maintenance (*rizq*) 120
Canal 119
Mamlūk 186, 187, 190, 212, 213n, 214
Archive 189
Chancery 188n, 214
Document 193, 214
Empire 186, 189, 192
Era 130, 131, 133
Jerusalem 136n
Layout 214
Treaty with Aragon 185, 187, 213, 215
al-Manṣūr 108
Manuscript 12, 28n, 29, 33, 43, 46, 47, 48, 49, 65, 66, 68, 88, 103, 111, 112, 127, 138, 186, 212
Ancient South Arabian 38
Aramaic 12
Kharoṣṭi 12
Paper 110, 111
of ḥadīth collections 108
Writing 26, 27, 28n, 39n, 48
Mārib 28n, 30, 44
Marriage
Delayed marriage gift 171
Delayed marriage payment 155
Delayed marriage settlement 156, 169, 171
Jewish marriage contract (*ketubba*) 159
Marwān I 108
Mason (*bannā'*) 121
matn 75, 76, 87
Memoranda 4, 5
Merchant 117, 131, 137, 152, 159, 161
Catalan 187

Mesopotamia 3, 4, 6, 20, 26
al-Miqdām b. Zā'ida 106
Miṣr, see Cairo; Egypt
misthosis, see rent
Monumental
  Epigraphy 27, 35
  Inscription 26, 28, 35n, 39n, 40n, 43, 44, 47n
  Letter 28
  Script 28, 29, 109
mu'akhkhar, see delayed marriage settlement
muḥaddith 79, 87, 111
muhmal 79, 109, 110
muṣannaf 76, 79, 80, 87, 88, 110, 111, 113, 114
musawwad, see draft
muṣḥaf 25n
Muslim
  Court 136, 137
  Family law 138
  Legal document 142
  Slave 191
  Muslim-Christian treaty 213
musnad 28n, 76, 79, 80, 110, 111, 113, 114
mustanad 188
muwaṭṭa' 104, 113

Nāfi' 86, 88
Nahray (Nehoray) b. Nissīm 131, 137, 161n
Naqsh-i Rustam 14, 15
Narration 62, 186, 188, 189
naskhī, see script
Nashshān (al-Sawdā') 29, 46, 47n, 48
Network 155, 158
  Business 143
  Commercial 158n
  Communication 160
  Social 158n, 163
  Scholarly 75
Northwest Semitic
  Palaeography 6
  Script 3
Nu'aym b. Ḥammād 104
al-Nuwayrī 133

Obligation 132, 153, 154n, 158n, 161, 162
  Financial 43
  Written 185

Orthography 60, 103
  Practice 20
Ostracon 4, 66
  Assur 3
Overseer (*khawlī*) 119, 120, 121, 122

Pahlavi 13, 14, 15
Palestinian 169, 174
  Yeshiva 153, 160n, 161n
Palm
  Grove 119
  Leaf 24, 25, 36, 49n
  Leaf-stalk (*'asīb*) 25, 27, 29, 30, 32n, 33, 35, 37, 47, 50
Paper
  Coptic letter 61, 66, 68
  Letter 60
  Manuscript 110, 111
Papyrus
  Account 59
  Aramaic 4, 5, 12
  Coptic 57, 60
  Documentary 74, 75
  Ḥadīth 74, 75, 79, 109, 110, 112, 113
  Hermopolis 10
  Letter 60
  Literary 74, 75, 109, 110, 111, 112
  Passover 5
  Scroll 33, 89
  Temple 5
Parchment 25n, 57, 108, 113
parnas, see communal official
Parthian (Arsacid) 14, 15
  Rule 15
Patron-client relation 157, 158
Pedro, governor of Barcelona 188
Pen 33, 68, 102
  Kalamos 31
  qalam 31n
  Stylos 26, 27, 31
Persepolis 4, 8
Persian
  Middle 14, 15, 16, 17
  Modern 13
  Old 4, 5
  Script 4, 5
  Persian-Jewish heritage 6
Petition 70, 71, 138, 155n, 158n
Pilgrimage 73, 191, 192, 210, 213

Planting 118, 121, 122
Porter (*ḥammāl*) 120
Portugal 188
Protocol 153, 188, 189
Psalm book 25

qalam, *see* pen
Qalāwūn 186
al-Qalqashandī 186, 187, 188, 193, 211, 212, 213, 214, 215

Radiocarbon 48n
Real estate 130, 133, 134, 136
  Price 118
  Transaction 136
Receipt (*apodeixis*) 59
Registry remark 188, 189
Rent 117, 118
  payment of a rent (*misthosis*) 59
Requisition 59
Rescript 61
Responsa 154, 155n, 158n, 163
Reuse 133, 134, 136, 139, 142
rizq, *see* maintenance

Sabaic
  Amiritic dialect of 32
  Early Sabaic period 29
  Late Sabaic period 30, 40
  Middle Sabaic letter 42
  Middle Sabaic period 39, 42
  Wooden stick viii
Sabaean kingdom 44
Sahidic 61, 66
ṣaḥīḥ 73, 76
Saʿīd b. Abī Ayyūb Miqlāṣ Abū Yaḥyā al-Khuzāʿī al-Miṣrī 106, 108
Saʿīd b. Djubayr 86, 87
Sailor (*nūtī*) 120, 121, 207
Sale
  Bill of 127, 130, 132, 136, 137, 138, 139, 143
  Deed of 139
Salmān 78
Sancho, king of Castile 188
Sanaa 30, 31n, 34n, 47
al-Ṣayrafī 133, 136
School
  Exercise 33, 60
  Practice 34
Signature 40, 42, 43, 171
Scribal
  Fāṭimid culture 138
  Practice 112, 128, 133, 136, 137, 138
  Training 19n, 20
Scribe
  Akkadian 4
  Aramaic 4
  Elamite 8
  Jewish 137, 138, 142
Script
  Aramaic 3, 19
  Chancellery 109
  Cursive 28, 109
  Document 128, 133, 138
  Ethiopic 25
  Ḥidjāzī 109
  Kharosṭi 12
  Kūfī 109
  Majuscule 28, 59n, 65
  Minuscule 28
  Monumental 4, 28, 29, 109
  Naskhī 109
  Northwest Semitic 3
  Old Persian 4, 5
  zabūr 25, 26, 28n, 31, 38, 39, 40, 49
Seal 5, 38, 210
Secretary 8, 108, 185, 186, 187, 212
Settlement 34, 162
  Delayed marriage gift (*mu'akhkhar*) 156, 169, 171
shurūṭ, *see* contract stipulation
Ṣila b. Zufar al-ʿAbsī 87, 88
Silk Road 12, 19
Ṣirwāḥ 44, 45
Slave
  Muslim 191
  of Nubian origin (*djins*) 136
Slavery 128n, 142, 143
Social
  Consideration 154
  Embeddedness 152n, 155, 162, 163, 164
  History 142, 147, 155
  Network 158n
Sogdian 15
Sovereignty (*kafāla*) 188
Stonecutter (*naqqāṭ*) 121
Stylos, *see* pen

Sugarcane 119, 121
Sulaymān 86
Supplementary deed (*faṣl*) 130, 133, 134, 136, 137, 138, 139, 142, 147
Susa 11, 15, 18
Syene, *see* Aswan
Syria 187, 192

Tablet
  Cuneiform 3, 12
  Persepolis fortification 5, 13
  Wax 31n, 32
  Writing 32
Tafsīr Furāt 89, 93
Taṣliya 192
Tax
  Document 75
  Payer 59
  Rate 123, 192n
  Receipt 59
al-Tirmidhī 76, 94, 95, 102, 103
Trade
  Embargo 187, 190
  Levantine 187
  Trans-Mediterranean 190
Trade agreement
  Arabic-Frankish 187
Transmission
  History 74n, 89, 93, 112
  Line 76
  Literary 188
  Oral/written 111, 112
Transmitter
  Chain of (*isnād*) 73, 75
  Genealogy (*ʿilm al-nasab*) 73
  Prosopography (*ʿilm al-ridjāl*) 73
Tyre 153

ʿUbayd Allāh b. Abī Djaʿfar al-Miṣrī 106, 108
ʿUmar b. Muḥammad b. Zayd b. ʿAbd Allāh b. ʿUmar b. al-Khaṭṭāb 86, 88
ʿushar (*Calotropis procera*) 30
al-Ushmūnayn 58, 59, 61, 121
  Hermoupolis 10, 58, 59

Valencia 188
Venice 190

Wādī al-Ğawf 30, 31, 48
Wage 118, 119, 120, 121, 122
Warranty 42, 130
  Clause 132, 133, 138, 139n
  darak 131, 133, 138
  Formulae 132
Watchman (*ḥāris*) 119, 120
Wax 38
  Inlay 32
  Tablet 31, 32
Wheat 119, 120
Wine 59
Witness clause 130, 132, 138
Wood 27, 28, 29, 30, 31, 32, 46, 47, 190
  Wooden stick viii, 6, 25, 28, 31, 32, 33, 35, 40, 43, 49
Writing
  Angular style of 109, 110n
  Mode of 24, 27, 32, 49
  Manuscript 26, 27, 28n, 38, 39n, 48
  South Arabian 27, 33
  System 13, 20, 28
  Tablet 32

Yazīd b. Abī Ḥabīb 110, 114
Yemen 25, 26, 48, 49, 50
  Ancient 25, 32, 49
  Pre-Islamic 24, 26, 30

Ẓafār 30
zabūr, *see* script

Printed in the United States
By Bookmasters